Cases in Enterprise Information Systems Implementation

Volume 1

Edited by Amir Manzoor

Cases in Enterprise Information Systems Implementation
Volume 1

ISBN-13: 9798858975311

DEDICATION

To the faculty and students dedicated to advance the knowledge of
information systems.

ABOUT THE EDITOR

Engr. Dr. Amir Manzoor holds a PhD in management sciences. He is a graduate of NED University, Pakistan, Lahore University of Management Sciences (LUMS), Pakistan, and Bangor University, United Kingdom. He has more than 20 years of diverse professional and teaching experience working at many renowned national and internal organizations and higher education institutions. His research interests include Information Technology, E-commerce, Strategic Management, Enterprise Resource Planning (ERP), Project Management, Supply Chain Management, and Business Analytics. He has published books that have been adopted as text/reference books in curriculum of undergraduate and graduate programs of large and reputed Asian and European universities. Amir can be contacted at engr.dr.amir@gmail.com.

ABOUT THE CONTRIBUTORS

Zakaria Soomro is an experienced Oracle Functional Consultant with a demonstrated history of working in manufacturing, educational institutes, media, and e-commerce industries. He is skilled in Oracle Fusion Cloud, e-Business Suite, PeopleSoft, Management Accounting, and Microsoft Office. He graduated from the Institute of Cost and Management Accountants of Pakistan. He is pursuing a master's degree from the Karachi School of Business and Leadership (KSBL), Karachi, Pakistan.

Muhammad Faizan is a Treasury Accountant with more than ten years of experience, a strong SAP migration background, and expertise in SAP S4 HANA. He holds a Chartered Management Accountant qualification from ICMA-Pakistan and is pursuing a master's degree from an MBA in FINTECH from the Karachi School of Business and Leadership (KSBL).

Karim Bux is a Chartered Accountant with over 15 years of experience as a business finance partner, inspiring leadership and delivering project finance, with expertise in FP&A and reporting & controlling. He is an associate member of the Institute of Chartered Accountants of Pakistan and also holds a Master's degree from the Karachi School of Business and Leadership (KSBL), Karachi, Pakistan. He is a chartered member of the Chartered Institute of Logistics and Transport, United Kingdom. Before working in PIBT, a World Bank project in Karachi, Karim Bux worked at Ernst & Young Pakistan in the Audit & Assurance department.

Aatika Sohail is a dynamic professional with an MBA specializing in Human Resources from the Karachi School of Business and Leadership (KSBL). Aatika's journey unfolds through a tapestry of experiences. From her impactful roles at multinational corporations like Pakistan Beverage Limited and GfK Etilize to her selection for the prestigious McKinsey Forward program, her strategic thinking and hands-on expertise shine. A self-starter with proficiency in content creation, social media management, and marketing, Aatika is a multi-talented individual with a keen understanding of the corporate world and remarkable business acumen.

Maheen Kamal is a professional digital marketer with over eight months of experience. She holds a Bachelor's degree from Bahria University (Karachi) and a Master's from the Karachi School of Business and Leadership (KSBL), Karachi, Pakistan. Her expertise includes SEO and backlinking. She has received multiple awards for her exceptional academic and corporate work.

Muhammad Rehan is a professional banker with over nine years of experience in top banks in Pakistan. He holds a master's degree from the Karachi School of Business and Leadership (KSBL), Karachi, Pakistan, and is also a Professional Body ACCA (Association of Chartered Certified Accountants) member. His expertise includes finance and risk management. He has received multiple awards for his exceptional work in academia and the corporate world in a short time.

Muhammad Arslan is a proficient accountant with over three years of professional expertise. He holds a bachelor's degree in accounting and finance from Sukkur IBA University and a master's in Fintech from Karachi School of Business and Leadership (KSBL) in Karachi, Pakistan. His expertise includes auditing, financial reporting, and financial analysis. He is a recipient of the Sindh Endowment Educational Fund (SEEF) Scholarship.

Jahanzeb Qadeer is a professional accountant with over 12 years of experience. He is a Chartered Accountant and a Certified Public Accountant. He also holds a bachelor's degree from the University of Karachi, Pakistan, and is pursuing a master's degree from the Karachi School of Business and Leadership (KSBL), Karachi, Pakistan. His expertise includes auditing and accounting, and he is currently working with a Big4 audit firm in Ireland.

Owais Ahmed is an aspirational, motivated individual with over three years of banking experience. He has performed in branch banking's different departments like daily operations, remittances, and audits, and was also responsible for monthly reporting to the area office. He holds a bachelor's degree in finance and a Master's from KSBL. Constantly learning and updating his skillset and knowledge base, he aspires to be a problem solver and improve our society.

Muhammad Usman Khan is a chartered accountant and a member of the Institute of Chartered Accountants in England and Wales and the Institute of Chartered Accountants of Pakistan. He is a seasoned finance professional with over ten years of experience ranging from assurance and financial advisory services at PwC to managerial and leadership positions across various manufacturing corporations. He specializes in financial planning & analysis, financial management, and business partnering. While pursuing his Master's degree from the Karachi School of Business Leadership, he led the University's team to victory in the CFA Institute Research Challenge Pakistan 2023.

Syed Gulraiz Haider Naqvi is a professional Sales Manager with over six years of experience. He holds a bachelor's degree from the Institute of Business Administration (IBA, Karachi) and a master's degree from the Karachi School of Business and Leadership (KSBL), Karachi, Pakistan. His expertise includes B2B sales, retail sales, and digital marketing. He has received multiple awards for his exceptional corporate work and is also a trainer on soft skills.

Ilsa Abdullah is a creative and passionate marketeer. She holds a bachelor's in business administration (BBA) degree from the Institute of Business Administration (IBA), Karachi, and a master's in business administration (MBA) degree from the Karachi School of Business and Leadership (KSBL), Karachi, Pakistan. Her interests lie in social media, client services, and digital marketing. She has received multiple certifications for her exceptional work in academia.

Marium Ali is an Assistant Manager - Brand Marketing at Pakistan State Oil. She holds a bachelor's degree in marketing from Karachi University Business School (KUBS). She is pursuing her master's degree from the Karachi School of Business and Leadership (KSBL).

Sumaira Sultan is an experienced marketing, outreach, corporate social responsibility, and admissions professional. She is pursuing a Master of Business Administration (MBA) major in Talent Acquisition and Marketing from the Karachi School of Business and Leadership (KSBL).

Mohammad Ali Imran is a member of ACCA and holds a master's degree from the Karachi School of Business and Leadership (KSBL). He is an experiences supply chain professional currently working as Procurementr Spcialist at Dawlance Pakistan.

Shazib Khalil is an experienced corporate banker with over four years of experience. He has exposure to diverse industries such as Textile, Pharmaceuticals, Trading, Distributors, Modarabas, Manufacturing, Energy, Construction, and Plastic Films. He holds a bachelor's degree in accounting and finance from the Institute of Business Administration (IBA) and a master's degree from the Karachi School of Business and Leadership (KSBL).

Suleman Imran is a banking professional with over four years of Corporate Finance experience. He has diverse experience in business development, client organization, relationship/ account management, corporate debt, deal and credit structuring, loan syndication, trade finance, and business, financial, and industry analysis. He possesses strong knowledge of International Trade, Credit, Treasury, and Transaction banking products. He holds a bachelor's degree from Oxford Brooks University and a master's degree from Karachi School of Business and Leadership (KSBL).

Muhammad Ali Qureshi is an experienced marketing professional currently working as a Content and channel Specialist at Pfizer. He holds a bachelor's degree in business administration from the Institute of Business Administration (IBA) and a master's degree from the Karachi School of Business and Leadership (KSBL).

Muhammad Nasarullah is an experienced accounting professional working as Deputy Manager of Costing and Budgeting at TATA Pakistan. He holds a CMA from the Institute of Cost and Management Accountants of Pakistan (ICMA Pakistan) and a master's degree from the Karachi School of Business and Leadership (KSBL).

Muhammad Saad is an experienced supply chain professional currently working as a senior planner at Hutchison Ports. He holds a bachelor's degree from Iqra University and a master's from Karachi School of Business and Leadership (KSBL).

Muhammad Maaz Siraj is an experienced supply chain professional working as Skin Care's inventory coordinator. He holds a bachelor's degree from Iqra University and a master's from Karachi School of Business and Leadership (KSBL).

Syed Ahmed Hasan is currently working as a managing partner at Syed Fuels. He is a passionate marketer specializing in selling commercial and industrial petroleum products. He holds a bachelor's degree from Shaheed Zulfikar Ali Bhutto Institute of Science and Technology and a master's from the Karachi School of Business and Leadership (KSBL).

Jawwad Ur Rehman is a passionate E-commerce specialist working to enable industry leaders in Pakistan to sell globally via platforms like Amazon and eBay - helping industries add new channels to increase their sales. He holds a bachelor's degree from the Institute of Business Management and a master's from the Karachi School of Business and Leadership (KSBL).

Waleed Uz Zaman Siddiqui is a well-established warehouse supervisor with a proven track record of optimizing operations and maximizing efficiency in fast-paced distribution environments. He is passionate about driving productivity and maintaining high-quality standards while ensuring a safe and organized working environment. He holds a bachelor's degree from the Institute of Business Management and a master's from the Karachi School of Business and Leadership (KSBL).

Syed Saad Mansoor is an experienced finance professional currently working as assistant manager of finance at Power Cement Ltd. He holds a bachelor's degree from the Institute of Business Management and a master's from the Karachi School of Business and Leadership (KSBL).

Ayaz Shaukat is a highly accomplished and tech-savvy finance professional with a proven track record in corporate finance, complemented by strong leadership and management skills. He has managed core corporate functions, including Financial Reporting and fund management. He graduated from the Institute of Cost and Management Accountants of Pakistan. He holds a master's degree from the Karachi School of Business and Leadership (KSBL).

Shankar Talreja is a passionate and diligent investment specialist. Currently, he works as the Senior Manager - Investments (M&A & VC) at Lucky Cement Limited. He holds a bachelor's degree from the Sukkur Institute of Business Administration and a master's from the Karachi School of Business and Leadership (KSBL).

PREFACE

In the ever-evolving landscape of modern business, effective implementation of Enterprise Information Systems (EIS) effectively has become a pivotal factor in determining an organization's success. Worldwide, companies strive to harness EIS's power to streamline processes, enhance decision-making, and achieve competitive advantage. In this context, the role of EIS has gained paramount significance. This book delves into the experiences, challenges, and triumphs encountered in the pursuit of deploying EIS within the context of a developing country.

Developing countries present unique circumstances and complexities that demand innovative approaches to EIS implementation. Through the lens of various industries, including oil, banking, Fast-Moving Consumer Goods (FMCG), Small and Medium Enterprises (SMEs), pharmaceuticals, shipping, and more, this book explores the journey of organizations striving to leverage EIS as a transformative tool. The case studies of this book are not merely accounts of technological endeavors. The authors provide readers with the opportunity to go through the strategic decision-making processes, technical dilemmas, organizational changes, and unforeseen challenges that arise during EIS implementation.

The knowledge encapsulated in this book contributes to the growing body of literature on EIS implementation, offering a fresh perspective from the viewpoint of the developing world. Lessons learned from successes and failures provide valuable guidance to practitioners, academicians, and policymakers seeking to navigate the complex landscape of EIS deployment. Furthermore, the diverse range of industries explored underscores the universal applicability of these insights, transcending geographical boundaries. Each case study not only offers a glimpse into the challenges faced by these organizations but also illuminates the strategies, methodologies, and innovations that have paved the way for their achievements.

Amir Manzoor

CONTENTS

VEHICLE TRACKING & INTEGRATION AT EAGLE EYE

Karim Bux Soomro, Zakaria Soomro, and Muhammad Faizan Qadeer of Karachi School for Business and Leadership (KSBL) prepared this case under the supervision of Dr. Amir Manzoor. The case was prepared solely to provide material for class discussion. The authors do not intend to illustrate either effective or ineffective handling of a managerial situation. Certain names and other identifying information have been disguised to protect confidentiality.

Ahmed Raza, the Finance Manager of Eagle Eye Tracking Solutions (Private) Limited (Eagle Eye), a logistics company primarily dealing in vehicle tracking and fleet management, was anxiously collecting his thoughts and the papers on his desk when he was called-for at the CEO's office in an evening of March 2019. It was his third visit to the management along with his CFO, Parvez Abbasi, for the same agenda – reconciliation of vehicle tracking billing by Oracle EBS with CRM. Customer complaints had been overwhelming, and with revenue leakages now increasing due to untimely invoicing, the problem seemed to persist and augment further.

Ahmed had already been working on a solution and proposed it to Parvez. According to Ahmed, cloud-based ERP was the most suitable solution in the current situation, which will align CRM with the billing software. However, the CFO hesitated to present this to the management for two reasons. First, their focus (both in terms of time and resources) was on launching new products and services. Second, Eagle Eye had already incurred considerable costs in procuring Oracle EBS just eighteen months ago. Hence, the proposition of a new ERP at this time did require audacity.

Eagle Eye Tracking (Private) Limited

Eagle Eye is Pakistan's largest privately held Fleet Management company. Founded in 2001 as a privately owned business, the Company has grown by investing in technology. It now has over 180,000 customers and corporate clients to secure and monitor assets of over US$ 2 Billion. Eagle Eye positioned itself to provide affordable security and vehicle tracking solutions nationwide.

Eagle Eye is headquartered in Karachi and has a regional presence in major Pakistani cities, including Multan, Lahore, Rawalpindi, and Faisalabad. The company employs more than 500 people. The company imported assembly parts for the tracking device(s) installed in vehicles primarily from Europe. Eagle Eye has collaborated with around a dozen tech partners to maintain faster connectivity, deploy the latest technology, and achieve vehicle monitoring accuracy. The Company has achieved significant growth in revenue in recent years (Exhibit 1) due to the quality of services, excellent customer support, and aggressive marketing efforts. The company earns most of its revenue from fresh installations and repeated renewals by existing customers (Exhibit 2).

Chief Executive Officer Syed Salman Hyder owns 75% of the company's shareholding and has been Eagle Eye's CEO for eight years. He played a pivotal role in the company's remodeling. A BBA and a CFA, Saad had eight years of directorship and investment banking experience before joining Eagle Eye.

The leadership also includes Mr. Shankar Talreja. He holds a Master's in telecommunication and software engineering and a Ph.D. in Computer Science. Currently, the Chief Operating Officer of Eagle Eye, Shankar, has an overall experience of more than ten years in project management and technology. At Eagle Eye, he has accelerated growth by making significant tech changes and instilling a progressive culture and mindset. Shankar was also the team leader in developing the company's operation management software, Customer Relationship Management (CRM).

Business Operations

Eagle Eye operates in a segmented market for vehicle tracking and related IT services, primarily covered by two or three leading players. TPL Tracker is another major publicly-held company that competes with Eagle Eye. With this pretext, news about billing malfunctions would be disastrous for Eagle Eye's reputation, especially since around 70% of the business clients utilizing the fleet management services are Corporate, including renowned insurance and banking companies.

A complete fleet tracking and monitoring solution involves innovative technology that instantly tracks or monitors the vehicle's location at any time. The tracking system consists of a GPS device that sends periodic updates of its location to the route station through the network server. The server hosts the Eagle Eye web application, which stores and represents the information sent by these gadgets in a meaningful and user-friendly format and is displayed on maps and transferred to users via SMS, e-mail, or application interface to provide the location of the vehicles geographically along with various other parameters like vehicle speed, idle time, etc.

The order process starts with the marketing team promoting Eagle Eye's products and services through careful ad placements, social media campaigns, and partnerships with car dealers. Customers can order online, via the call center, or by visiting the premises. After that, technicians visit the customer's premises to install the tracking devices.

The management is now planning to venture into other allied products and services, which would add value to the targeted corporate clients by providing customized solutions to enhance the efficiency of their operations. Higher productivity is possible by using insights on resource utilization, such as optimal vehicle path, data on fuel usage and detecting fuel pilferage, alerts for over-speeding movement, and idle time. Specialized industries such as cold storage vehicles (where temperature monitoring is essential) or agriculture vehicles (where yield measurement is critical) were interested in these services. Eagle Eye was also working on Logistics Optimization that offers remote logistics management for efficient order management and delivery. Fleet care provides automation of the maintenance process with better planning and cost management.

The Legacy Environment

Customer Relationship Management (CRM)

Eagle Eye's complex technical operations necessitated the development of a well-designed and easy-to-use software that would meet the Company's requirements. Shankar led this task, and his team developed CRM software in two years. CRM deployed on Oracle database, with an on-premises server for operations and backup. The software had been working for a long time, so the most staff was well-versed in CRM. Further, in-house development allowed Eagle Eye to modify CRM per changing business needs and operations and refine it with improved functionalities and interface, all at no additional cost to the Company (except for the fixed costs of IT person-hours). All the business locations of Eagle Eye provide access to CRM for their employees, and around 200 of them were CRM users, including technicians who upload vehicle tracking jobs in CRM, billing staff who use CRM for billing reconciliation, sales staff who use CRM for recovery and call center personnel, who provide 24/7 support to customers.

Oracle E-Business Suite (EBS)

Oracle E-Business Suite (EBS) is a complete set of business applications for managing and automating business processes. The Oracle E-Business Suite Architecture is a framework for multi-tiered, distributed computing that supports Oracle E-Business Suite products. Eagle Eye, realizing the need for automation in its support functions and operations, selected EBS primarily because its finance module had an excellent reputation in the market. Like CRM, EBS deployed an Oracle-based database with an on-premises server for operations and backup and a Java-based application for the user interface. Implementation of EBS took almost a year, with active involvement from employees, and it has been operational for around eighteen months now, with the finance and supply chain management modules including General Ledger, Accounts Payable, Inventory, and Procurement working as per desire.

Complications in Legacy Environment

During the implementation stages of EBS, the team highlighted CRM and EBS integration issues. Despite software integration, the Application Program Interfaces (APIs) for data fetching by EBS and data provision by CRM were incompatible due to system incompatibility. Due to this, CRM operational data forming the basis of billing, such as vehicle details, tracker and other jobs/services details, customer details, etc., was being incorrectly communicated to EBS. There were occasional data integration and interfacing delays due to the system's slow response time. As a result, customer billing from EBS was either delayed, incorrect, or incompatible with actual jobs and services performed. This situation caused reconciliation issues for the billing team, with monthly sales figures differing by around 20%. It also created difficulties for the sales recovery team, whose job was to chase customers after billing, and erroneous billing was frustrating both the customers and the recovery staff.

In addition, as EBS was an on-premises software, the employees at locations other than the head office had to access it using a VPN, which was not only causing lags in operations but was also creating troubleshooting nightmares as user support was usually late. Connectivity issues were causing location-based recovery staff troubles reconciling their recoveries with billed invoices. The technical staff faced problems maintaining and updating tracking devices installed on vehicles. The CEO was alarmed as this situation was damaging the company's reputation.

Selection of Solution: Oracle Fusion Cloud

Ahmed Raza was already in discussion with his friends at IX, a Company specialization in ERP implementation of all types, for a solution for Eagle Eye. Ahmed had worked closely with IX for an ERP implementation assignment in his previous company and knew about the team's competency and working methods. They selected Oracle Fusion Cloud, a renowned next-generation enterprise application suite from Oracle Corporation (Fusion Cloud). Due to many standard open APIs and the ability to develop custom APIs, Fusion Cloud will be effective in fetching the billing data from CRM and ending Eagle Eye's billing problems. Furthermore, since it is a cloud-based application accessible worldwide, location-based staff will have no connectivity issues. Ahmed pitched the solution to Salman, and the project was approved. IX was selected as the software implementation consultant because it had implemented the most Fusion Cloud Projects in Pakistan, and Ahmed Raza was made the Project Manager from Eagle Eye.

Project Implementation

IX and Eagle Eye agreed on a Rapid implementation methodology for Fusion Cloud, targeting effective implementation within four months. They decided to implement the following modules at Eagle Eye:

- General Ledger

- Cash Management
- Inventory Management
- Account Payables
- Asset Management
- Procurement
- Account Receivables

Even though all of these modules, except for Receivables, were working satisfactorily in EBS, they had to be re-implemented in Fusion Cloud because Fusion Cloud provided the software as a package containing all modules. Some users of these modules were pretty comfortable using the EBS. These users showed resistance to system change. However, clear and stern directions from management and advocacy from the project team that Fusion Cloud would provide better functionality and enhanced efficiency in performing routine tasks for these modules with a similar operating interface were persuasive enough for users to accept and contribute to project implementation.

Implementation Teams

Eagle Eye and IX had decided to use two teams to manage the project. While senior management on the steering committee would decide on strategic issues relating to the implementation, the Project team would be responsible for tackling operational obstacles. Table 1 shows the project teams, their composition, issues addressed, and time devoted.

Table 1: Project Team Structure

Team Name	Team Composition and time commitment	Issues addressed by the team	% of total Issues addressed by them
Steering Committee	Division VPs Eight people Monthly meetings	Business Strategy (e.g., sequence of site installations and planned changes in strategy).	10%
Project Team	Operations employees (e.g., Planners, Buyers, Financial Accountants, and Consultants) 15 people, Full Time	Implementations issues	80%
Special Technicians	Support for SOAP Web Services for implementation of Fusion I-Cloud. Two people (Full Time)	Mapping of CRM to Fusion I-Cloud through XML-based web services.	10%

Project Plan

IX and Ahmed developed a Project Plan (Exhibit 3) which covered the following activities:

1. Conference Room Piloting (CRP) & Required Outputs
2. Solution Design and Gap Analysis
3. Training

4. User Acceptance Testing (UAT)

5. Go-Live

CONFERENCE ROOM PILOTING (CRP) & REQUIRED OUTPUTS

A Conference Room Pilot (CRP) is a process used in the real world to help progress communication and collaboration, particularly while choosing and executing software solutions. CRP is a process that validates system expectations and allows end-users to have a look-and-feel experience of the system. CRP benefits organizations by enabling businesses to test new systems before fully committing to them. CRP results can identify system loopholes the company must address before the new system goes live.

Integration Experts adopted the CRP in three-phases:

1. Scope
2. Design
3. Build

Scope: In this phase, the implementation team sets the project's scope, i.e., to what extent the output must be attained and what the final results would be. This project aimed to integrate CRM with Fusion Cloud and eliminate connectivity and business billing process issues.

Design: The team transforms the requirements into system design in this phase. In the design phase, the team with technical and functional expertise starts designing the project. An adequately prepared CRP, in this case, would validate an understanding of the critical elements of the business scope. IX team had thoroughly analyzed the current business processes and involved related Head of departments to map the business processes and authority matrix to distinct the user interface as per the specific This is achieved by experts stepping in the roles of the Organization's key personnel to utilize the system for smooth business processes optimally.

Build: In this phase, the IX team starts configuration to translate the design elements developed into a fully functional application. Therefore, a live demo i.e., "a look and feel" experience of the system process and interface with total team participation, is essential during this phase. This process requires timely collaboration from team members to finalize the requirements and parameters of the system. Eagle Eye's employees already worked on Oracle-based software and had hands-on experience. They were better in a better position to assess system behaviors and migrate from Oracle EBS to Oracle Fusion Cloud.

SOLUTION DESIGN AND GAP ANALYSIS

Gap analysis compares where we are against where we would like to be. Gap analysis helps identify the gaps between these two states and develop an action plan to close them. The IX and Eagle Eye teams were very clear about the system's requirements; therefore, based on requirement gathering, the solution design document was confirmed, which finalized the processes for capturing business transactions, design & architecture of the system. The team prepared a high-level structured design document. In this document, the team mapped the organizational structure of Eagle Eye. It covered the 4Cs (functional currency, calendar convention, chart of accounts, and accounting conventions) to configure the Primary ledger of Eagle Eye. After thorough discussions with users and prototyping sessions, the IX and Eagle Eye teams prepared this document. The solution design document for Eagle Eye contained multiple business process flow charts (See Exhibit 4).

TRAINING

After confirmation of detailed Solution Design Documents, IX trained users to get hands-on experience with the system. It is the stage where IX introduces the client to the standard procedure set. The previous Oracle experience of Eagle Eye made the imparting of training swifter.

USER ACCEPTANCE TESTING (UAT)

After training, IX gave users access to the Test System for data entry and scenario testing. During UAT, issues identified are listed and categorized as per priority and addressed to rectify the system functions or reports. Here again, the previous Oracle experience of Eagle Eye meant that users were spending less time on overlapping functions, significantly increasing UAT's pace.

Experts of SOAP Web Services

The implementation team had agreed to utilize XML-based web services to integrate CRM with Oracle Fusion cloud to accomplish the desired results of integrated billing. However, while integrating CRM and Fusion Cloud, the team faced a new challenge whereby the SOAP web services, the XML-based protocol for accessing web services, used by Fusion Cloud's APIs to collect CRM data was behaving irrationally and malfunctioning. Since the internal IT resources of Eagle Eye did not have the expertise in XML web services, IX suggested hiring third-party SOAP experts to work on the solution and overcome this challenge. This hurdle cost the project a lag of July 2019 and additional resources, but the project continued towards going live.

GO-LIVE

The final stage of implementation is when the system application is made available for user operations. The team implemented the system with the authority matrix where users input the data to be approved by the supervisor. The strategic partners used the reports generated for decision-making. To train the users of the respective modules, IX issued user IDs after UAT. After all the necessary assurance, the system went live in August 2019.

The Way Forward

Following implementation, the implementation team resolved customer billing and remote connectivity issues. The success factors for the effective implementation of Fusion Cloud at Eagle Eye included;

- Employee dedication and an overall motivation drive initiated by management to get through the implementation

- Precise requirement analysis of system needs and documented expectations

- Previous experience of employees with similar Oracle environment and therefore focus on pain areas

- Effective project management, using third-party resources when needed.

- Effective team management: At the Project Kick-off meeting, Ahmed (Project Team Lead) established principal accountabilities of the implementation teams and ensured their roles.

With this spirit in mind, Eagle Eye aims to enhance its cyber security protocols and adopt excellence in inventory management standards.

Exhibit 1
Yearly Sales Figures

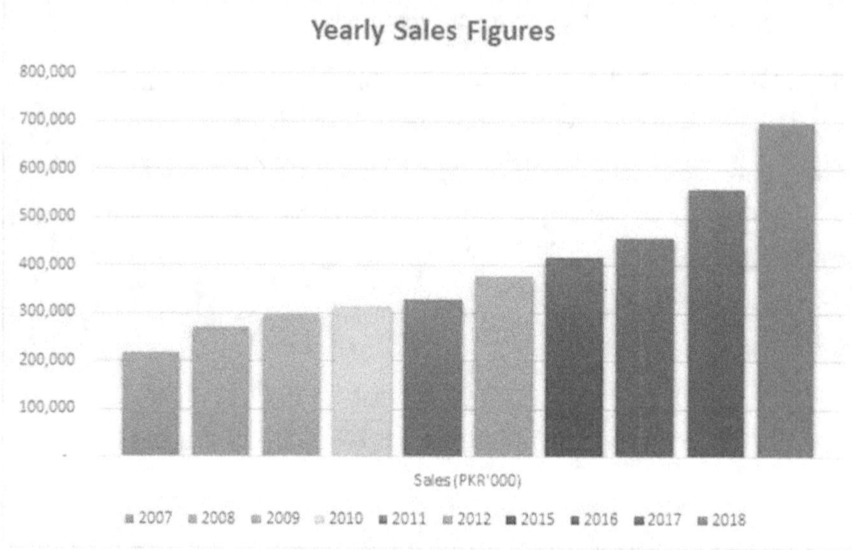

Exhibit 2
Breakup of Sales by Service Lines

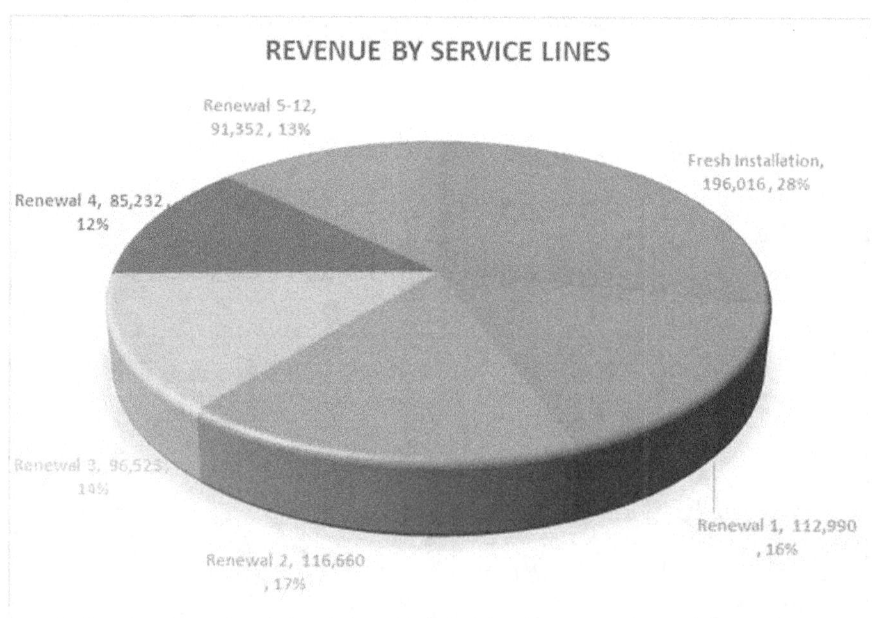

Exhibit 3
Project Plan

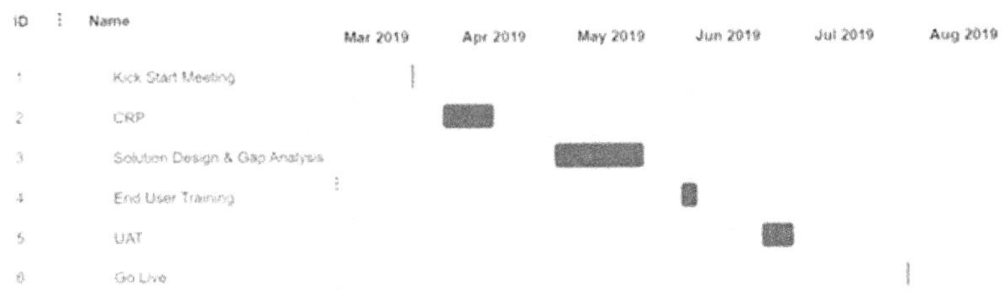

Exhibit 4
Business Process Flow Charts

Procurement

Procedure Title

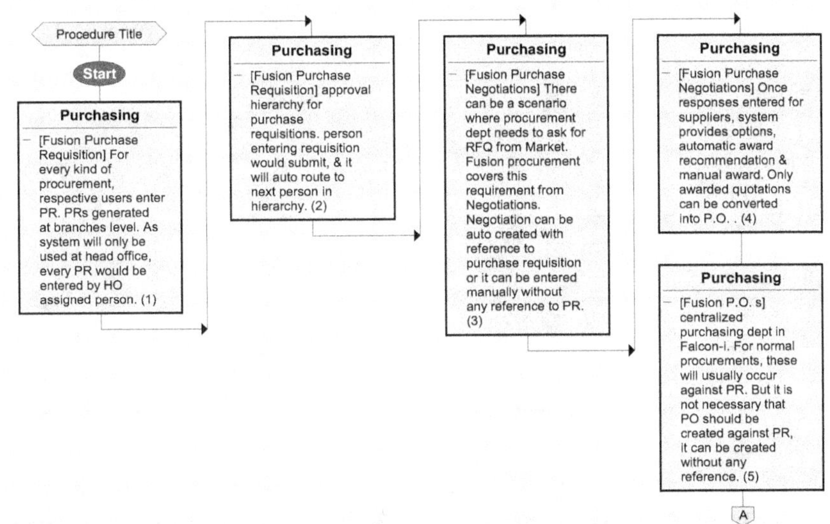

Inventory Management:

Procedure Title

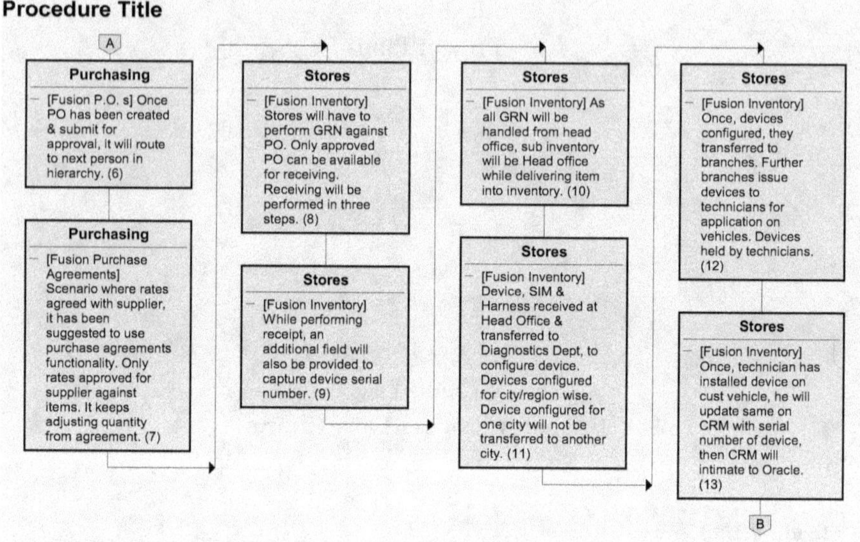

Accounts Payables

Procedure Title

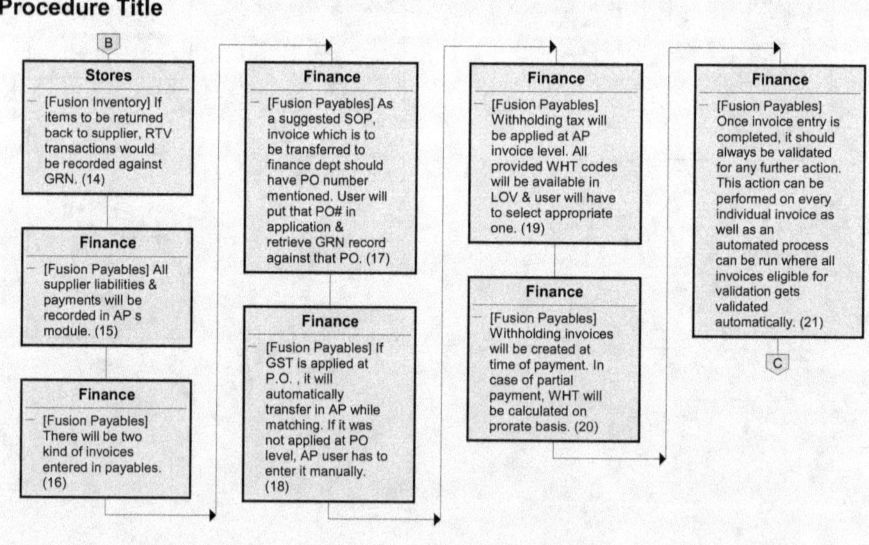

Procedure Title

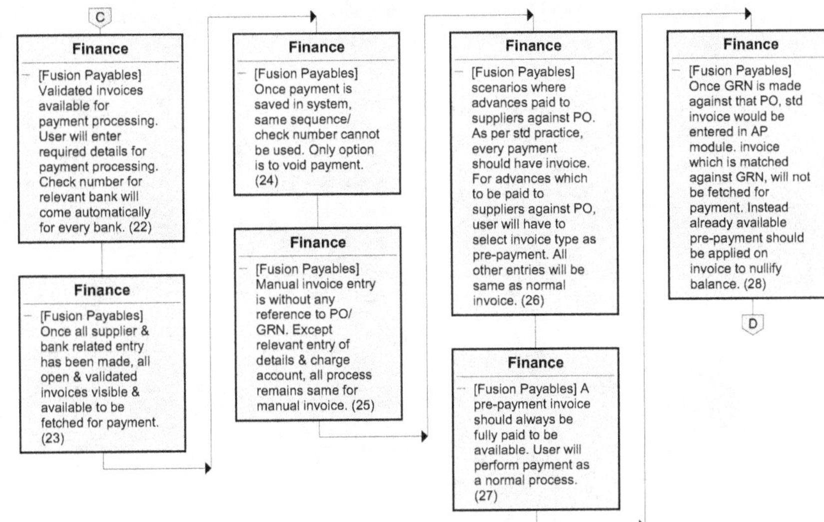

Accounts Receivables

Procedure Title

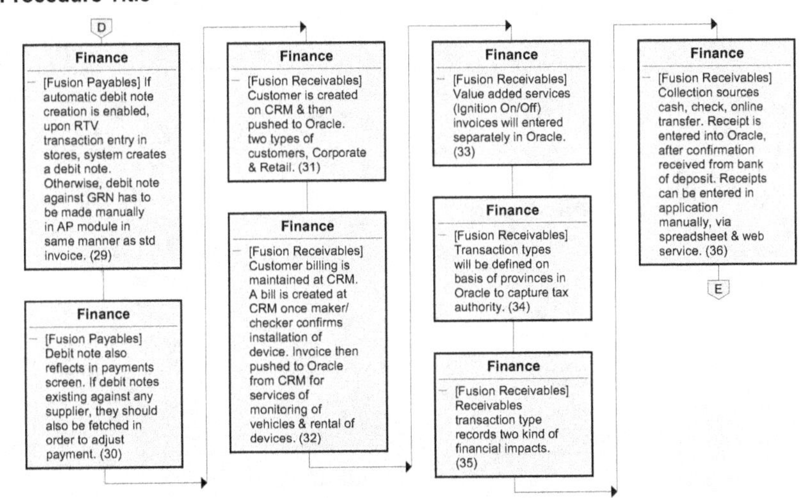

15

Asset Management

Procedure Title

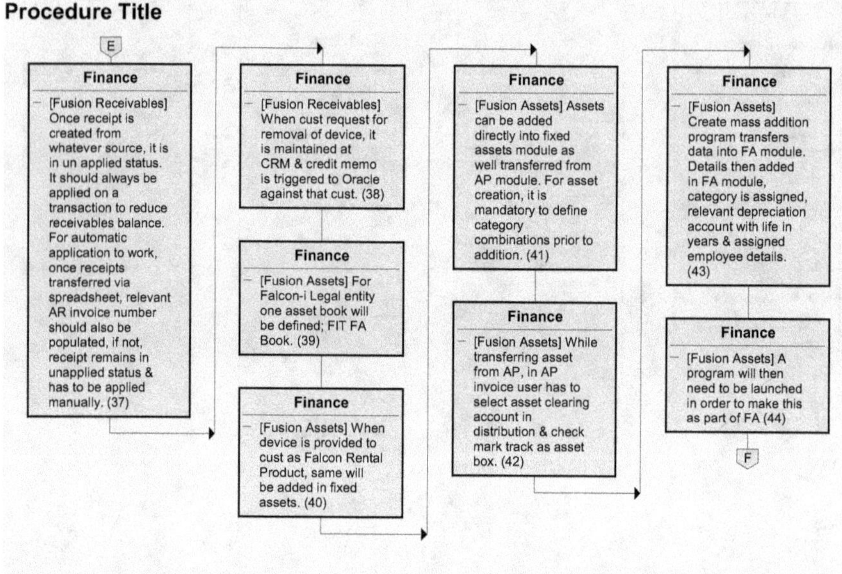

General Ledger

Procedure Title

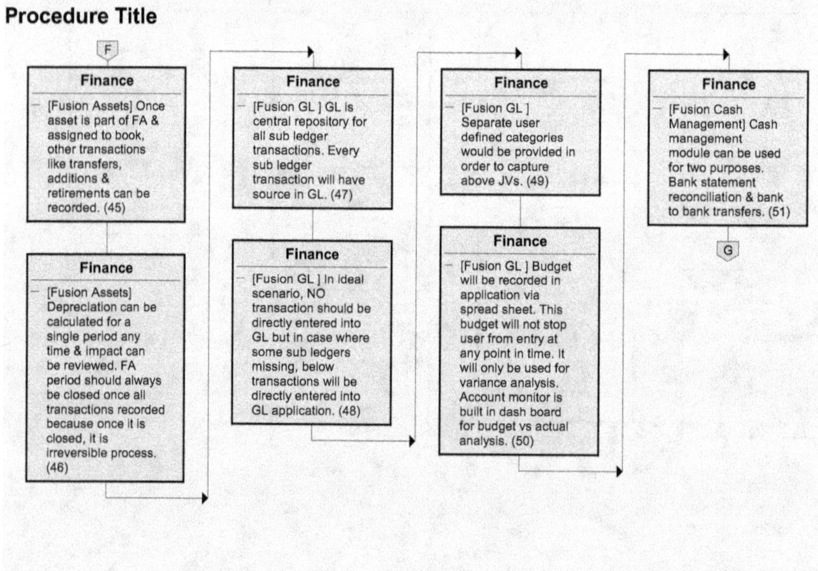

Cash Management

Procedure Title

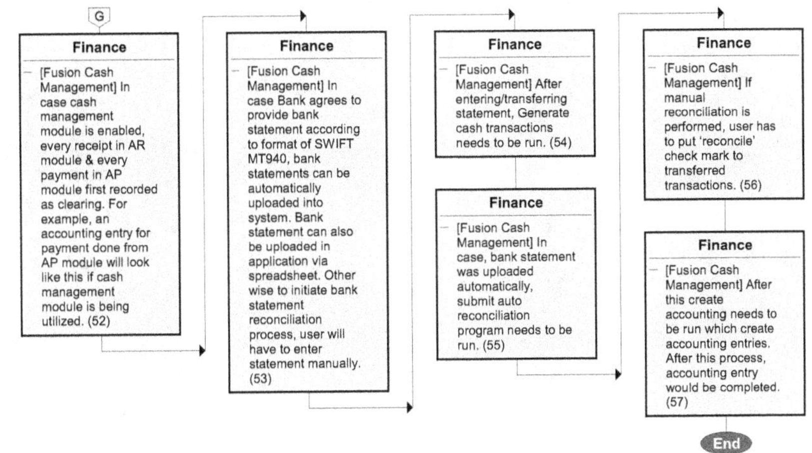

This page was intentionally left blank.

IMPLEMENTATION OF HUMAN RESOURCE MANAGEMENT SYSTEM (HRMS) AT PAK PACKAGES LTD.

Ayaz Shoukat and Muhammad Usman Khan of Karachi School for Business and Leadership (KSBL) prepared this case under the supervision of Dr. Amir Manzoor. The case was prepared solely to provide material for class discussion. The authors do not intend to illustrate either effective or ineffective handling of a managerial situation. Certain names and other identifying information have been disguised to protect confidentiality.

Introduction

"How did it come to this?" the new Chief Financial Officer of Pak Packages Limited contemplated as he stared at the audit report on his laptop screen.

Danish Iftikhar had just taken over as the CFO. The management of Pak Packages recently changed due to a change in the company's ownership. Danish had over 15 years of experience working at several multinational corporations. He had been working with the new management for the past several years. Due to his strong standing and experience, he led the rehabilitation of Pak Packages, which had been at a loss for several years.

The audit report depicted the company's complete failure of human resource information systems for the past several years, resulting in massive losses to Pak Packages due to fraud. The failure of information systems had allowed personnel from the human resource department to create ghost employees for systematic misappropriation of funds.

Danish stood up from his chair and instinctively began pacing across his room as he gathered his thoughts. He did not know precisely how deep the fraud went and whether other information systems were compromised. A few minutes later, as he gazed across the office hall from his window, he concluded that one thing was sure. The current information systems had to go, and there was a critical need for massive upheavals of human resources. He finally sat at his desk and began preparing a plan to present to the Board of Directors.

Global Landscape of the Packaging Industry

The global industrial packaging market can be segmented along three primary criteria: 1) material, 2) product, and 3) application. In terms of materials used in packaging, plastics, glass, metal, paper & board, and wood are employed to deliver packaging solutions, available in multiple product formats such as drums, sacks, pouches, and wraps catering to the needs of numerous industry applications including foods, beverages, and pharmaceuticals.

The global demand for packaging reached US$ 914.7bn in 2019 and was expected to grow in the coming years. Despite the COVID-19 outbreak in 2020, consumer spending was in recovery mode internationally, and the growth of home care and personal care demand was a catalyst for the recovery of the global packaging industry in 2021. Paperboard is the most used packaging material, accounting for around a third of the world's packaging market consumption, followed by flexible packaging at 25.5%, rigid plastics at 18.7%, metal at 12.1%, glass at 5.8%, and other packaging types at 4.7%. Pak Packages Limited operates in the flexible and rigid packaging segment in Pakistan. This market mirrors the accelerants driving Asia-Pacific regional growth, where 41% of industry growth will originate over the next five years.

In this regard, key growth markets of China and India were expected to outpace the growth of advanced economies. Central to the industry's growth expectations was the increased demand for pharmaceuticals, food, beverages, personal, household, and retail products, with numerous flexible packaging applications deployed. Thus, increasing diversification and penetration of these industries will have positive spillovers for the demand for flexible packaging solutions. From a broad perspective, high growth in these regions is due to the global shifts in demographics, such as increasing urbanization, growing number of small households, and rising middle-class population. Consequently, these demographic shifts have changed consumer buying behavior and taste and preference, thereby leading to an increase in demand for packaged products.

Additionally, the role played by modern trade channels, e-commerce platforms, and other specialized sales channels is essential in driving demand for packaging solutions. Food packaging was expected to account for the largest share of the end-user segment for flexible packaging over the near term. The potential for growth in packaged food sales was slated to drive demand for packaging globally. Changing lifestyles and food habits were significant factors underlying the growth of the packaged food industry worldwide. Regarding sustainability, flexible packaging offered lower wastage and was less energy-intensive while significantly reducing food wastage. Besides food packaging purposes, the flexible packaging market was expected to ride on the tailwinds of solid cosmetics and personal care segment growth as the prevalence of smaller, more economical product variants (pouches, sachets) was likely to replace rigid plastic packaging.

Domestic Flexible Packaging Landscape

Three main channels cater to Pakistan's packaging film industry demand: 1) locally manufactured films, 2) imported films, and 3) smuggled and grey market products. Locally manufactured films dominate Pakistan's packaging film industry. Locally manufactured films have a market share of 98% of the total flexible packaging demand. The remaining need is primarily met by imported films and grey suppliers, including smuggled and below-standard products. In recent years, the confluence of more formidable import barriers, stringent food quality enforcement measures, and an increased range of products from locally manufactured players has reduced the share of the grey market in this product segment.

Pakistan's packaging industry had an approximate size of USD 5.86 billion (PKR 1,219 billion) in the financial year 2021, compared to approximately USD 5.53 billion (PKR 1,150 billion) in the previous year, representing a growth of 6%. The local packaging industry comprises four major segments: paper, plastic, tinplate, and glass. Paper and plastic segments occupy a significant share of the total market, while other materials, such as tinplate and glass, occupy relatively more minor shares.

Margin & Cost Structure of the Plastic Packaging Segment

The segment's direct costs consist mainly of imported raw materials (approximately 70%). Therefore, volatility in exchange rates and international price trends significantly impact costs.

The average margins of the plastic packaging segment have declined since 2016, with average gross margins falling from 14% in 2016 to 9% in 2021. In addition, net margins fell from 6% in 2016 to 2% in 2021. One plausible explanation is rising raw material costs, which many small players struggle to pass on promptly.

Competitive Landscape of the Domestic Packaging Sector

There were few major players in the industry and an intense competitive rivalry among them. The entire industry depends on imported raw materials from abroad, so the rivalry is in front of efficient procurement management, bulk buying, maintaining cost, and satisfying customer needs.

History of the Company and Information Systems

Pak Packages Limited was incorporated in 2007 and had its head office and production facilities in Karachi. Over the years, it had grown rapidly and established four production divisions by 2015: Plastic Bags, Bottles, Cups, and PVC. Its customers included large corporations in Pakistan, including several renowned multinational companies operating across multiple industries.

The Company's organizational structure has the Board of Directors, who are also the key shareholders at the top. The Chief Executive Officer reports to the Board of Directors and is himself one of the key shareholders. Under the CEO are heads of departments. These include the Chief Financial Officer, Human Resources, Internal Audit, and Chief Operating Officer for its four production divisions, each with a General Manager working under them. Managers work under the General Managers. These managers looked after the day-to-day affairs of the Company. Any decision taken by the Board is effectively final.

For the last few years, the Company has been suffering from losses. The previous management had been unable to reliably identify the reasons for those losses since the information systems were capable enough. These information systems were out-of-date. It forced many departments and functions to bypass the information systems frequently to complete a task. In many cases, manual work was also performed to corroborate the information generated by the information systems, resulting in duplication of work and the requirement of excessive employees. As a result, there was no coherent system for delivering information to the management, and any request for information required department managers to collect data both from the information system and manually on spreadsheets on a case-to-case basis. The administration knew that something was amiss with the labor costs as they were pretty high. Still, they could not pinpoint the reasons or establish a trail of accountability using the available information system. Due to persistent losses and the inability to do anything about it, the management sold the business.

The new management that took over the company in October 2015 had been operating their family-owned businesses for decades. They started their business in India, owning a plastic manufacturing business that they had been running for generations. They migrated to Pakistan in 1975 and entered the textile and plastic industries, where they operated multiple companies, including one with the exact nature of business as Pak Packages. Their extensive experience in the industry made them confident that they could turn around the loss-making company.

They kept a similar organizational structure as the previous management with family members who were also shareholders on the Board of Directors, one of them being the Chief Executive Officer. Since the packaging industry operates on very slim margins, the previous management had focused on growth and increase in sales. Information systems had taken a backseat. Expenditure on a sound information system was considered an unnecessary expense that would increase the costs of the products without a corresponding increase in sales.

The result was an in-house developed information system comprising separate systems for production, finance, and human resources. These systems lack integration. As a result, there were always differences between the information generated from each system that was reconciled manually.

However, such reconciliations presented their challenges due to the organization's culture. The organization had a "closed-door" culture where departments were reluctant to share information. Each department considered itself an independent entity instead of being part of a single organization. The heads of departments were considered absolute authorities for their departments and reportable only to the CEO and there was no "internal customer" concept at work. This situation resulted in each department looking after its interests instead of working towards the organization's growth. A lack of an integrated information system helped foster this culture by allowing department heads to keep critical information under their control.

Due to this, it had become almost impossible to reconcile any data being generated by any of the information systems except where the CEO directly intervened to acquire some information and have it reconciled. It also presented a severe hindrance to the operation of the finance department as its role inherently required dependency on data generated by various departments with no way to verify its authenticity.

The developer of the information systems left the company in 2013. Since there was no IT department, maintenance of the systems fell squarely on the departments using them. Since the systems had been in use for a long time, the front-end users could perform routine operations. However, none of the employees understood the inner workings of the systems, so there was no way to update the system in line with the latest developments as the business grew. Some minor changes in configurations were possible via the trial-and-error method. However, no logs were maintained for any changes to the system, and senior employees would make changes as they deemed fit to manage their operations. Where any situation required information the system could not generate, there was no choice but to maintain the relevant data for generating that information on spreadsheets and even physical registers. As the new CEO said, "It was a recipe for disaster."

The Fraud

Tasked with pulling the company out of losses, Danish started digging into the financial numbers. It was apparent that expenditure for direct labor had increased substantially over the years, disproportionately to the increase in sales. As he analyzed the trend of increase in expenses for direct wages, he noticed that labor hours and, therefore, the total expense for wages had increased sharply from 2014 without a corresponding increase in production of one of its divisions, WPP (Exhibit 2). This situation occurred soon after the developer who developed and maintained the human resource management system resigned. The human resource department received complete discretion to modify the system as they wanted. He realized that a detailed investigation into the system was required.

The Head of Human Resources was reluctant to answer the CFO's queries and allow him to investigate, as was the deep-set culture of the organization. Therefore, the CEO provided the CFO and the Head of Internal Audit with complete authority and autonomy to do whatever it took to investigate the matter and get to the bottom of it.

Their investigation highlighted glaring deficiencies in the HR system. There were no validation checks in the system. An employee could be added to the payroll with the same CNIC number multiple times. Further, since shift rosters were manual, the same employee could be recorded as having worked numerous shifts on the same day while having worked only a single shift.

There was also a lack of segregation of duties. The human resource department was responsible for maintaining the information system, adding new employees, and disbursing salaries, making the situation ripe for cooperation between employees. While an RFID system was in place to mark the attendance of employees, the human resource department was responsible for issuing new RFID cards. There were no checks to prevent the unauthorized issuance of cards.

Further, scanning an RFID card did not guarantee an employee's physical presence, as anybody having physical custody of the card could mark attendance. The CFO and Head of Internal Audit knew, courtesy of their experience, that usually, in organizations that use RFID systems for marking attendance, an employee of the administration department is always present to keep an eye on the scanner to ensure that each person scans only one card. Further, it is common practice that a buzzer sounds or light is activated when any card is scanned, alerting the people nearby in case a single person scans multiple cards. This mechanism, while not fool-proof, is usually adequate.

However, no such mechanism was in place at Pak Packages, and there was nobody present to monitor the RFID scanner and deter employees from scanning the RFID cards of multiple employees.

The CFO and Head of Internal Audit interviewed several employees across various departments. They also set up whistleblowing boxes and an email ID to encourage employees with knowledge of the matter to come forward anonymously and without going through multiple levels of hierarchy. The interviews and whistleblowing pointed towards collusion between human resource department employees, including the Head of Human Resources.

The audit report concluded that the weaknesses of the information system, coupled with the lack of segregation of duties, allowed the Head of Human Resources to conspire with his subordinates to create ghost employees and fictitiously work the same people in multiple shifts to misappropriate funds.

The Response

The CFO and Head of Internal Audit presented the internal audit report to the Chief Executive Officer. The report recommended that the Company replace its entire Information Management System and procure a new system from a renowned vendor. The matter was eventually escalated to the Board of Directors.

Despite the available evidence, the head of Human Resources refused to accept the charges. The Board concluded that there was substantial evidence of collusion by employees, including the Head of Human Resources, and it was impossible to determine precisely how many employees were compromised. Consequently, the Board terminated the entire Human Resource Department immediately. The Board agreed with the CFO's recommendation that a new integrated Management Information System was required. However, they argued that implementing such a system across the entire company would require a long time, whereas the Human Resources information system had to be replaced immediately.

Further, the company had been operating on a very unsophisticated and outdated system for a long time, and the employees were used to it. Additionally, many employees had developed manual workarounds as an alternative to information systems. Therefore, the Board members were doubtful that the employees of the Company were prepared or capable of such a huge endeavor and were worried that such a radical change would lead to significant resistance. That was something the Board was not prepared to risk at the moment. There had already been massive upheavals due to the change of management. The firing of the Human Resource department would add to uncertainty and reduce the morale of the entire workforce. In such a situation, a complete change in how the organization works by introducing a new information system across the company could push the people to the breaking point. That could have severe consequences in the form of mass resignations, strikes that could shut down the operations, and even deliberate sabotage of the new system by frustrated employees.

Therefore, it was decided that, for the time being, only the Human Resource Management System would be replaced. The entire Human Resource Department was already being built from scratch, so there wouldn't be resistance from within the Department as the new team would be working on the new system from the beginning.

The new Board was aware of the importance of a sound information system. After the existing fiasco, they had already seen that failure to implement a proper information system had resulted in the Company not achieving its business objectives and going into losses. Therefore, it was decided that the new system be procured from a mainstream and experienced vendor and should have all the features of a modern human resource management system to protect the interests of the Company.

Further, it was decided to establish a dedicated Information Technology department with a Head of Information Technology. The Head of IT would report directly to the CEO. The IT department would be responsible for implementing a new human resource management system, its maintenance, and security and providing technical support across the organization. As part of its long-term objectives, this department would also implement a complete ERP that would integrate all the organization's functions, including the new human resource management system.

This situation led to the appointment of Mr. Fawad Bukhari as the Head of Information Technology. Mr. Fawad had an experience of over six years in implementing information systems while working at one of the largest IT consulting firms in Pakistan. Mr. Umar Mirza, a graduate with over five years of experience working at a large multinational organization as a Human Resource Business Partner, was appointed the Head of Human Resources. He was tasked with building the entire Human resources department from scratch, training them in the organization's procedures, and integrating them with the other departments. That was a daunting task considering the closed culture of other departments and the fact that he was new to the Organization.

The Board of Directors also faced another key decision critical to selecting and implementing the new information system: who should they appoint to lead the process. The newly appointed Head of Information Technology could be a logical choice because implementing the system was part of his job description and because he had the technical knowledge and industry connections to make it happen. It would also make it easier to get the Head of Information Technology to "own" the system during day-to-day operations and while implementing an ERP later on.

However, the Chief Financial Officer had worked with the Board of Directors for a long time, even before they took over Pak Packages. They knew well about his competence, capabilities, and leadership skills. Further, in the wake of the ongoing crisis, they wanted someone they could trust to lead this critical task. In addition, after his extensive investigation to uncover the fraud, the CFO was already familiar with the workings of the organization and all the practical issues faced by the human resource function. Further, Danish also had experience working with information systems.

The Board wanted someone who not only knew the technical aspects of implementation but also how the entire business operates and how decisions regarding the information system would impact the business. They wanted somebody who knew other department heads to be able to take them on board while implementing the system. Further, they did not want to overburden the new Head of Information Technology with business complications and organizational politics so that he could focus better on the technical aspects of implementing the new system. Therefore, they entrusted this task to the CFO. The CFO created and led a team comprising the newly appointed Head of IT and Head of HR to search for and implement a new Human Resource Management System.

Search for a New HRMS

The CFO, the Head of Human Resources, and the Head of Information Technology drafted the Human Resources Policy and standard operating procedures. The following points were part of these documents about the requirements that the new system would have to fulfill:

- Every employee's computerized National Identity Card (CNIC) will be the employee ID in the new system and a primary field in the employee master table. That requirement would conclusively prevent any duplication of CNIC numbers.

- No user can enter the CNIC number into the system manually. Instead, a barcode reader would scan and upload the CNIC into the system to prevent false CNIC numbers from being entered into the database.

- Attendance should be marked using face recognition and not through the RFID System.

- Biometric verification of every employee will be mandatory and utilized at the time of disbursement of wages.

- There must be proper segregation of duties and approval of leaves, overtime, induction of new employees, etc., that the information system should enforce

With these guidelines, the team started to search for a new human resource management system. They asked their colleagues at various companies about the systems they were using and discussed whether they met the requirements outlined in the HR Policy and standard operating procedures. Further, they posted on LinkedIn to invite vendors to express their interest in providing the required solution to the company. They received expressions of interest from several companies, including those based outside Pakistan.

After extensive searches, deliberations, and recommendations from other companies using human resource management systems, three systems were shortlisted. License costs and annual maintenance fees for all these systems were more or less comparable, and all these systems supported roster management. Further, all these systems had the option of being integrated with other systems, which was critical since the implementation of a new ERP was planned for the future.

Timetrax: This system was in use at several organizations. Installation of this system would require purchasing a new server as it was incompatible with the company's existing hardware. Online and on-site technical support was available. However, it was decided that the new system to be implemented must acquire data about the CNIC of employees directly by scanning the barcode on the CNIC. Further, it should not be possible for a CNIC to be repeated. These validation checks were not available on Timetrax. Therefore, this option was eventually dropped.

PayPeople: This system was also in use across the industry. The system was cloud-based, eliminating the need to have physical servers at the Company's premises. It had all the validation checks required by the new HR policy and standard operating procedures. In addition, it had advanced human resource management features, including management of training of employees, analysis of productivity, and an online portal allowing employees to view and manage their information. However, no onsite technical support was available as the vendor company was based in Lahore. The Head of IT was worried that if they ran into any major problem after implementation, it would be difficult and time-consuming to diagnose and resolve the issue. Therefore, it was decided not to move forward with this option.

FlowHCM: This Python-based system was used by some of Pakistan's largest and most renowned multinational organizations. It fulfilled all the requirements of the HR policy and standard operating procedures regarding validation checks. Its personnel could physically visit the company's premises to deploy it and provide technical assistance in the future since they were based in the city. Instead of using an RFID system, FlowHCM used biometric identification. It allowed the use of both facial recognition and fingerprint recognition. That would eliminate the chances of marking employees' attendance when they were absent.

Further, it used barcode readers to scan the CNICs of employees and input them directly into the system. Payment of wages to workers required them to scan their fingerprints at the human resources department to acquire a system-generated token. They could then submit this token to the finance department for their paycheck. The reduction of manual intervention and the segregation of payment responsibilities was desirable for the CFO and the new Head of Human resources.

The Head of IT was also very comfortable with this system. While Timetrax and PayPeople maintained separate databases in the attendance machines and on the central servers/cloud, FlowHCM maintained only a single database on the cloud. That would reduce the possibility of compromising data integrity due to synchronization errors and reduce data security risks associated with databases being directly accessible at multiple locations. Further, FlowHCM would be providing its proprietary hardware. Both Timetrax and PayPeople would be using third-party providers. That would make it much easier to implement FlowHCM by preventing compatibility issues during deployment and when the hardware/software needs to be updated.

There was one downside to this, too. FlowHCM would provide all the hardware, resulting in a vendor lock-in. In the future, there was a risk that the vendor might exploit this to charge high prices for replacement hardware. Further, if the required hardware were unavailable, the company would have no choice but to wait as long as it took for the vendor to replenish its inventory. In addition, keeping the database in the cloud introduced its own risk of reliance on the cloud service provider. The company would have to trust the integrity, security, and reliability of the cloud service provider that wasn't even present in Pakistan. However, considering all the benefits and the excellent reputation of FlowHCM and its vendor, it was decided that these risks were acceptable. It was, therefore, decided to go forward with FlowHCM. (Exhibit 3)

New System's Implementation

FlowHCM's vendor provided a complete solution with the hardware and software and would be deploying the system at the company's premises so the management did not have to worry. However, the CFO and the team know that the transition would require great care and organization, especially in the case of data collection.

The firing of the entire human resource department, while creating uncertainty and a bit of demoralization among the company's ranks,, had one advantage. Having seen the strict and decisive action by the top management, every department was eager to cooperate with implementing the new system, which overcame the traditional reluctance to collaborate with other departments.

The CFO chaired a series of meetings to develop an implementation plan. The CFO knew that to implement the new system successfully; he would need to take all departments on board as part of change management. That would create a sense of ownership in all the departments, and giving them a say in the matter would also raise morale and invest the people in the successful implementation of the new system. After all, no department would want the system to fail after having created a joint implantation plan and putting in extensive efforts in implementation. Further, a new human resource management system would affect all the employees, not just the Human Resource Department, so it would only be logical for all departments to expect a say.

Therefore, all the heads of departments and general managers were present. Further, each department was directed to appoint one manager to act as coordinator and use their business knowledge to act as business analysts for assisting with implementing the system. Therefore, these managers were also present in all the meetings. Further, system analysts from FlowHCM's vendor were also present. A phase-wise approach was developed.

Phase 1 – Infrastructure deployment and training

The first logical step was to deploy the hardware and software. It was also the easiest step. All facial recognition attendance machines and fingerprint recognition machines were deployed. Necessary software was installed on the user's computers. Once everything was in place, the vendor and the users extensively tested the system for bugs.

While testing, some practical issues were also discovered. For one, it was found that one of the face recognition machines could not correctly identify faces during nighttime as flood lights shone directly into the employees' faces while standing in front of the facial recognition machine. This issue was overlooked during installation, which was done during the day. That prompted an adjustment in the angle of the attendance machine.

Several training sessions were held with all employees during system deployment to take them on board and familiarize them with the system. Sessions were conducted by department heads, focusing on employee benefits to get them invested in the system's success. They highlighted that a reduction in manual work and verification would result in earlier disbursement of salaries and prevent errors in calculations that would occasionally occur previously. Further, it was highlighted that the employees could access their data, including the status of leaves, and apply for leaves online. Previously, the employees would have to run after their department heads to get manual leave forms signed. With the new system, not only could the employees file the leaves online, but the system could also track how long it took for their line managers to approve (or deny) the leaves, encouraging them to dispose of the leave decisions on time.

The vendor's personnel held sessions focused on using the hardware and the software and included live on-field demonstrations and training videos. One of the vendor's representatives was always at the company's premises to resolve any issues and respond to any questions the users might have.

The CEO also knew that they were attempting to implement a new system and a fundamental change in the organization's culture. He planned on using this project to break down the walls between departments by forcing them to cooperate and coordinate. Further, the employees had previously been treating the information systems as a hindrance to their operations due to various limitations of the old systems. The CEO wanted the employees to realize that proper maintenance of information systems was critical to the business's operation and the users' facilitation. He, therefore, frequently visited all the departments to follow up on the status of the implementation of the system and also to address the employees and inform them of the importance of information systems. That was also part of his plan to prepare the people for implementing a full-fledged ERP in the future.

Phase 2 – Data collection

This phase was considered the most sensitive. The CFO and Head of HR knew they couldn't rely on any of the data in the previous system as it was all considered compromised. Relevant data was collected jointly by the IT department and vendor's personnel. CNICs of all employees were scanned via barcode readers, and the biometric machines captured their facial images and fingerprints. The barcode readers provided the employees' names and CNIC numbers, which were uploaded live into the database.

The remaining data (for example, the date of birth) was acquired from respective departments, and the manual records were available with the Human Resources Department and compiled in spreadsheets. All this data was verified from physical documents in the presence of representatives from the Finance and Internal Audit departments. After verification, the data entry operators of the Human Resource Department would upload the data into the system. A report containing all the details of the employees whose records were recently uploaded would be generated from the system at regular intervals. The Human Resource Manager would then compare it with the spreadsheets given initially to the data entry operators to correct any errors.

Phase 3: Implementation

After gathering and uploading all the data onto the system, the system was made live one department at a time. In case of failure, the problem would affect only one department instead of hindering operations across the entire organization.

Since it had already been established that the old system would no longer be used, the CFO and Head of Human Resources recognized that payroll was the most critical function needed for smooth functioning, even if there were problems during implementation of the new system. Regardless of any implementation difficulties, the Company needed to ensure that the employees' salaries were disbursed correctly and on time.

It was decided that the finance department would maintain the necessary data of all employees for processing payroll for three months on spreadsheets in parallel with the new system. That was a very time-consuming task as the attendance status of all employees had to be collected from all departments and verified manually by the Finance Department. Further, these spreadsheets would need reconciliation with the data produced by the new system to ensure that the new system was functioning correctly.

Some human resources were temporarily transferred to the Finance Department for workload management. Further, specific non-essential tasks were identified, and it was decided to suspend or delay these tasks temporarily for the duration of the implementation.

The Resistance

Before the implementation began, several training sessions were held to prepare the workforce to transition to the new system. Coordinators/business analysts were appointed in each department to ensure a smooth transition and all departments' involvement and ownership. The CFO and the CEO were confident that due to all these measures, there would be minimal resistance to implementing the new system. However, once the implementation began, the Chief Operating Officers and the General Managers of all the businesses approached the CFO and the CEO with complaints.

They were worried that the new system was creating too much unrest and uncertainty in the workforce. The workforce, mainly comprised of low-skilled and low-paid resources, had become used to the relaxed (and lack of) controls in the old system and could earn substantially by charging excessive overtime by working inefficiently. That had been going on for years. The stringent biometric-based controls ensured that only workers physically present would be paid overtime.

Further, the managers were not used to the level of accountability that the new system established for overtime. The new system could generate daily reports of attendance, overtime, average normal hourly rate, and average overtime hourly rates for each shop for each business. That meant that the CFO and the CEO could now question the Chief Operating Officers, the General Managers, and the line managers about overtime in their respective areas by comparing overtime hours with trends in previous months.

Further, the finance department could calculate the total hours worked at each shop. Using the number of units produced and the standard hours required to make those units, the finance department calculated the number of production hours required and compared it with the actual hours worked at each shop. The finance department would send a "Labor Productivity Report" to the CEO daily showing the hours worked at each shop, the number of standard hours required, the excess hours worked, and the extra cost incurred. The report would also show the per unit labor cost of all shops for each day over the last thirty days plotted on a line graph highlighting anomalies at a glance. All Chief Operating Officers we/re required to explain reasons for excessive overtime to the CEO fortnightly.

This accountability put severe pressure on the Chief Operating Officers to cut overtime, eventually cascading to line managers. The line managers, therefore, began to establish strict schedules and production targets for each worker and made floor supervisors strictly monitor the workforce to minimize the wastage of time.

Whenever a worker resigned, the shop manager approached the Human Resources Department for a replacement. The Human Resource Department would request the Finance Department for the Labor Productivity Report for the respective shop for the last thirty days. If the report shows excessive hours worked at the shop, any new hiring would require approval from the CFO, who would only permit the hiring if the shop manager could provide sufficient justification.

The Chief Operating Officers explained to the CFO and CEO that this sudden increase in monitoring of the workforce and the resulting reduction in overtime created unrest amongst the workforce. Most of the company's production workforce was comprised of low-paid workers. Even small reductions in their paychecks resulted in a significant effect on their earnings. As a result, the Chief Operating Officers and their managers feared that the workers would go on strike or resign in masses, resulting in production loss. They also explained that many line managers, under high pressure, were close to quitting. They recommended the CEO delay implementation of the new system. The CFO and CEO knew that any delay would probably turn permanent. No matter what steps they took to facilitate implantation, there would always be resistance as it involved a major cultural change in the Company and reduced earnings.

The CEO then called a special meeting of all department heads and managers. He informed them that the Company could not survive with the current payroll costs, which had made the products of the Company highly uncompetitive. He categorically told them that the new system and its accountability would be implemented at any cost. He informed them that all efforts were being made to facilitate implementation. In case of any technical problems, they could refer to their department's coordinating managers, who could escalate them to the vendor's implementation team for a swift resolution. Explicitly addressing the managers, the CEO explained that going through the system implementation process and analyzing and improving their workers' productivity was an excellent opportunity for their professional development as managers. He also informed them that the resulting performance bonuses would benefit everyone if the company made profits.

Although there were mixed opinions, the people realized there was no going back as the CEO was determined. The company was ready to bear all consequences, including temporary loss of production. That effectively ended the resistance.

Results

The system was extensively tested before implementation. The employees were taken on board and trained to use the new system. Further, the system was implemented one department at a time and continuously reconciled with spreadsheets maintained at the finance department. Despite some initial resistance, the deployment of the system went smoothly. Right at the end of the first month of complete implementation across all the departments, Danish, Umar, and Fawad looked over the new numbers for payroll in delight. Despite annual increments and the addition of employees, payroll costs had declined by almost 15% over the previous month.

At the end of 2016, the total payroll cost stood at PKR 376 million compared to PKR 421 million in 2015. That represented a decline of 10.7% despite the addition of employees and annual increments. Further, the possibility of integrating FlowHCM with other systems also opened up many opportunities that the Company took advantage of occasionally. For example, (fast-forwarding to the year 2022) it has allowed the Company to sign a contract with the vendor for a mobile app called "Abhi" (translated as "Now" in English). The vendor of this app also has a contract with the vendor of FlowHCM to make the integration between their systems possible. The app allows employees to access their FlowHCM account via mobile phones. With a single tap, the employees can obtain advance salary for fifteen days and their monthly payroll directly into their bank accounts. That benefited the employees and reduced the chances of payment to incorrect persons (and therefore fraud) by eliminating manual intervention and reducing the workload at the Finance and Human Resource departments.

The Way Forward

The previous management made the fatal mistake of ignoring management information systems while their business flourished. As a result, things went out of their control, and the company suffered losses due to fraud. Investment in acquiring a new information system and professional deployment enabled the new management to turn the company around, initiate a positive cultural change, and make the Company profitable once again.

Do you think the management took the correct approach to select and implementing the new Human Resource Management System? Do you believe this implementation has prepared the employees for an ERP?

Exhibit 1
Organizational Structure of Pak Packages Ltd.

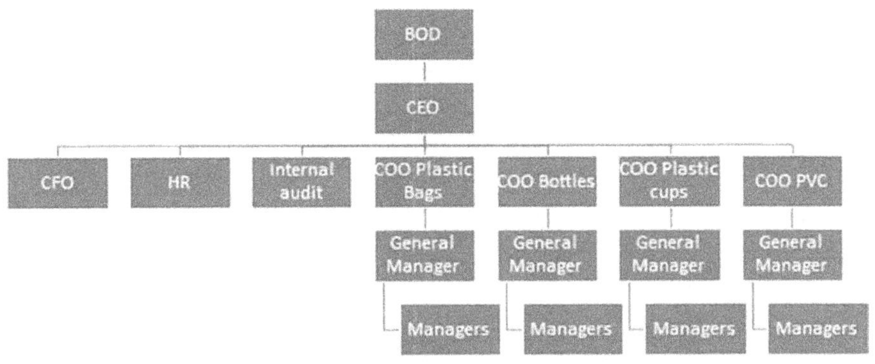

Exhibit 2
Key Performance Indicators

| | | | | | | | RS '000' | |
| DEPT. | WPP | | RIGID BOTTLE | | EPS CUPS | | PVC | |
YEARS	PRODUCTION(KGS)	WAGES EXP(RS)	PRODUCTION(KGS)	WAGES EXP(RS)	PRODUCTION(KGS)	WAGES EXP(RS)	PRODUCTION(KGS)	WAGES EXP(RS)
2010	127,364.00	129,311.00	38,209.20	38,793.90	11,462.76	12,332.00	3,438.83	4,103.00
2011	140,100.40	169,423.00	42,030.12	43,449.17	12,952.92	13,811.84	3,817.10	4,595.36
2012	154,110.44	198,433.00	46,233.13	48,663.07	14,636.80	15,469.26	4,236.98	5,146.80
2013	169,521.48	237,903.00	50,856.45	54,502.64	16,539.58	17,325.57	4,703.05	5,764.42
2014	186,473.63	319,732.00	55,942.09	61,042.95	18,689.73	19,404.64	5,220.38	6,456.15
2015	205,121.00	324,413.00	61,536.30	68,368.11	21,119.39	21,733.20	5,794.63	7,230.89
2016	225,633.10	267,394.00	67,689.93	76,572.28	23,864.91	24,341.18	6,432.03	8,098.59
2017	248,196.40	278,533.00	74,458.92	85,760.95	26,967.36	27,262.12	7,139.56	9,070.43

WPP DEPT.

BOTTLE DEPT

Exhibit 3
Comparison of Available Options

Description	Timetrax	PayPeople	FlowHCM
Can be used on existing server	No Rs 900,000	Not required	Not required
Cloud	No	Yes	Yes
License cost	Rs 700,000	USD 1,100 per master user (3 needed) Plus USD 500 per data entry operator (8 needed)	Rs 800,000
License renewal	Rs 200,000 per year	20% of cost per year	Rs 250,000 per year
SLA cost	Rs 100,000 per year	10% per year	Rs 150,000 per year
Peripheral devices	Third party	Third party	FlowHCM's own
Attendance machines	RFID	RFID	Face recognition and biometric
Attendance and server databases	Separate	Separate	Single (only on server)
Required validation checks	**No**	**Yes**	**Yes**
Advanced HRM (eg. Training, productivity, online portal)	No	Yes	Yes
Online technical support	Yes	Yes	Yes
On-site technical support	**Yes**	**No**	**Yes**
Rostar management	**Yes**	**Yes**	**Yes**

ENGRO CORPORATION'S ONE SAP PROJECT

Sumaira Sultan, Mohammad Ali, and Sheeraz Shaukat of Karachi School for Business and Leadership (KSBL) prepared this case under the supervision of Dr. Amir Manzoor. The case was prepared solely to provide material for class discussion. The authors do not intend to illustrate either effective or ineffective handling of a managerial situation. Certain names and other identifying information have been disguised to protect confidentiality.

Mr. Khalil, VP Group Head Engro Corporation for SAP Transformation, was sitting in his office drafting names for SAP Quality Awards and was reflecting on how almost 51,000 person-hours have helped streamline and unify the group systems and ensure Engro's leadership commitment to transparency, data intelligence, efficiency, simplicity, and accuracy.

Conditions prevalent before the project's inception included an environment with no unified system or consolidated master data. There was no end-to-end SAP process. Only a few modules of ERP were being used. Hence, Mr. Khalil saw tremendous room to implement system-based controls and implement a system that was not people-dependent but system-led and governed per current best industry practices, which will cater to front-line needs, reduce workload, and help swiftly escalate pain point resolution.

Company History

Engro Corporation Limited is a conglomerate headquartered in Karachi. Founded as a fertilizer business in 1965, it is one of the largest companies in the country that employs over 2,600 individuals across the Group and has operations in a diverse range of businesses. With a core purpose of solving the pressing issues in Pakistan, Engro operates through the following four verticals: Food and agriculture, Energy and related Infrastructure, Petrochemicals, and Telecommunication Infrastructure.

Engro Corporation has come a long way since its inception as a fertilizer manufacturing and marketing company to emerging into the largest diversified conglomerate in Pakistan with Engro Corporation as the holding company (See

Exhibit 1). Significant Engro subsidiaries include Engro Fertilizers, Engro Eximp Agriproducts, Engro Eximp FZE, Engro Energy, Engro Powergen Qadirpur, Engro Powergen Thar, Engro Elengy Terminal, Engro Vopak Terminal, Engro Polymer & Chemicals, and Engro Enfrashare. (Exhibit 2).

Engro Corporation provides world-class governance through capital allocation, corporate performance management, people development, and deployment. The company offers conglomerate value addition for its subsidiary businesses through Centralized Strategy, Technology, Procurement, M&A, Treasury and legal, Government and Public Relations, talent access, and financial capital.

Information Systems at Engro Corp.

The company runs the SAP R/3 version and wants to upgrade to SAP HANA to standardize and unify functions across group companies. In the words of Mr. Khalil, the initial intention was, "I feel the system should deliver a common set of business processes, standard master data, and quality information in a timely fashion, all of which should improve the speed of decision making."

Engro Corp and related companies were facing unique challenges and dire need of innovative changes in ERP systems to ensure business excellence and continuity of ever-expanding business operations. Hence, this led to an in-depth analysis of Engro's current systems and associated challenges. These challenges included UNSPSC classification for detailed spend visibility and analysis in the supply chain and redesigning the entire procurement structure to leverage SAP best practices. That, in turn, laid the foundation for centralized procurement to leverage group buying opportunities.

Senior management can benefit immensely from the Planning feature available in SAP BPC by encouraging automation, transparency, accuracy, and governance in corporate planning and enabling precise decision-making. Faster month-end closings with 98% accuracy will allow holding companies, especially Engro Corp, early access to subsidiaries and associates' financial statements.

Complex product costing design involves amalgamating PP-MM-CO & material ledger and redefining MRP and ROP formulas to eradicate excessive ordering. One of the primary factors considered during the choice of solution was consolidating finances across 30+ legal entities using BPC. BPC was initially implemented on ECC 6 and then rolled out on SAP S/4HANA.

Information on COPA reports enabled profitability analysis on multiple dimensions and made sound business decisions. That included the deployment of Fiori in 106 sales warehouses, which helped mitigate connectivity risks and helped business continuity, especially in remote locations.

Innovative areas stem from business needs, and Engro's management team must ensure business needs are fulfilled correctly. All external consultants were interviewed by the IT head and CFOs to ensure that they have sufficient experience to understand the complexity of Engro's business and are the right fit for the project. The senior leadership performed a detailed analysis of hiring the right implementation partners. After visiting clients for feedback & also obtaining feedback from SAP Pakistan, Engro decided to hire EY as the implementation partner.

Detail of the Solution

All business requirements were incorporated into the system to make it more effective and efficient. The system should be effective enough to improve the organization's productivity and fulfill the vision and mission of the organization. In many organizations, if any other system is introduced, many heads of the company tend to lower their workforce to lessen or control their expenses, e.g., salaries. So, after the decision to implement the new system, the business users need to be educated that their jobs will be safe. On the other hand, after implementing the system in the organization, their skills will be used for analysis, creative thinking, decision making, adding value and problem-solving rather than manual work. This task was more time-consuming and energy-consuming. That will not only be beneficial for the organization but also benefit individuals' career and professional development.

A full dress rehearsal (FDR) was conducted with SITF with actual system data and authorizations. Furthermore, end-to-end processes were executed in the presence of the project team to ensure smooth integration between modules and, if error and mishandling occur, could be resolved immediately with the help of professionals. End users play a vital role in the implementation and succession of any system because, in the end, they are the ones who would use the system first and give feedback to the department for maintenance of the system to ensure the maximum output of the system. Business SITF provided training to all the end users. This training helped the end users and the organization to make the most of the system in which they have added so much planning, investment, team, time, and research.

All licensing requirements were fulfilled to avoid possible legal issues impacting the system's productivity and reliability. The training was crucial not only for the end users but also for the other teams that were associated with the system. After go-live, the requisite SLAs to ensure support by EY were ensured and approved by Steercom. Mock Runs & transactional data readiness were ensured through Full Dress Rehearsals. For example, cost estimate simulations for all products were done on the Production System before Go-Live. That ensured all master data was complete & correct. The professional teams were with them all the time to handle all the bugs in the systems.

As the training completed with the site implementation task force, which was very productive and fruitful in understanding the system's objectives, the team made the material for later use. So, to ensure the best result of the training, all training material have been delivered to End Users through SAP Enable Now so that they can review all the content and important information after the sessions and make the most out of the system.

After completing training and ensuring all the needful was done, the confirmation from all relevant heads in the BPR Committee to commence go-live took place. In an organization, all the departmental heads must be on one page to get the maximum output and ensure productivity and results for which the whole team worked hard. That is to confirm if any incident occurs during the go-live, everyone would know how to react and resolve the issue.

Implementation Plan

The project team's approach to stakeholder management used the ADKAR model. Table 1 depicts the elements of the ADKAR model and how this engagement model was effective in building rapport among the team and, most importantly, stakeholders affected by this change. Key stakeholders were engaged as part of the governance structure to ensure the process ran smoothly during the pre-implementation and implementation phases.

The ADKAR model

Table 1: ADKAR Model

Phase	Explanation
Awareness	Announcing the need for an end-to-end integrated ERP system, talking about the current challenges entities face, and explaining the reasoning behind the massive transformation
Desire	Gauge through feedback business users' reactions to the change. Identify and establish a Site Implementation Task Force that shall champion the change and address the concerns of business users.
Knowledge	Provide training in 2 iterations, address any skill gaps, and share resources that users can reference.
Ability	Full dress rehearsal before going live
Reinforcement	Monitor the change and use feedback, rewards, and recognition to encourage employees to continue to use the new system.

Key Stakeholders and Governance Structure

For successful system implementation, project governance, and maximum ROI, three separate committees were formed to look after the different stages of project deployment. For details on these teams, see Exhibit 3.

1. Steering Committee (STEERCOM) chaired by Group CEO and Chairman Ghias Khan to provide leadership oversight, guidance, and objectives, to confirm success criteria, review processes, and provide crucial approvals on the major development plan of the project.

2. Business Process Re-Engineering Committee (BPR), which the Group CFO chaired. This committee's purpose was to confirm direction and objectives, confirm success criteria, review processes, and provide approvals.

3. The Project Team comprised Engro's core user team (representatives from all departments) and the service provider's team. The core function of this committee was to design and test the system as per the Business Process Documents.

SITF Nomination, Orientation, and Engagement Plan

The Site Implementation Taskforce (SITF) was formed to work alongside the One SAP team in administering, managing, and enriching the implementation of the One SAP program in their respective entities. The following roles were defined.

Change Agents were the champions of change and played out the steps necessary to realize One SAP's vision.

Deployment assured timely, well-spread, and thorough implementation of One SAP project across their respective entities.

Business Risk identified business risks, created mitigating plans, and managed risk response activities.

Master Data assisted in aligning, managing, and consolidating data to create standardization across their respective entities.

As the One SAP implementation phase went along, SITF got more and more responsibilities, with the One SAP project team relieved from the implementation until entirely in the post hyper care period (Exhibit 5).

Implementation Process

A comprehensive cut-over strategy was developed in collaboration with EY. The strategy involved planning, executing, and monitoring a successful Go-Live. Full Dress Rehearsal (FDR) was conducted to ensure all end-to-end processes with authorizations were in place. A blackout (freeze) period was agreed upon with the approval of each company's Engro executive committee and CFOs.

It was decided that all business and financial processes in the system would be handled manually under the approved BCP so that data could be transferred to the newly deployed system. Finalization of a predefined cutover date from where onwards, new operating procedures/processes come into effect, and pre-go live systems/portals will become redundant. Operating instructions, in the form of a user manual, must be available during the handholding and Post-go-live support process. The go / No-Go decision was based on a documented criterion where all critical activities were required before the system was marked as production-ready and monitored live (Exhibit 4).

To closely follow up on this critical implementation phase, the company decided to have meetings at regular intervals for close follow-up on issues. Meeting agendas are clear and concise, with post-meeting minutes shared with the attendees to track the issues' progress.

Meeting	Objectives	Materials	Frequency	Attendees
Steering Committee	Provide leadership/oversight/ guidance and make critical decisions.	Steering Committee Presentation	Monthly	Committee members
BPR Committee	Provide leadership/oversight/ guidance, make critical decisions/ flag challenges and risks.	BPR Committee Presentation	Fortnightly	Committee members
Project Status Meetings	Discuss workstream status, progress against milestones, and any issues or delays.	Status report and workstream status report	Weekly	Project Managers, Business leads, and Workstream leads
Workstream Status Meetings	Discuss day-to-day status of tasks and progress towards workstream milestones	Tracker	Daily/Weekly	Business Lead and Workstream team

Project Team Motivation and Progress

VP had made a tremendous achievement in getting the best out of the project team. All critical business users were identified before initiating One SAP project from various entities and engaged in the project right from the beginning. The roles and responsibilities of stakeholders were clearly defined and empowering. VP had instructed and made it mandatory for leaders and business managers from the group to use One SAP as their principal objective for the year, based on which their performance appraisal was gauged and marked.

Business users were educated on how their skills will be of assistance for analysis rather than manual data entry work and to keep the motivational level high of the project team, a dedicated custom-built workspace keeping in mind the nature of the project and the scope was designed to promote the culture of design thinking, openness, transparency, and the will to innovate.

In addition, constant interaction with the Steering and BPR Committee, including the CEOs and CFOs of all entities chaired by the Group CEO and CFO, proved significant learning for the project team and the group. Project bonuses were introduced and linked to timely project completion, where high achievers and members with innovative ideas to incorporate in One SAP were recognized with additional bonuses. Giveaways were distributed among SITF members for their immense support for the One SAP project team.

The project progress was tracked and communicated to the entire One SAP team in fortnightly sessions with the One SAP Project Lead. In these sessions, progress, issues, and challenges were discussed. Regular updates (such as videos of senior leadership describing major milestones achieved) were provided at the workplace to encourage out-of-the-box thinking. End-user surveys were introduced to gauge user engagement and take necessary actions if required. This approach was helpful in proactive data gathering on issues and proved to be instrumental in meeting project deadlines.

Implementation Team

One SAP and Business team was required to define the scope, processes, and training manuals and to conduct necessary UAT and training. The primary responsibility of the Implementation Team was to ensure that the system was configured as per business requirements and addressed all pain points. Additionally, a Site Implementation Task Force was developed, comprising business users to work alongside the project team to design and deploy the system in their respective entities.

A comprehensive UAT plan and test cases were developed. Users were required to test all scenarios. Before going live, a full dress rehearsal (FDR) of end-to-end processes was done with business users from multiple functions to assist them in adapting new system processes. However, the acceptance was subject to quality review by EY Global on the implementation process.

Implementation Issues

Scale and Complexity of Business Transformation

Engro's One SAP project is a one-of-a-kind transformation journey of a conglomerate in Pakistan. Such a large-scale deployment of a conglomerate running businesses in 4 different verticals was never witnessed in Pakistan before. Being the first to undergo a massive transformation in the country was challenging. Hiring international consultants for BPC and Employee Central proved to play a vital role in combating this challenge. Onboarding EY Global with tremendous success stories and stringent compliance and processes was also a major step towards successful implementation. One SAP project, due to its complex nature and large-scale transformation project, building a dedicated project team of highly skilled and knowledgeable employees from all Engro entities was successful in creating a governance structure comprising of all CEOs, CFOs, Manufacturing, Supply Chain and Sales heads of all Engro entities was to cater and safeguard objectives of One SAP project. That led to extensive change management at all levels.

Standardization of Processes and Data

Before the implementation of SAP, all entities of Engro were adhering to their own business practices and data structures. To standardize all entities in One SAP business environment was a daunting task. However, many useful measures were taken due to the VP's sheer commitment in delivering this project. SITF members were motivated to align their business processes and practices as per the SAP standards. Strong change management was done at all levels where C-level executives were involved. An iterative training plan was developed to ensure that new standard processes were understood and followed. Users realized how One SAP would make the work process easy and transparent. Day-to-day tasks were automated so that users could focus on the actual job of why they are with Engro. Processes that required special attention and were important for entities were red-flagged and highlighted proactively. Separate regular workshops were conducted for these processes.

Need for Futuristic Design

Being Pakistan's leading company in multiple sectors, Engro is continuously exploring new business ventures. Implementing SAP at Engro involved seven legal entities in Wave 1 and 13 entities in Wave 2, which were quite diverse from one another. Engro's design needed to be futuristic enough to incorporate new businesses with different models. Therefore, the project team gave special attention to aligning the system with the requirements of all business models. Standard processes were implemented, and customization was not encouraged. Each process was benchmarked with companies with similar complex models like Engro, and regular sessions were held with senior leadership of Engro entities.

Overall Cut Over Strategy and Management

Data cleansing is an important aspect of all digital transformation and change. Data cleansing on the part of the business was lacking, i.e., Long Outstanding open POs and non-availability of Customer / Vendor-wise balance in various cases resulted in manual GLs. That seems to be the case for one of the group's entities, where humongous data transfer and subsequent transformation for a large manufacturing entity were done on MS Excel. Engro Fertilizers (EFERT) has been in existence for over 50 years.

Going live with seven legal entities was challenging to handle from a cut-over perspective. Extensive mapping was required for old to new vendors, storage locations, plants, warehouses, material codes, and other related issues. These challenges were mitigated by undertaking and providing training and extensive support to the business team on how to fill the templates as per the requirement of the new system. EY and One SAP Engro team conducted a comprehensive review to identify shortcomings in upload templates to avoid reuploading and wasting precious time.

PwC performed an independent review of entire cut-over templates to speed the process and provide support on data accuracy. To further facilitate the deadline of the One SAP project and to ensure operational readiness for go-live and run phase cutover timelines are also introduced in four major areas, i.e., Configuration readiness PRD system, Trail balance submission, ABAP object status cutovers, and master data submission cutover (Exhibit 6).

The following were considered as the pre-requisites of the Cut-over strategy:

- All business requirements have been incorporated into the system.

- Business users were educated that their job role would not be redundant and their skills would be used for analysis rather than manual work.

- Full dress rehearsal (FDR) was conducted with SITF with actual system data and authorizations. End-to-end processes were executed in the presence of the project team to ensure smooth integration between modules.

- Training of all the end users was completed by business SITF.

- Whether all licensing requirements have been met

- Whether all training materials have been delivered to end users.

- Furthermore, Post-Go-Live organization, i.e., the IT team readiness and requisite SLAs to ensure support by EY, were ensured and in place. These were also approved by Steercom.

- Mock Runs & transactional data readiness were ensured through Full Dress Rehearsals and mock runs on the actual live system as well. For example, cost estimate simulations for all products were done on the Production System before Go-Live, which ensured all master data completeness & correctness.

- Confirmation from all relevant heads in the BPR Committee to commence go-live.

BPC implementation

That is the first-ever implementation of BPC on such a large scale in Pakistan; hence, there was a limited reference for consultation and guidance available in the local market. Many factors contributed to the complexity of the BPC implementation at Engro One SAP. There was 30 disparate Chart of Accounts with four reporting currencies: PKR, USD, NGN, and AED. Each entity within the group has different subsidiaries and associate structures. There are nine different SAP clients on 5 SAP ECC 6 version systems.

Steps were undertaken to mitigate these challenges. First, an international consultant was hired to inform and devise strategy. In order to engage competent and motivated resources for the project, a thorough training plan and change management plan were implemented. All the pre-work was done on mapping 30 separate charts of accounts. The major step taken to mitigate the challenges was implementing BPC first on ECC before rolling it out on SAP S/4 HANA.

Data Confidentiality

One SAP project at Engro comprised various listed legal entities operating in a diverse business segment, i.e., fertilizers, infrastructure, and terminal businesses. Engro is the market leader in most segments. Most companies in the group were listed on the Pakistan Stock Exchange, and few are on the PSX 100 Index. That added responsibility on the project team to ensure that all sensitive financial information is safeguarded and to ensure this mitigates the risk of data breach Engro information systems policy was enacted to ensure that data for development and quality assurance server shared with the consultant and end users will be till last published financial results.

All users who had access to financial information were added to the respective entity's Securities Exchange Commission of Pakistan ITR (insider trading register). Users were only allowed access to their specific company data with the approval of their respective data owners and later with the line managers. Non-disclosure agreements were signed with all external consultants to ensure all stakeholders were covered for safe data handling.

Data Migration in Employee Central

Legacy Data of around 1500 employees had to be enriched, cleansed, and uploaded on Employee Central Tools using specific formats as per compatibility. Configuring the system according to Engro-specific policies with the limitation that no customization was possible in Employee Central proved difficult. Integration of data with SAP S4 HANA data was a risky task. That was because S4 HANA was already live and running, and integration could override data in S4 HANA. Online UAT of 50 power users from business and later conducting online training for around 1500 employees given the fact that due to the pandemic, Engro was completely on the Work from the Home roster, making it more difficult to chase the team.

In order to tackle these issues, data was uploaded by the One SAP team for successful validation and then shared with consultants for upload to avoid delays. The One SAP team tried to find substitute solutions available with Employee Central (EC) to fulfill the need. They consulted SAP global for a solution and advic where no solution was available. In case of no solution in EC, standard Engro policy was to align with the system—extensive testing for checking integration scenarios and consulting SAP Global where integration was causing issues. Training and extensive support were provided to the business team on how to run Employee Central, with a detailed user manual prepared for end users.

The Way Forward

After the successful implementation of S4 HANA, the next step would be to capitalize more on the uncapped potential of the existing S4 HANA features. New areas will be considered to realize more out of this. In the beginning, the automation of Shared Services, Success Factors, and Fiori apps will be planned for implementation. S4 HANA can help provide real-time data in the form of dashboards, thereby facilitating decision-making.

Not only this, but the successful implementation of SuccessFactors Suite across Engro will herald the dawn of a new era whereby employees can easily access all relevant information about employee life cycles, HR policies, leave management systems, talent acquisition, and payroll data. That will reduce the time to cover routine tasks and significantly lessen the time to deliver results. A transparent system for existing employees to not only access their data on the go through a self-service portal, increasing greater employee engagement while minimizing the burden on the concerned department. The availability of Fiori Applications will enable swift, systematic, structured, and dynamic access to information on the go (Exhibit 5).

Exhibit 1
Engro Corporation as a conglomerate

Fertilizers

Top 50 fertilizer manufacturer in the world; 5 decades of operations as a world class business

Energy & Mining

Operating Pakistan's first 217 MW power plant on permeate gas;

Operating first ever 2 x 330 MW mine-mouth coal power plant;

Managing Pakistan's first open-pit coal mine at Thar

Dairy

12mn consumer base; market leader in Pakistan's UHT segment and number 2 dairy dessert brand

Petrochemicals

The only fully integrated chlor-vinyl chemical complex in Pakistan producing PVC and other chlorine byproducts

Telecom Infrastructure

Operating the largest independent tower company in the country catering to the network deployment requirements of all 4 MNOs

Chemical Storage & Handling

Pakistan's first LNG receiving terminal, and an integrated bulk liquid chemicals and LPG terminal

Exhibit 2
Engro Corp. Organizational Structure

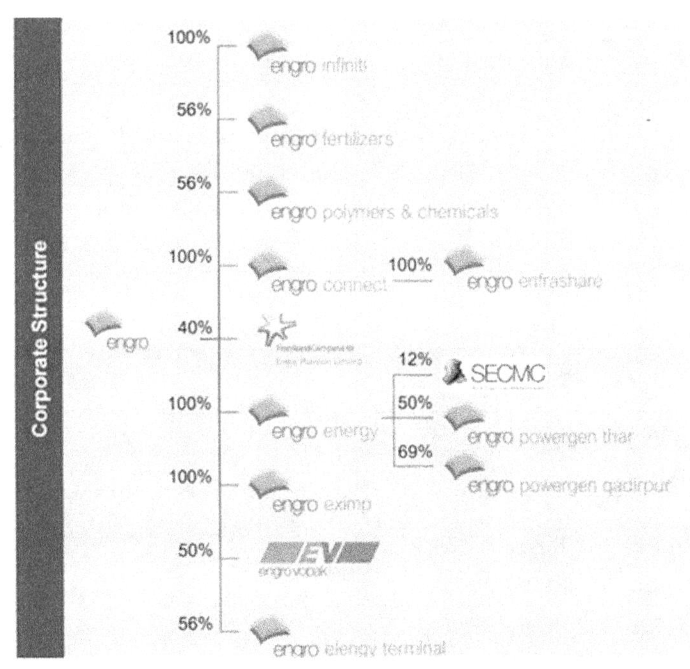

Exhibit 3
Project Committees

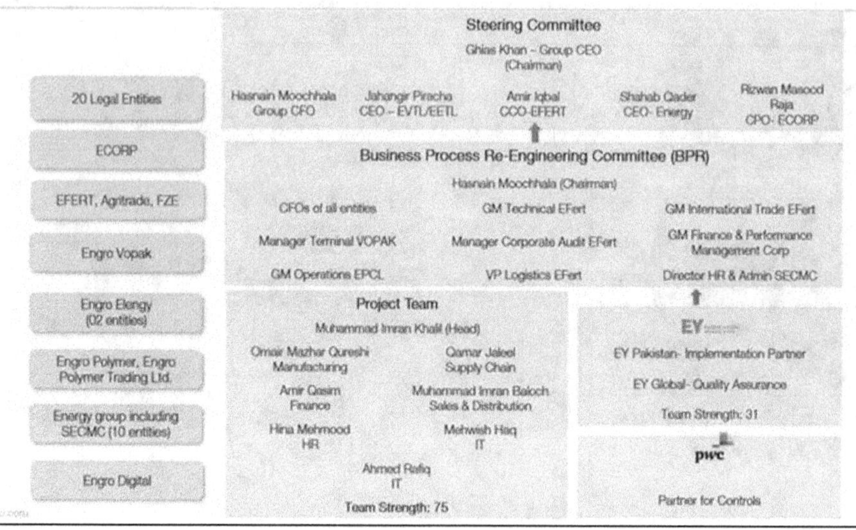

Exhibit 4
One SAP Go Live / No-Go Live Criterion

S.#	Go-Live Requirement	Criteria
1	Define the Cut over strategy	100% complete and approved by BPR committee
2	System readiness	Hardware and Software installations with relevant patches applied
3	Control process	Thorough review and external evaluation done
4	Transport to Production	100% completed
5	Initialization of the system	Complete
6	User's creation	Relevant users from each entity with their access and task profiles defined
7	Roles / Responsibility / Profiles by Users	

8	Job Scheduling (excluding system jobs)	Backups for the HANA database are automatically scheduled and tested for restoration.
9	UAT Completed	All UAT test cases are passed by end users and signed off before going live.
10	Sign-offs on UATs	

Exhibit 5
SITF Engagement Plan

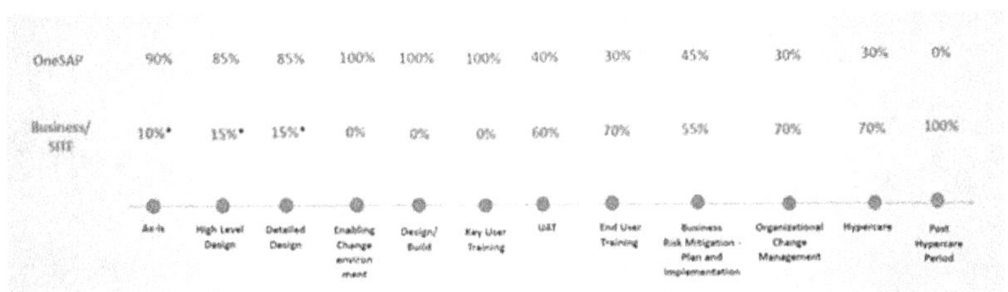

Exhibit 6
Cutover Timelines

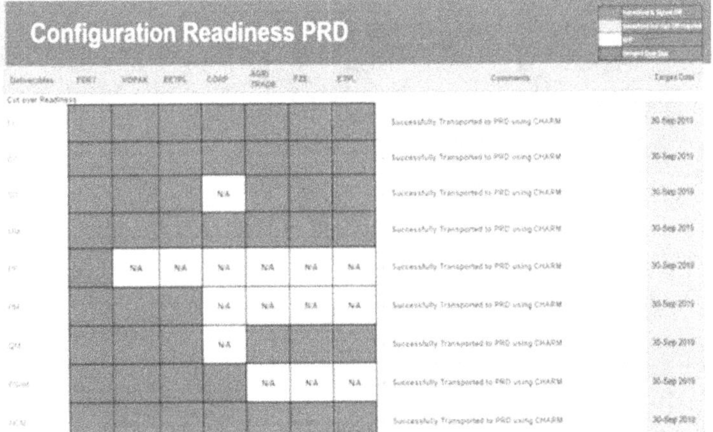

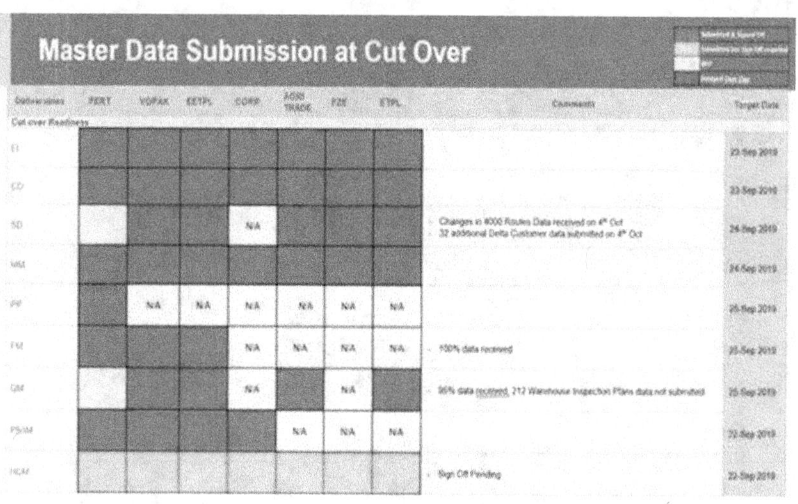

Trial Balance Submission for Cut Over

Deliverables	FERT	VOPAK	EETPL	CORP	AGRI TRADE	FZE	ETPL	Comments	Target Date
Cut over Readiness									
A/R Open Items				N/A		N/A	N/A	Fert. 37 TAR Customer's Master Data not provided in delta. Will be roll out post Go-Live	04-Oct 2019
A/P Open Items							N/A		03-Oct 2019
Stock (Stores & Spares)				N/A	N/A	N/A	N/A		01-Oct 2019
Stocks in Trade			N/A	N/A		N/A	N/A	Seed & Pesticide UoM Issues rectification in progress. Urea, Zarkhez & Agri Trade resubmitted after rectification of locations on 7th Oct 4AM.	04-Oct 2019
P&L Line Items (Retained Earnings)									10-Oct 2019
GA Balances									10-Oct 2019
Fixed Assets									10-Oct 2019
GR/IR via Open POs		N/A	N/A	N/A	N/A	N/A	N/A	Data Submitted. Corrections in Foreign POs data in progress, exchange rates pending	04-Oct 2019

Master Data Submission at Cut Over

Deliverables	FERT	VOPAK	EETPL	CORP	AGRI TRADE	FZE	ETPL	Comments	Target Date
Cut over Readiness									
FI									23-Sep 2019
CO									23-Sep 2019
SD				N/A				Changes in 4000 Routes Data received on 4th Oct; 32 additional Delta Customer data submitted on 4th Oct	24-Sep 2019
MM									24-Sep 2019
PP		N/A	N/A	N/A	N/A	N/A	N/A		25-Sep 2019
FM				N/A	N/A	N/A	N/A	100% data received	25-Sep 2019
QM				N/A		N/A		96% data received, 212 Warehouse Inspection Plans data not submitted	25-Sep 2019
PS/M					N/A	N/A	N/A		22-Sep 2019
HCM								Sign Off Pending	22-Sep 2019

CUSTOMER RELATIONSHIP MANAGEMENT (CRM) / SALES FORCE AUTOMATION (SFA) IMPLEMENTATION AT CANDOR PHARMA

Muhammad Ali Qureshi, Waleed uz Zaman, and Muhammad Nasarullah of Karachi School for Business and Leadership (KSBL) prepared this case under the supervision of Dr. Amir Manzoor. The case was prepared solely to provide material for class discussion. The authors do not intend to illustrate either effective or ineffective handling of a managerial situation. Certain names and other identifying information have been disguised to protect confidentiality.

Company's History

Pakistan's Pharmaceutical industry is valued at approximately PKR 600 billion and is growing at a rate of 22% annually. Both National and Multinational Companies dominate the industry. Public-private Partnerships in the health industry have also increased, with several Pharmaceutical companies working with government and NGOs to provide necessary access to medicines.

The growth of national companies is observed to be higher than that of multinational companies. In the perception-based drug industry, relative substitute is low because of the undifferentiated characteristics of products in the market. Approximately 650 companies are operating in this industry, out of which less than 30 are multinational companies, and this industry contributes approximately 1% to the GDP of Pakistan annually[2]

The government strictly regulates the pharmaceutical sector. The Drug Regulatory Authority of Pakistan (DRAP) controls all the registration of new medicines, renewal of licenses for manufacturing pricing and inflationary indexation, hardship cases, post-registration variations, and approvals of pharmaceutical products and manufacturing sites. It also regulates the prices (MRP) for all the medicines that are marketed in Pakistan. The marketing of drugs is strictly regulated and monitored.

Candor is a leading research-based biopharmaceutical Multinational Company based in the US, working globally for around 150 years. It started distribution with a local distributor in 1959 in Pakistan and began manufacturing in 1961. They aim to provide high-quality pharmaceutical medicines at affordable prices. Candor gradually captured market share in the Pakistan pharma industry of 6.5% (2020-2021) and has a 3500+ employee workforce in Pakistan to support business activities and create value in the business line by giving efficient performance and providing quality services. Candor strictly follows the rules maintained by the Drug Regulatory Authority of Pakistan. Since Candor is working in Pakistan, its revenue is growing yearly with a massive growth rate of 8-12% annually, along with capturing the biopharmaceutical product market. In 2021, Candor will have an annual revenue of Rs. 40 billion (see Exhibit 2) with annual sales growth of approx. 12 %(2021).

Candor ensures the health and safety of its employees and encompasses the best policies and procedures by performing proactively in the market. Candor follows a proactive approach and is always ready for continuous improvement. The KAIZEN principle evolves the entire value chain and adoption of new technology. Its objective is to achieve optimum utilization of resources, effectively follow the procedures, and take new steps with the objective of profit maximization. Candor ensures that the sales force is trained scientifically and technically about the products they are dealing with and aligns their goals with the organization's vision and mission.

History of Information Systems at Candor Pharma

Candor Pharma is one of the most advanced research-based biopharmaceutical Multinational Companies. The Company focuses on maximizing return on technology investment by assuring that all planned activities are delivered as per agreed achievable targets. Organizations invest in different Software and information systems to adopt innovation (see Exhibit 1). The Company has implemented multiple successful Information Systems for several reasons, including better record management, compliance, and transparency of transactions. Pharmaceutical companies use data/reports provided by systems to develop their commercial plans and portfolio strategies. Artificial Intelligence, Digital Transformation, and Machine learning are being adopted to bring innovation to the Pharmaceutical Industry.

In the past, Candor Pharma implemented some major Enterprise Information Systems.

SAP: In 2017, for better record management, performance efficiency, and automation of the business process and reporting areas, Candor Pharma successfully implemented SAP which cost around Rs.85,000,000, to enhance the ability of decision-making based on reports, cut the repetitive tasks efficiently use of time and resources of an organization. That benefits the overall organization in different areas.

IMS Plus: In 2013, to track the performance of brands against the competitors in terms of sales & to make innovation in the product line organization IMS Plus software, which helps provide information solutions to health care and pharma industry.

Pharmacy Level Data: In 2015, to track the units sold in a particular pharmacy, control inventory at each pharmacy, the history of purchasing trends of specific pharmacies, and also track the performance of brands against competitors at the pharmacy level.

MAPP Navigator: Organizations use the MAPP navigator to track and manage events to be compliant and fulfill all the policies and procedures.

Cvent: In 2009, Cvnet was used to ease the booking of hotels, International flight booking, and ground transport for internal and external meetings and traveling of marketing teams on national & international visits.

CRM and SFA Implementation: The Issues

Candor Pharma has many issues to resolve for implementing CRM and SFA.

The Implementation Process

Modern SFA tool, a CRM cloud-based application, will likely enable sales representatives to be more productive and transparent in the Field force visits to pharmacies and to track the performance of individual medical reps, promotional material approvals, and other factors much more efficiently. This data helps in Customer relationship management history of orders by setting KPIs to monitor the implementation process and develop an information system team along with department key personnel engaged in overall CRM cloud-based application implementation.

Benefits and Drawbacks of SFA/CRM

Candor Pharms needed to determine the benefits and drawbacks of SFA/CRM using multiple strategy models. Table 1 presents a SWOT analysis of CRM/SFA implementation.

Table 1: SWOT analysis

	Opportunities	**Threats**
Strengths	Using CRM increases Sales by rectifying the areas where sales are low, and other brands will reach strengths to consolidate and expand their market position.	CRM helps with two approaches - Strengthen the present market, analyze the trend, and create a strategy for market penetration approach.
Weaknesses	Through CRM building strategies based on consumer-oriented product development, record visits to doctors and pharmacies, and make marketing strategy accordingly.	CRM Sales should get out of these business areas and focus on strengths and weaknesses through feedback from doctors and pharmacists.

Steps of Implementation

Before adopting Veeva Systems, the organization evaluates the efficiency level required by tan organization and asses the current procedures and practices followed by the medical reps. The main departments involved in the implementation phase are the Information technology and the marketing department. Then, they identify the deriving forces of the project who are willing to succeed in this project, and the other one is restraining forces who, in this case, maybe reps because it is the primary duty of reps to collect the information from doctors and pharmacists.

Continuous Monitoring and Measurement of Multiple Key Performance Indicators

Digital Sales Presentation: In this modern world where technology is growing very fast and the impact of the pandemic is also affecting, virtually engaging doctors and pharmacists without physical interaction through connectivity online is needed. One option was a cloud-based application. It is convenient for doctors and sales teams to engage multiple doctors at a time, give briefings on products they are selling, and take any feedback.

Field Force Calls: CRM cloud-based application is linked with reps' iPads, mobile phones, and laptops, which track their performance as well as the time they spend with doctors and pharmacies. It includes physical visits and phone calls with doctors and maintaining relationships with them to attain the customer and enhance sales.

E-Detailing of Pharmacy Visits: When reps visit doctors and pharmacies, they record details of medicines electronically through their devices online from anywhere. Also, track the delivery record of specific orders and update their pharmacy accordingly regarding their delivery of orders.

Rep-Triggered Emails: Emails are triggered by reps. They can pop up easily on those emails, which is making hurdles in delivering on-time orders, and the sales team in the office can easily follow up through the supply chain department or inventory department.

Healthcare Professionals Coverage: Tracking the number of healthcare professionals' coverage by each sales representative weekly or monthly and how many healthcare professionals are in those regions or areas where our medical reps are covering.

Pharmacy coverage: Tracking Pharmacies, which are organizations' regular customers. This application allows reps and team members to monitor the visits or plan visits according to their timeline and schedule of visits to each pharmacy in their region.

Monthly Sales Targets: Monthly sales target achievement tracking and active monitoring from day-to-day sales and the pre-set target from the start of the month. Compare those targets with customer, product, and region-wise and share on every dashboard to clear their targets vs. achievements. Also helps to analyze the performance of each rep toward achieving the target.

Search for a Suitable System

When adopting the cloud-based software CRM system, a handful of companies provide extensive service. Candor Pharma sells its products in more than 125 countries. Veeva System is one of the leading CRM providers in the pharmaceutical industry landscape.

Veeva System is the only company that provides Software-as-a-service (SaaS) with vast applications of offering. The company offers service to over 160 customers and over 60,000 users worldwide, even though they provide services for various departments like clinical, regulatory, quality, safety, medical, commercial, and others.

Candor Pharma (Pakistan) was searching for a cloud cloud-based global CRM that provides high-tech software. It allows flexible and agile integration between laptops, mobile, and iPads and international harmonization. Monitoring and measuring multiple KPIs is another factor in adopting this cloud-based application. Marketing managers, sales managers, and other stakeholders will now be able to track the performance of individual medical reps, promotional material approvals, and other factors much more efficiently. A cross-functional IT team was designed to identify and evaluate multiple options for Veeva Vault Promo Mats, Veeva's end-to-end promotional materials management solution for the life sciences industry.

The company followed the Outside In approach to determine which solution to implement. With the Outside In approach, companies usually analyze the performance of software implemented in the industry and then implement it in their own company. Firstly, it can be analyzed that Veeva System is one of the leading cloud-based CRM providers. They provide services to a number of multinational pharmaceutical companies. In Pakistan, many national and multinational pharmaceutical company uses this service. If Candor Pharma is considered, it is operated in more than 125 countries. The global team implemented this software in multiple markets. As the solution is reliable, efficient, and agile, the global team assigned a timeline to implement the software in the Pakistani market.

Before adopting Veeva Systems, the approval, review, and distribution method was very complicated. The draft of promotional material was taken manually for revision between the stakeholders. The process was inefficient, as the corrections were missed in pieces, and multiple duplicate files were created. This method of approvals between marketing, medical, legal, and regulatory took 40 days or more on average, reducing the material owner's productivity.

Veeva Systems

To monitor and measure the KPIs, Candor Pharma implemented one of the services of *Veeva Systems*. Veeva is one of the world's most successful and innovative cloud software companies. It was founded in 2007 and provided solutions for regulated industries such as companies in the consumer, chemical, cosmetics, and life sciences sectors. Veeva Systems provides 360 cloud solutions to its clients with the help of multiple services. The headquarters of Veeva is in the San Francisco Bay Area, and different offices are located in North America, Europe, Asia, and Latin America.

Candor Pharma implemented Veeva Medical Suite, which consisted of three major services.

----

1) MEDICAL CRM

Medical CRM allows an organization to build key relationships and engage with key stakeholders across channels. In Candor Pharma, this service is mainly used to interact with Healthcare Professionals. Along with interaction, it also allows the company to track scientific engagement, understand scientific observation, and plan & align objectives with cross-functional departments.

Key features of medical CRM are as follows:

Strategic Account Planning and Engagement: The feature enables different stakeholders to access meaningful interactive tools. They can plan, execute, and track the performance of pieces across channels. Medical Reps can plan and prioritize their HCP engagement with the integrated cloud system.

Healthcare Professional Engagement: Engagement with HCP positively affected after the implementation of Medical CRM. The pool of doctors increased significantly. The medical reps could connect doctors remotely and show the relevant content in a very short time. Doctors who used to practice in far-flung areas of Pakistan were targeted and conversed with virtually. Along with that, doctors who had busy routines in the ICU were also targeted.

Medical compliant and approved content: Content tracking was made easy after the implementation of Medical CRM. Each promotional material had to go through MLR review, i.e., Medical, Legal, and Regulatory review. An integrated system was provided where a soft copy of the project was uploaded. Marketing managers initially approve it, then the medical lead, regulatory, and legal departments. Once it is fully approved, it can be disseminated to the field force.

Actionable real-time data for managers: The sweet spot of Medical CRM is that it provides real-time, actionable data for multiple stakeholders. Promotional materials can easily be tracked, the expiry date can be checked, and whether the piece is compliant or not can also be checked. Key Performance Indicators (KPIs) can also be tracked for medical reps, pharmacy coverage of the products, and many other factors that can be evaluated.

Streamlined content from cross-functional departments: Integrating and harmonizing this software with multiple other software is also an important element that makes it unique from others. The pieces uploaded on the platform are always available to multiple stakeholders. For example, medical reps can access the material from their iPads, while managers can access the piece from their laptops.

---

2) VEEVA LINK

Veeva Link provides the Field force control to prioritize and identify their key Healthcare professional. It also improves coordination across field force teams, channels, and regions. It also assists the field force with tailored and precise customer communication.

Veeva Link provides insightful data regarding medical and scientific experts. This data is used by different stakeholders within the organization. For example, medical reps prioritize their engagement time with the doctors using this data. They are engaging HCPs much more efficiently by planning across geographies and functions. Stakeholders are now able to measure their product's visibility across the market. Analyze the performance of their brands with the market and other competitors.

Veeva Vault is the major system implemented in Candor Pharma. Vault manages both scientific and nonscientific content that is published to any stakeholder. The content is reviewed at multiple stages, including marketing, regulatory, medical, and legal departments, before it is published.

Previously, the company was much dependent upon manual signing and approval of promotional material. Pieces used to travel from one desk to another for signing. If there was any mistake in the piece, it was sent back to the material owner, and the approval process was started again. According to one of the marketing managers, a single piece used to take 40 to 50 days for approval. If the piece was large, it also took up to 6 months for approval only.

After the Veeva Vault was implemented, the way of working changed in the company. All the approvals were streamlined. The approval time was reduced to as low as four working days for the pieces that previously took 40 days for approval. Multiple features were also introduced with time. Features like audit trail and reuse of global material brought ease to the workload of marketing managers. With the help of Audit Trail, the content owner can easily track all the comments marked by the approving party in just a single window. The other feature, like the reuse of global material, is that the content owner can use the material published by the global team for the local markets.

Vault is a global cloud-based solution. One of the features is that it equips the local market with global content. Local markets can also create content from global assets. It helps in tracing sources, the approval process, and adapting content in the local language. It provides easy-to-use dashboards and reports to analyze and set KPIs.

Moreover, Vault offers controlled distribution, access, and expiration of content. It is directly linked with other services of Veeva, i.e., 'Medical CRM.' It allows content to be delivered to the relevant team with the help of Veeva mapping. Teams are developed as per the business unit by the Sales Force Execution Lead.

System Approval

Being a multinational pharmaceutical company, Candor had to go through a strict and compliant way to get the solution approved for use in the local market. Even though a global team in another region initially implemented this solution, it had to go through approvals before it was implemented in the local region of Pakistan.

A cross-functional team was created within the existing organizational structure, which had the job of approvals and software implementation. The cross-functional team consisted of IT, regulatory, legal, marketing, and medical team members. This team reported to the Country Manager, who had all the rights to approve or disapprove the software implementation. The cross-functional team prepared the budget, testing dates, phased launch dates, and final launch dates. The summary was presented to the country manager, which was approved.

In the initial testing phase, two marketing personnel and one IT expert had permission to use the application. They tested all the features of the Veeva, which would be deployed in the local market. Soon, this was launched with a phased approach. Which means only one business unit had the right to use this application. If the bugs were detected, they were reported to the IT manager, which was further escalated in the region. A client service personnel from Veeva was actively working with the local market in case of any issues. Soon the software was launched within 50 days of testing days to the whole local company.

As part of the global implementation of the software, global stakeholders initially approved this software. The software was launched in every market at the given time frame. Once the regional team provided the approval and deadlines, the approval of the lead team was given and assigned to subject matter experts for the deployment of the solution.

Implementation of System

The implementation of the software was broken into multiple Work Breakdown Structures. The project management task was available on Gantt Chart and managed by the Project Manager. Access to the Gantt Chart was available to all the relevant stakeholders, i.e., the cross-functional team.

The HR team was involved during this process as hiring a Software specialist was required. This person played a pivotal role during and after the implementation of the software. This person had strong knowledge acumen about software, hardware, and implementation of software. After the launch of the software, the role of the employee shifted towards managing and keeping track of all the matters related to Veeva.

A phased approach was used to implement the software across the organization. Initially, the software was only tested in a testing environment by a cross-functional team. Once the approval of the team was given, it was launched for selected stakeholders, including the marketing manager, the lead team, and the cross-functional team. Within 50 days, the software was available for the entire company.

Glitches and bugs were detected, like the limit on the file size, the webpage's freeze, and the software's sudden crash. However, the issues were resolved in the updates that came later that month. Constant client service personnel were available to assist the team and anyone with software-related problems.

Implementation Team

Cross-Functional Team: A cross-functional team was formed within the current organizational structure to handle software approvals and implementation. Members of the project, regulatory, legal, marketing, and medical teams made up the cross-functional team. This team reported to the Country Manager, who had complete authority over the software installation. The cross-functional team prepared the budget, testing dates, phased launch dates, and ultimate launch dates. The country manager authorized the summary submitted to him.

Project Team: The team, comprised of top executives, guaranteed proper performance and capital assistance and was active in the project for a few hours each week. The project manager possessed business operations and technical competence and operated on the software installation daily. During the conception stage, a team of end users was committed to providing feedback to the project manager; they also compared the performance during the planning and implementation stages, involved in the project 2-five hours each week.

Regulatory Team: Regulatory operations teams have completed the submission assembly process. Their distinct, all-encompassing perspective spanned from content creation to submission. This viewpoint enabled regulatory processes to more efficiently manage initiatives, such as synchronizing diverse workflows to handle cross-functional requirements. With actual statistics on the progress of each department's records, regulatory administration knew which divisions were performing effectively and which were jeopardizing corporate schedules. The team identified and solved patterns before they became an issue, allowing timelines and subsequent entities to be satisfied. Tactically, regulatory operations did not only collect a report and get that out the doorway, but they also contributed strategic significance by assisting the organization in planning future filings and successfully executing to fulfill business goals.

Legal Team: They work with compliance requirements such as corporate law, trading regulations, investor contracts, and compliance standards, as well as support the decision-making bodies that comprise the organization's system of governance so the firm may operate legally. This ensured that the corporate body was constituted and existed legally, allowing it to continue to do business.

Marketing Team: Most systematic implementations started with sales but ultimately expanded to cover marketing and services. It was prudent to include a marketing representative in the planning discussions. Their criteria were not implemented immediately, but understanding what they would require aided the program's future trajectory.

Challenges Faced During Implementation

Analyzing Current Processes

The operational sales teams already have a sales procedure in place. This process can be relatively informal and controlled by individual salespersons, or it can be quite explicit with sales cycles and goals. Evaluating the preexisting sales process was a critical first step in Candor Pharma's effective installation of solutions. Company management discovered shortcomings and made improvements by reviewing the old sales process before being pushed by their latest software to integrate an unsuccessful sales funnel into an effective program. The chosen software allowed for the definition and tracking of sales phases, sales achievements, actions, and more. Most of them have some well-designed preset procedures. However, Candor Pharma originally did not comprehend its own process. It was forced to use the software's built-in procedure, which may not correspond to what the company's sales staff is doing and can cause instability and dissatisfaction. Organizations should search for software to personalize the sales phases and other sales process details. If a firm invests time, energy, and money in reviewing and improving its sales process, looking for software that will allow them to implement "their own" method seems sensible. While most systems on the market provide well-designed and productive sales processes, a firm should not be forced to use that process if it does not meet its needs.

Resistance to Change

The most difficult problem in integrating new sales software was resistance to change. People found it incredibly difficult to modify their practices. Typically, roughly 25% of medical reps resisted so hard that they were on the verge of abandoning their employment if compelled to make changes they did not desire. Most medical reps initially fought the change, but gradually embraced it. The others were ready for change and were frequently eager partners in the process. This group was a critical component in ensuring the success of this implementation. After seeing the positive sides of the software, the medical reps quickly tilted their behaviors towards adopting the software. It allowed them to connect with their clients from their homes, offices, or café. The organization leveraged its zeal and involvement to help create a favorable environment around the initiative.

Not every team member initially participated, especially if the sales team was huge. Completing a questionnaire about how medical reps sell was sometimes enough to make them feel involved. The company also sought volunteers to help with some of the research and efforts needed in software reviews. This provided unexpectedly favorable outcomes, as the sales crew was able to provide information that management had not considered. It was critical to raise awareness of the project and provide the essential knowledge to recognize the benefits of the shift. Never confuse the sales staff with modifications. A major mistake during this period was "telling" the sales staff that they were getting a new software package. It simply became another item on a busy medical rep's extensive to-do list. The firm should have requested feedback and help from the sales team in picking the software. Management should have avoided asking them if they wanted an SFA program; instead, ask the team what needs they had for an SFA program. In this approach, the organization could empower the sales staff to own what the new software is and achieves. Knowledge is power, and so was the engagement in this situation.

Use of Memory

Like the rest of us, medical reps usually run their businesses and tasks in their brains. Each medical rep was well-versed in the specifics of their client's current sales connections and potential. The data was frequently minimal, such as the names of the principal connections for a certain profile. Nevertheless, it may have included more specific data, such as the items in which the client is now intrigued. The more complicated the connections and sales prospects got, the more difficult it was to organize everything in the medical rep's thoughts. This software was inputting and evaluating customer information virtually as simply as putting it into or out of their minds to function properly. The organization should have discovered techniques to make it simple to transfer critical information from a medical rep's thoughts to a digital medium. Suppose a sales force utilizes a tool like Microsoft Outlook to gather contact information and e-mail prospects. In that case, an SFA program using an existing Outlook customer database will make it much easier. They should engage a card scanner to enter the contact details into the system as swiftly as possible. If the firm receives e-mail queries from clients regularly, it should choose a feature that would allow it to establish a link and a selling prospect from such e-mail communications with the tap of a button. That removes the need for the sales staff to enter or record the data and helps them to track their sales actions immediately. The firm should have established procedures for recording critical customer and sales data. It will be beneficial only if the sales staff adds useful insights into the application. The classic saying "trash in, trash out" is applicable here. Most solutions make it simple to take notes, check e-mail, arrange appointments, and keep track of sales. When management examined and polished the company's sales cycle, they established standards for what the sales staff is required to perform to monitor their sales.

One Step at a Time

Most individuals underestimated the complexity of the cloud-based CRM/SFA tool. For most businesses, the sales and marketing process progresses in lockstep with the business, beginning with crawling, then walking, and finally running. The firm was over the crawling phase while exploring programs, but it should never have decided to break into a sprint. That may have resulted in a significant decline and was a primary reason the newly established system nearly collapsed. It wasn't until the last moment that people discovered how much work went into effectively implementing such a program. Putting in the work and time to correctly deploy and build up the application and educate the employees might mean the difference between good execution and becoming a stat in the 70% rate of failure. Deployment should be meticulously planned and given adequate time. The firm must have planned for deployment, education, and a go-live date. The organization should have also tried to be practical rather than idealistic. Sufficient duration must be provided to finish each step before moving on to the next through using available resources. Several SFA and CRM software vendors offer deployment and education packages. The firm should have utilized them.

Furthermore, the vendors understand their product better than anyone else, so they will likely have expertise with nearly any network arrangement. A firm should contemplate executing a pilot program of its selected SFA/CRM product if the intended installation is big. This pilot program might give valuable information on how the sales force and marketing stakeholders will use the system and the outcomes. That allows the sales management and staff to take charge. By testing the system on a smaller scale, the IT department would have had the opportunity to test how it would perform in the company's distributed system. That might be an excellent opportunity for the corporation to iron out any hitches while also getting exposure from the entire organization. Many businesses are astonished to discover that there is a higher requirement than they anticipated.

Exhibit 1
Organizational Structure of Candor Pharma

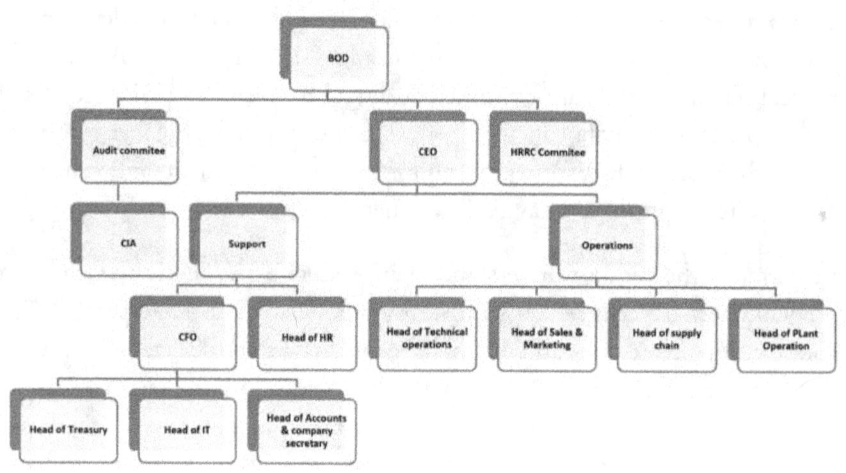

Exhibit 2
Sales Revenue (In PKR Billion)

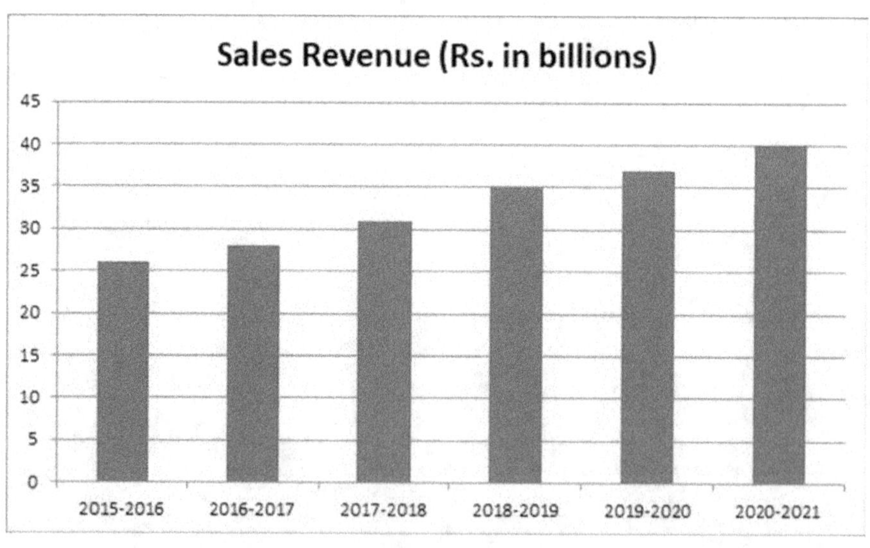

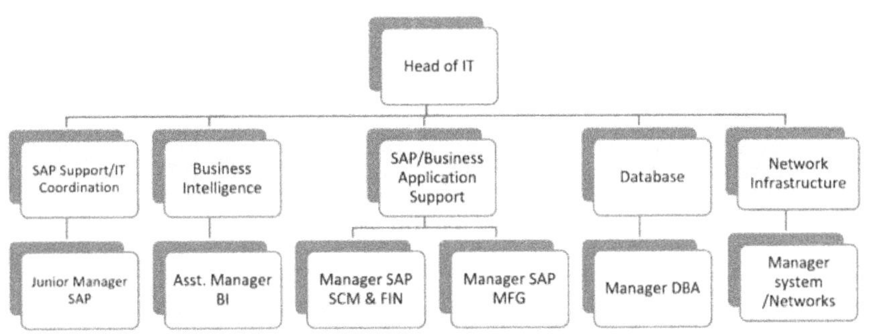

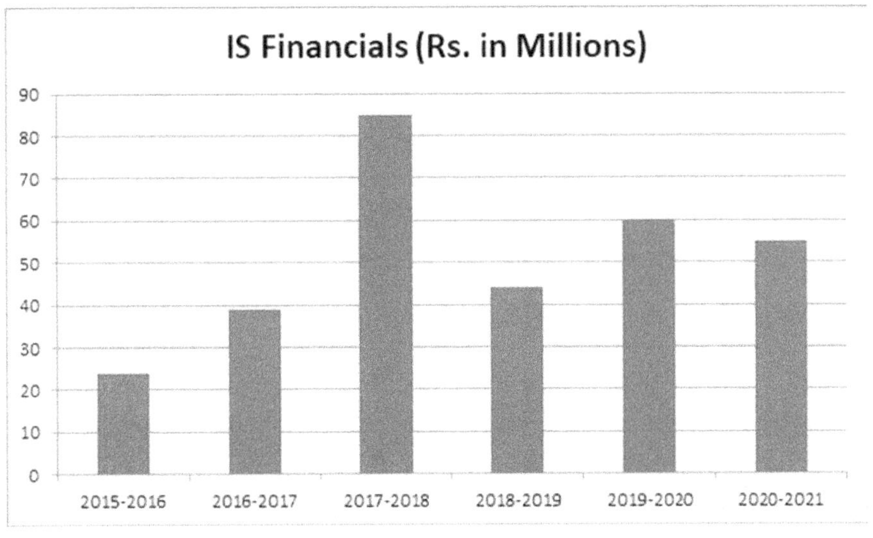
IS Financials (Rs. in Millions)
90
80
70
60
50
40
30
20
10
0
2015-2016
2016-2017
2017-2018
2018-2019
2019-2020
2020-2021

Exhibit 5
Cross Functional Team

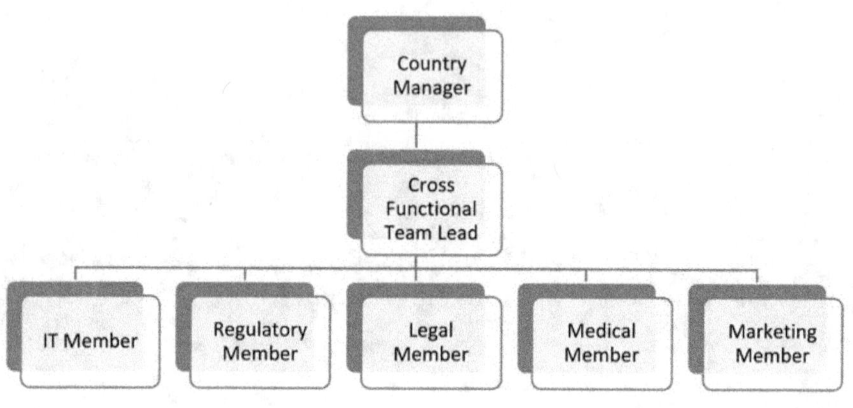

INTEGRATION OF NGEN WITH DATA AND DIGITIZATION AT HUTCHISON PORTS

Muhammad Saad, Muhammad Maaz Siraj, and Syed Ahmed Hasan of Karachi School for Business and Leadership (KSBL) prepared this case under the supervision of Dr. Amir Manzoor. The case was prepared solely to provide material for class discussion. The authors do not intend to illustrate either effective or ineffective handling of a managerial situation. Certain names and other identifying information have been disguised to protect confidentiality.

Mr. Danial, an Assistant Manager at the Regional Operations Center of Hutchison ports, faced several issues in his current system. Port operations have several stages, which include allocation, preplanning, planning, execution, and departure of the vessel. The Department of Regional Operations Center does not only give its services to local ports. They are associated with five ports for which they carry out operations remotely. The department consists of almost 31 people, primarily those under 30. The reason which is given to us by Ray Xing, the head of the department who initially started this project, said it is much easier to train a younger mind as they are much more tech-savvy and open to taking challenges rather than experienced individuals. (See Exhibit 1).

There are several issues that ROC is facing right now. Firstly, the process of allocation is a serious issue. Allocation refers to a list of containers that must be onboard the vessel. Shipping lines provide the allocation list. The allocation list plays an essential role in the planning procedure. It lets the port analyze how many containers are already on the port and how many need to be gated in. The allocation list has frequent changes due to customs clearance and the credibility of the goods. The allocation list is usually sent by e-mail, which causes issues as most of the emails are repeatedly sent and useless. Secondly, a number of other operations correspondence is being done through email. Finding the relevant specific email takes a lot of time.

Furthermore, the other major issue is accountability. A port works 24 hours a day, and the berthing schedule can be at any time. At ROC, there are two shifts, day and night. There is no electronic medium to leave handover remarks; thus, the errors during planning make it tough to find out how and for whom the error was. Moreover, ROC has to coordinate with the execution team based solely on call. There is no documentation for that. If an error occurs by the execution team, they never accept it. Instead, they blame the planner and the planning team for it. For operations to go smoothly, coordination with other departments is very much obligatory. ROC must coordinate with the commercial department as they are in direct contact with the shipping line. For execution purposes, proper documentation needs to be followed, which can be saved and used for future reference.

Because of these issues, several losses have been borne by the company. Several times, the port has to make several re-stows. Re-stows are actually a relocation of containers, which causes the quay crane to have extra movement. Usually, for re-stows, the port charges 150$ to the shipping line if shipping lines request to make it, but if re-stows are to be made during the operation, the terminal has to bear the cost. Moreover, KPT gives a particular window. If that window exceeds, KPT puts heavy fines. If berthing is delayed due to negligence of port operations, shipping lines pass the penalty to the terminal. The terminal has to face it. In 2019, a fine of 400,000 was passed to the terminal by one of the shipping lines, which was caused by the negligence of the operations team. Due to lack of accountability, planners are very skeptical about whether to work in the operation department or not, as most of the time, they are held responsible, as there is a lack of evidence to accuse other departments. Most of the individuals working at ROC has master's degree, and they have pitched the idea to bring a new system, as the other ports, such as DP World (Dubai-based port network), are using a system named NAVIOS, which is very user-friendly.

According to Mr. Danial, they wanted a system that could synchronize well with their current planning system and boost the correspondence method. He also wanted documents to be standardized, which are hatch prints, the move of the QCs, yard performance, and which can tell the overall efficiency. They were making these reports by themselves as the vessel operations. To save time and start working on other vessels, he wants a system that can auto-generate all the reports after the operations so they can forward it to the quality assurance and audit department.

Company History

Hutchison Ports Holding owns Hutchison Ports Pakistan. Globally, Hutchison Ports has 52 ports in 26 countries and 319 berths. Hutchison Ports has the biggest port network in the world. The port industry is vital for a nation to survive economically. Hutchison ports have two major ports in Karachi: KICT and SAPT. Both are located in the Keamari basin. The Ports are under the supervision of the Hong Kong board. The CK Hutchison group mostly takes the apex decisions. As per the global resource journal, in 2005, Hutchison Ports was the leading operator with a market share of almost 8.3%. In 2006, Hutchison Holding sold 20% of the share to PSA International for US$ 4.4 billion. In September 2016, Hutchison Port Holding rebranded itself as Hutchison Ports.

Hutchison Ports believes in investing where there are expected returns. SAPT is a deep sea port, whereas KICT has a lot of berthing traffic as it has been a center port of Karachi for several years. The company is now expanding its operations in the UAE and Africa. Recently, Hutchison acquired a new port in Saudia Arabia known as Jazan Port and Ports El Dekhelia in Egypt. Refer to Exhibit 2 for port assets. SAPT (South Asia Pakistan Terminal) came into operation in 2016, investing in Hutchison Holdings and KPT. It is considered to be Pakistan's only deep-sea port that can hold apex vessels with a draft of more than 360M. SAPT welcomed its first mother vessel CV, COSCO BELGIUM, in 2019, which had 13000(TEUs) almost 6500 40HQ.

Hutchison Port has a vision of bringing innovation to the port industry. They try to execute new and advanced methods in port operations. For example, rubber tire gantry, remote cranes, executing remote operations, and developing AI-based systems to bring efficiency to their current port operations. Advanced scanners are being installed at various ports, to bring efficiency in customs clearance, especially scanners are very much necessary for the cargo that has to be shipped to the United States, several procedures in port operations need to be followed, and the port has to tailor their SOPs accordingly as every country has different criteria of cargo clearance, they need to make sure that shipping lines do not get affected due to any issues that the port can create. Hutchison Ports tries to give their shipping partners quality service so they are not affected throughout the voyage.

Hutchison Port's major competitors include PSA Singapore, LF Logistics, COSCO Shipping ports, and DP World. In Karachi, a major competitor is considered to be DP World, also known as QICT. As per the forecast, SAPT will be competing QICT in terms of volume and handling TEUs within five years. Hutchison Port also focuses on working through a hybrid approach, as they also give services to COSCO Hong Kong terminal by providing their services by giving them a whole planning solution in terms of the port. According to one of the reports, Hutchison Ports globally impair Price Waterhouse Cooper, meaning that in accounting terms, PWC accumulates more than 10% of its revenue from Hutchison Group.

During the press conference, the directors of the Hutchison group were asked why they were investing in another port in Karachi. They already had a running port, KICT, which has a rich history. KICT was previously used as the primary port during British Raj. The directors gave it because SAPT has a natural deep water berth, which is not easily found in the world, and the convenience that SAPT will provide to shipping lines and businesses is far more exceptional. Secondly, the import volume of Pakistan has increased over the past few years. The company saw a huge financial and profitable prospect while investing in Pakistan. Moreover, the company saw far more exceptional talent in Pakistan in terms of workforce. While quoting the employee performance of KICT, he said it is exceptional and surprising how employees are showing adaptability to new port methods.

SAPT has almost 800 employees varying from labor to management positions, and almost 600 employees are on daily wages, which are on third-party contracts. Whereas the IT department has almost 20 employees, the rest of the IT services are taken from outsourced staff, which are third-party contracts too. Operation, commercial, and Customer support are all the major departments involved in the port operation, and all employees are under Hutchison Ports, which means no employees are on third-party contracts.

History of Information System at the Company

Hutchison Ports (SAPT) is open to experimenting with new methods to bring efficiency to its current operations. As discussed with Mr. Danial, he mentioned that they follow only two criteria they follow for hiring. They have clearly mentioned to HR that a candidate should be good with numbers and be open to challenges in learning new systems. He said the dynamics of port operations are changing very frequently, technology is taking over, and traditional methods are being replaced, it is necessary for us always to learn new systems as Hutchison Group will not compromise on their standard and practices and the overall staff and culture of the company are just like that, they always try to bring new methods on the table to bring efficiency and growth to the business. The issue that is thoroughly being discussed is mainly related to operations, but other departments also have a role in it. That's why, as per HR policy, quarterly training is being done to enhance their familiarity with information systems and new techniques.

NGEN is the current system that all the 56 ports of Hutchison are using. NGEN is a complete solution for planning. It consists of a simulator called Guider, in which 3D pictures of vessels are seen. The operations department uses NGEN, although other departments also have an idea of how to use it and what functions are in it. The berthing schedule of the vessels is also accessible, which can be seen which vessels are on hold and which are the top priority. Before NGEN, all the planning was done manually. That caused errors. The most common error was over-stow. Every vessel has a route, which is called a voyage. For instance, a vessel will go first to Port Pusan, then Port Incheon, then Port Shekou, and then Karachi Port. If cargo that needs to be discharged on Karachi is on the cargo of Pusan, it is called over-stow. This is considered to be a serious error that increases the cost. That is because the port charges shipping lines per cargo movement. If the move is increased, the shipping line has to bear an extra cost. For this error to minimize guider has function if there is an over-stow on the vessel, it will show a red mark which states that the plan is unsuitable for further stages. There are various other functions as well. If the operations department is handling a mother vessel that tends to be huge in size and has a huge capacity to store, re-stows need to be made, as the Quay crane must penetrate the vessel's hold. A hold is actually the basement or the below compartment of the vessel. Thus, the planner can execute and can make re-stows through NGEN. According to Mr. Danial, NGEN is a lifeline for our operations. We cannot preplan, plan, or execute operations without it.

To understand the function of NGEN, an overview of the current operations is very much necessary. The operations department handles three stages in planning: Stowage Optimization, Crane Working Program, and Loading Sequence. There are two lists of containers that are being followed: the allocation list, which is given by shipping lines, and the other list, which is provided by customer support. The allocation list states the ideal number of containers that must be onboard the vessel. The customer support list gives the data on how many containers are gated in, which means how many containers are currently in the yard. The shipping lines give An initial color plan to the planning team, which gives the location of each container. The color plan is then amended by the planner on the guider by comparing it with the port's on-hand units. After the SO, color plans are generated, which gives the description of the cargo stowage. In other words, what will be the final stowage of the cargo? After that, the CWP stage is very tough to handle, in which quay cranes' movement must be decided. Quay cranes' function is to load and discharge the containers from vessels.

SAPT is one of the world's finest Quay Crane. It can perform 26 moves in an hour, making the operations very smooth. The problem arises when multiple vessels on the berth and cranes have to be used on both vessels. As per Mr. Danial, it is one the most difficult stage in the planning and takes most of the time as we have to plan it so efficiently that none of the cranes stays idle for a second, and we have to make sure they do not clash or in other words do not collide with each other. A few months ago, due to the negligence of QC operator, one QC of SAPT was damaged, which almost cost them around $300,000 for repairing that QC. The CWP stage is very sensitive and requires most of the time. Once CWP is finalized, the planning department can give the go-ahead to the execution department to proceed with discharging. The last stage is the loading sequence, in which the planner has to pick and adjust the right weight from the yard to maintain the stability of the vessel. Once the plan is finalized, it is sent to the vessel captain or chief officer to determine whether the current plan is giving them stability. If there is a request for a change in the plan, the planning department amends it and sends the plan within a few minutes. Another tool that is being used to find out crane intensity is an adjacent bay report (ABR), which is quite a common terminology in port operations. A vessel itself has two compartments: hold and deck. Every bay has a hold and a deck. Sometimes, it varies due to vessel structure. ABR report gives you an idea of how much loading and discharging is there in a vessel. Moves from every bay are written on ABR. ABR also shows a long bay. A long bay is two adjacent bays, showing that the most moves are in the vessel. It is an SOP to start the quay crane movement from Long Bay.

NGEN has several advanced functions as well, which are to generate the final reports, which include bay reports of the vessel, hatch prints, bay plans, the shuffle of the yard, hatch cover movements, mask list (allocation and customer service list), custom hold details, clearance hold details, container history, container condition and many other functions which are very much necessary not only for planning even after execution and departure of the vessel. A mask list is also a major tool. Without referring to the mask list, we can proceed further with stages. The number of units must be balanced with the loading and yard figures.

Selecting the System

In the operations department, there is a sub-department called Quality Assurance. The Quality Assurance department was monitoring for a long period, around 1.5 to 2 years, if the current system used in the organization could tackle or improve the in-efficiency errors occurring in the planning, commercial, and operations side. But they figured out that it wasn't possible to tackle the issues with the current system. The issue was released and taken to the upper management. A meeting was called to plan if a new system should be introduced in the organization, and every department had to participate in the meeting, including the planning, commercial, and operations departments, to finalize if it would be worthy or not. The conclusion of the meeting came, which was that a new system should be introduced. The main goal of the new system was to focus on real-time tracking, which should not include manual entries as large bulk should be tackled in less time, and AI should be used so that the forward processes can become trouble-free and run smoothly. To make it perfect and run smoothly, they had to go through other organizations where new systems were introduced and the issues they faced in the process and how they tackled or failed in it.

The conclusion was forwarded to CK Holdings group, which shortlisted two vendors for the IT system, Micro Focus, and Atos. They chose Micro Focus over Atos because this company had previously worked on logistics and port management-based IT solutions. Regarding the installation, the operations department was insecure as the operations couldn't be shut because of the berthing traffic on the port, as 80% of the trades (import and export) in the world are engaged on cargo vessels through shipping. So, they decided to focus on the parallel approach in which the current operations shouldn't have any leakage. The installation should go smoothly, and the installation of other systems should go through at the same time.

The System Approval Process

An in-depth proposal was developed for the consultation process with all the stakeholders, which included the context of the descriptions and details of the project as well as how it will affect a wide variety of stakeholders in the business. It was a consultation that involved the system's detailed overview followed by prompt and relevant feedback from all the stakeholders that would help identify and mitigate risks associated with the project. Initially, a meeting was held regarding the proposal, where it was presented in detail to all the departments, and all the departments conditionally agreed to the new Microfocus Software.

However, weekly meetings were conducted to get feedback from all the departments regarding their requirements and demands, where the relevant requirements and demands were accepted after detailed scrutiny. Work was done like a flat/Horizontal organization, and opinions from the relevant departments were taken as an essential part of the design. Also, other stakeholders such as shipping lines, clients, and central planners who were in charge of cargo operations of loadings and un-loading were also taken on board and were communicated in detail about the benefits of the system.

They were also informed about the system in detail and how it's going to assist them in data handling and operations through proper management of the Email system and allocation sheets. It was also mentioned that the new system would operate in line with artificial intelligence, which will initiate more automation, and all related businesses will eliminate mainstream systems.

However, they were initially reluctant to change from the old system, but they were initially reluctant and resisted change. Moreover, they referred to QICT - Port Qasim International container terminal, where they were also operating with the same mainstream system. However, later on, more sessions were conducted to create awareness about the importance of the system and how it would be helpful in time-saving and efficiency at work.

It was said that there would be more impact on vessel timings, and they would have more time to stay on the window, which would eventually protect them and safeguard them from different sorts of fines and penalties as well. They were further briefed about more benefits, such as during planning before the vessel's departure, there is a PDI (Pre-departure inspection), which is done, and a report is issued against it where the system tells the suitability and tells if it's ready to depart. This will give a dashboard facility that can be shared through the cloud with partner businesses, so it can also greatly help in correspondence with central planners and other clients. All the stakeholders agreed to implement software to benefit their departments collectively and gave a positive reply with the assurance that all the guidelines would be followed on a real basis.

Details of the Solution

The meetings were very fruitful, and the findings of issues were easily highlighted and noted throughout the process. Although the process was very long, they wanted to bring solutions that would not impact their current operations or their performances. Inputs were taken from operations, commercial, IT, human resource, customer support, and execution teams. All the departments put their valuable inputs on the table and demanded that these options and solutions be included in the new system.

The operation department was the one that was going to be directly impacted by the new system. They demanded that, firstly, a dashboard where all the details, correspondence, legal documentation, integrating with NGEN, handover remarks, and job details should be there for every vessel. Details of containers are usually done with manual paperwork that was being loaded on NGEN. They wanted an option where all the details of the container should be directly loaded into the system so that they do not have to cross-check the details of the container with paperwork. Secondly, the dashboard should contain the correspondence of every stakeholder that is being associated with the vessel which is requesting a change in the plan or any other operation-related tasks that should come through with this new system, as the method of e-mail is found to be very inefficient and taking a lot of time. The option legal documentation should also be there, which focuses on the condition of the container, i.e., whether the customs have cleared it, whether the owner's history is clear, and whether it is legal to be on-board or discharged on the port. According to Mr. Danial, the major demand was to integrate NGEN with the new system, which means they wanted to auto-load these data on NGEN. For instance, if a shipping line gives a list of container numbers that are to be excluded from planning, the system should be smart enough to auto-remove it from NGEN. Every container number is unique. Thus, if the shipping line gives the changes, there should be a button like auto-adjust that can remove and adjust the plan accordingly.

Moreover, the issue of handover remarks needs to be resolved. There should be an option for handover remarks that a planner or any other person who is associated with planning purposes can leave a comment for the next team to handle. To increase accountability and check the performance of employees, Mr. Danial also suggested that a portal is necessary that can show which person has done how many jobs can help him analyze and prepare performance reports. The data should be clear, and the portal should have less complexity.

The commercial department stated that they needed the tracking of the whole operation as they wanted to inform and give updates to their clients about their container stages. According to shipping lines, many irregularities were observed from the port commercial department, as they did not give them precise details about their units. A tracking process will help their clients and provide overall process transparency. The commercial department even argued that this would make their port unique as none of the ports in Karachi is helping their client in such ways. Secondly, there should be an integrated option where all the client's data can be stored.

The IT department was very much conscious of their role in the overall process, especially about the maintenance and quality control of the system. As initial planning and vendors have decided, the IT team of SAPT will also be on board during the implementation and integration of the new system. The management said local IT has a clearer idea of how the port works. They will assist the vendor with limitations and areas they can work out. Microfocus will provide Zoom training to IT staff about the new system, and the IT department itself will do the testing. Microfocus will be in the loop throughout the process if the IT team finds any bugs or uncertainty in the system. IT manager Mr. Shazaib planned and gave the IT team a daily schedule for internal meetings to ensure the new system was integrated successfully. The IT department also gave summaries to the vendors about their current system speed, the hardware that departments are using, and what expected manuals should include. They demanded that the vendor provide an easy go-to manual so that they can distribute it in the office so that they do not have to go to each person to tell the new environment of the system.

HR was very concerned about how many modules they had to add to their training. HR wanted to make sure that training should be easy to conduct, as employees are already following a current system, and they do not want it difficult for the employee to learn new options. Secondly, they wanted to know what sort of people will be best suitable now to work on the new system, if the system is user-friendly and does not require much training they will not change their recruitment techniques but if there are some limitations in the system and complexity is high they have to bring changes to their current recruitment process.

Customer support wanted a system to be quick and efficient. They wanted an option for the data of gate-in containers, which need to be entered manually in NGEN daily. They should add an option in a new system through which the container details are auto-updated once the container is gate-in. They do not have to send an adjustment list to operations, affecting their time and overall productivity.

The execution team requested to add another option in the handover remark section that they can give a reply to the planning team, as there is less accountability in the current system. The execution team wanted operations to be held smoothly. Each and every task that planners are asking should be written on the portal for future reference.

The Implementation Process

The state-of-the-art new system was built in March 2019, and DD (Data and Digitization) was ready for the trial run. After valuable consideration and requests of the departments, the system has various options that were not seen in any port information system. Hutchison Group planned to execute DD as their primary system throughout their 56 ports. Still, DD has to clear its trial period for that, and a significant impact should be seen in SAPT's overall performance. DD provides complete solutions not only to planners but all the stakeholders, which means it was helping out the organization as well as the external stakeholders, which were shipping lines.

The initial trial was conducted in Hong Kong it was done under the supervision of Microfocus and the technical staff of Hutchison group. The trial was conducted for 3-4 months. According to Mr. Danial, we were also informed about the testing of the new system. According to them, the system did not lag much and showed great quality while being used. According to Mr. Shahzaib, integrating or introducing a new system is not easy. They were lucky they did not face many bugs, and things went smoothly for Hutchison and Microfocus. Microfocus was very keen to help out by giving them manuals and instructions for training the new system.

SAPT went for a parallel approach. Mr. Daniel states that port operations are very sensitive and cannot be stopped. Almost 80% of trading is by sea. He said you could not stop air operations. Similarly, you cannot stop port operations. They used a parallel approach because they did not want to risk their current operations if the system failed. Even if the system has passed through several trials, once it is in production and shows bugs, the whole port operations will be affected. Secondly, through this new system, methods are going to be updated. They do not want to risk directly with their current system.

They used the DD strategy they used for implementing the system. In this strategy, the operations department will first use the system. From time to time, new options in DD will be live. Mr. Danial himself conducted the trial. He said DD is like a port ecosystem. The vendor has done thorough research while developing the information system. Once the Operations department has expertise in using the DD, other departments will be using DD, too. The whole value chain was under this new system, and secondly, the integration with the current system was so good it reduced the planning time to almost half, although the time varies from vessel to vessel. However, it was clear that the innovation of DD would have a huge impact on the overall port operations.

It was the first time artificial intelligence was used in a port system. AI was helping the system segregate reports by working on targeted words. For instance, if shipping lines or business units are forwarding an adjustment list, DD will automatically target the keywords of the file and ask the user to execute it or not. Once the user executes it, the DD will automatically adjust the changes in NGEN. The user does not have to make new plans and ask for approval from the business unit; rather, they execute the same instructions given to them, and according to Mr. Danial, we will see a huge decrease in discrepancies and errors due to this facility that DD is providing.

Moreover, DD included a very important option, which was IDOC. Which will be a dashboard (such as a portal), a planner who is working on whatever stage has to mention it on IDOC. It was very user-friendly. In the early stage, the option of IDOC was live. Within a month, the performance of employees increased as they now have a sense of ownership of whatever they do. It even decreases the number of errors within the first two months. When Mr. Danial saw the early outcome, he was very keen to launch another option of DD now. (See Exhibits 3 and 4). Task monitoring was also given to the user. They just have to go through and track where they are actually standing in the operations stage. For the job stages, the planning task was divided into three stages: Stowage optimization, CWP, and the loading sequence. For instance, if a user has done stowage optimization, he goes on IDOC and fills the SO of this particular vessel, the same for all the stages. Every user has an ID. Thus, while they are IDOC, the ID will confirm who has done this certain task.

Danial said during the implementation process, the role of IT was tremendous. They helped the operation team out in so many ways. Although they did not know the severity of the functions, as port operations are not their actual domain, they tried to help us by researching and learning about port operations themselves. The IT support also made their own manuals and provided an operations team. Mr. Danial put it on their file server so everyone could access it. Those manuals help them out during operations when they are stuck. They just have to open the file and search for the option; this way, users learn far more quickly.

The Implementation Team

Mr. Danial said many people were involved in implementing DD. He said it was necessary to include a few of the secondary departments in the implementation process. DD was a system that would bring innovation and change the working environment of the whole organization. Thus, vendors needed to take their input during implementation.

Individuals from Microfocus visited Hutchison group headquarters. They worked with their technical staff to develop the new system accordingly. Hutchison's strategy was executing the new system in all its 56 running ports.

So they wanted a system with generic options yet it covers all the aspects of port operations. Microfocus was very much focused on developing such a system and providing an information system that could bring value to Hutchison's group.

SAPT was the first terminal that would use Data and Digitization. The IT department was in the loop with the Hutchison group. They used to conduct meetings on Zoom and Google Meet to ensure the quality and relevancy of the system. Technical needs and support are critical while executing or implementing a new system. In the past, we have had a number of examples of technical support and needs that were not considered while implementing the new system, and we have seen the adverse consequences.

Operations must be tested first because the system focuses more on operations. They can clearly tell whether the implementation process is going successful. Senior planners with experience of more than three years also took part in the initial testing phase at SAPT. Most of them found great ease in their work. The task they were used to in 30 minutes they were doing now in 10 minutes. Secondly, the upper management who dx the head of departments asked implementation to be very conscious and sensitive during the whole process. They asked IT support to assist at the moment of the day as port operations are running throughout the day and night.

Implementation Issues

During the implementation, several issues were observed but eventually overcome by the organization. As we can see, DD was an innovative technology; it was new and obviously bringing value to the organization. During implementation, everyone was expecting the workforce, processes, and technology to all be challenged by the bringing of new systems. Moreover, a lot of time was consumed while creating DD. The whole process took almost a year and a half. That caused the overall project budget to rise. The strategy was to bring relevancy and quality to the processes, but because of this, complexity increased because many departments were involved in the project. The failure of the information system is not new in the industry. There were several incidents where ports suffered huge losses due to following the wrong procedures. The Hutchison group was very conscious during the implementation stage, although they were confident about the planning they had done before it.

During the initial implementation of DD, people were very skeptical about their future in the organization. This was also expected, and that's why the human resource department was part of the project. Most people related to the operation were smart and easily adapted to the new system. The inertia was being seen in the other departments, such as execution and customer support. Daily wage workers feared having their overtime cut off, and customer support was adjusting. The people in the department had the experience of almost 7-8 years in the port industry. Other ports were still following the traditional methods of client handling. For these, human resources took the initiative and conducted training programs for the department to show how much the new system was making. People from IT support provided them with their study manual to help them overcome their issues.

For daily wage people, management assured them overtime would not be changed. But if the working hours are affected, they will be compensated with allowances. Moreover, people were not in the habit of filling out IDOC, which is actually the recording of their tasks. In the beginning, people used to forget and write about their tasks. Later, when performance sheets were created and the ranking of employees with respect to their number of jobs was noted, people started to fill IDOC more seriously. Although performance reports were annual, for people to be motivated to fill out IDOC, the Head of the department suggested monthly performance reports. A celebration dinner was given at a local 5-star hotel to motivate employees. As per Mr. Danial, human management in the port industry is the toughest task to do. Firstly, because it's a niche industry, people who are willing to come into this industry need to understand the port operation from 0. Secondly, the growth is slow in the department.

Through DD, the whole process of port operations was coming under change. It was like mini restructuring; we can say the process, which took almost a day to execute properly, is being done in half a day. Due to changes in the process major increase in efficiency was observed, as we can see that time and resources are now being used very efficiently, the lag time was reduced, and productivity was seen. Secondly, accountability was increased. With the introduction of the IDOC option in DD, employees owned whatever jobs they had done. They cannot refuse or decline the tasks as they have left or fill the IDOC themselves. The number of errors was reduced as employees were now taking ownership of their tasks. A huge decrease in the number of errors was seen. Secondly auto-generated reports help them to keep focusing on the operations rather than generating reports by feeding data to NGEN. Red tapping was reduced as DD is a platform that is accessible by almost everyone in the organization. Reporting authorities can read and approve the plans by themselves rather than sending files to each and every stakeholder for their manual approval. The upper management can see the process themselves; the process tracking was easy. Now if there is lag or any stage of operations is taking extra time, upper management can see and question the problem. Stakeholders were satisfied and willing to work in the structure. They found it more convenient as the results showed the same. Data storage was also added to the process. All the data being recorded during the operation will be saved under the dashboard. It was very helpful for future references and auditing.

In terms of technology, various issues were seen during implementation. The new information system requires the latest Windows operating system, which must be installed or updated throughout the organization. The IT support was very helpful. They updated the operating system of all PCs. Another issue that was seen was that in the execution department, they were required to install a system. Before that, they only carried out the operations using ROC's printed plans. For accessing DD, it was necessary for them to install the systems. After the local IT support installed the system, they gave initial training. Commercial departments and customer support PCs also needed to be replaced, as DD was incompatible with their old computers.

Exhibit 1
Business Process

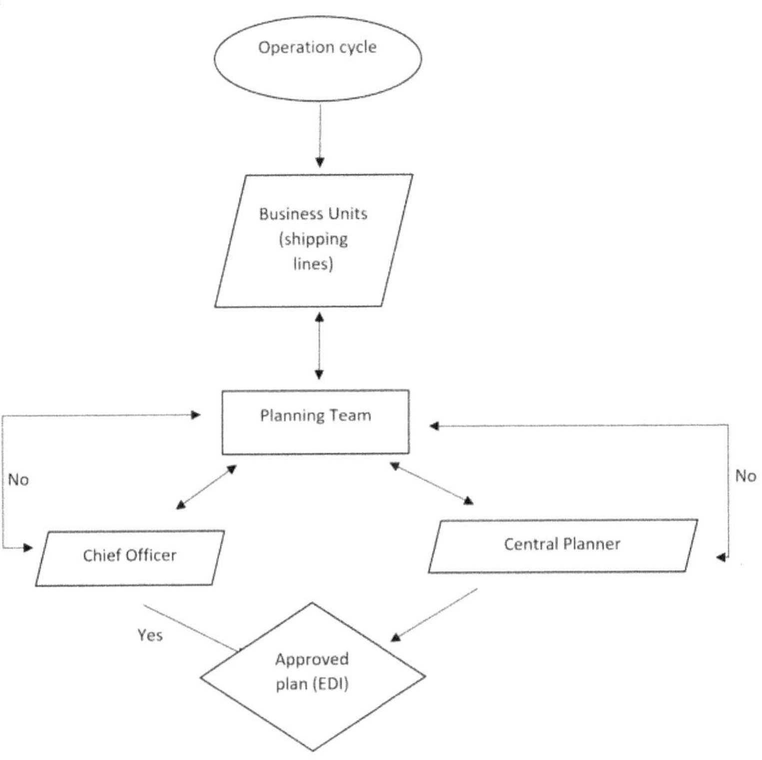

Exhibit 2

City	Country or Region	Name	Share
Barcelona	Spain	Barcelona Europe South Terminal (BEST) in Port of Barcelona	Wholly owned [13]
Buenos Aires	Argentina	Port of Buenos Aires (Terminal 5)	
Brisbane	Australia	Port of Brisbane (Berths 11 & 12)	Wholly owned subsidiary
Sydney		Port Botany (Terminal 3)	
Freeport	Bahamas	Freeport Container Port Limited	Joint Venture (51%)
Willebroek	Belgium	Trimodal Container Terminal Belgium	Subsidiary[x]
Alexandria El Dekheila	Egypt	Alexandria International Container Terminals Company Ltd.	Joint Venture (50%)
Duisburg	Germany	Duisburger Container Terminal GmbH	Subsidiary[x]
Hong Kong	Hong Kong SAR, PRC	Asia Port Services	Wholly owned subsidiary
Hong Kong (Kwai Tsing District)		Kwai Tsing Container Terminals (CT4, CT6, CT7, CT9N)	Subsidiary (66.5%)
Hong Kong (Kwai Tsing District)		Kwai Tsing Container Terminals (CT8)	2nd largest shares holder (33.3%) after COSCO Pacific
Hong Kong (Tuen Mun District)		River Trade Terminal	Joint venture (50%) with Sun Hung Kai Properties
Jakarta	Indonesia	Jakarta International Container Terminal	Joint Venture (51%)
Jakarta		Terminal Petikemas Koja	
Karachi	Pakistan	Karachi International Container Terminal	Subsidiary
Karachi		South Asia Pakistan Terminal	
Taranto	Italy	Taranto Container Terminal S.p.A.	Joint venture (50%)[14]
Busan	South Korea	Hutchison Busan Container Terminal	
Busan		Hutchison Gamman Container Terminal	Subsidiary
Gwangyang		Hutchison Kwangyang Container Terminal	
Gwangyang		Korea International Terminals (Port Phase II)	Subsidiary (89%)
Veracruz	Mexico	Internacional de Contenedores Asociados de Veracruz (ICAVE)	Subsidiary
Lazaro Cardenas		Lázaro Cardenas Terminal Portuaria de Contenedores (LCTPC)	
Port Klang	Malaysia	Westports Malaysia Sdn Bhd	2nd largest shares holder (30%) as of 2000[15]
Dar es Salaam	Tanzania	Tanzania International Container Terminal Services	Subsidiary (70%)[16]
Isle of Grain	United Kingdom	London Thamesport	
Harwich		Harwich International Port	
Felixstowe		Port of Felixstowe	Wholly owned subsidiary
Rotterdam	Netherlands	HUTCHISON PORTS ECT ROTTERDAM	
Yangon	Myanmar	Myanmar International Terminals Thilawa	

Exhibit 3

Exhibit 4

This page was intentionally left blank.

MEEZAN BANK'S BRISK: AUTOMATING THE RISK MANAGEMENT

Shazib Khalil, Suleman Imran, and Maheen Kamal of Karachi School for Business and Leadership (KSBL) prepared this case under the supervision of Dr. Amir Manzoor. The case was prepared solely to provide material for class discussion. The authors do not intend to illustrate either effective or ineffective handling of a managerial situation. Certain names and other identifying information have been disguised to protect confidentiality.

Background

The disruption brought about by new entrants (big technology giants and FinTech) entering the same market with new tools (latest technologies, data sharing, ample funding, lean structure) in their arsenal, having a unique competitive advantage over traditional banking methods, has created new challenges for the banking industry worldwide. The younger generation's technology-dominant lifestyle, purchasing patterns, and demographic changes have radically altered the financial scene. The dramatic change in the banking industry is partially due to globalization and technological advancements. In the banking services sector, "service-dominant reasoning" is quickly taking over the position previously played by "product-dominant logic."

Meezan Bank, Pakistan's first and largest bank, has recently signed an MoU with BenchMatrix to develop a digital platform called BRisk to digitize the Bank's compliance and ORM structure. This agreement was reached mainly as a result of the tireless efforts on the part of the key leads from the risk management group and the IT department, namely Mr. Asad Nouman and Mr. Saad Khilji, respectively. The arrangement can empower Meezan Bank to improve the risk and compliance functions by bringing potency to its process and minimizing risk. Additionally, it will facilitate the bank to meet regulatory requirements by conveyance of additional transparency through automation.

The Risk Management group, in collaboration with the IT department of Meezan Bank Limited, has recently implemented a new in-house software named BRisk for routing, processing, and approval of credit proposals, including but not limited to the annual renewal of accounts, interim approval,

NOC's and various deferrals. These credit proposals are comprehensive data reports which consist of the below-mentioned documents/information:

- Annual audited accounts, financial analysis of the company over the three years
- Industry analysis
- Lending/facility and collateral details
- Basic information about the company
- Shareholding patterns
- Business unit comments
- Risk Management Memo
- Approval chain
- Prudential regulation compliance
- Internal risk rating calculation and the documents tab

Previously, the approvals were processed on paper, consisting of Microsoft Word and Excel files printed and compiled in a box file. This process had its challenges and issues, which were addressed with the introduction of BRisk. Some of the paper-based method issues included unnecessary wastage of time due to the multiple reprinting of the approvals as per the recommendations of the key personnel in the approval process. Another issue was physically inquiring about the whereabouts of the approval, as there was no automated method to track the position of the request regarding the approval process. The paper-based approval process also went against the zero-paper policy of the bank.

Another major concern with the previous practice was that there was no centralized storage of approvals, and large files had to be maintained and stored, which was not feasible. The paper-based method also delayed the approval process due to a lack of accountability, as there wasn't any way to monitor the TAT (turnaround time) of each individual and department. Formatting all the documents/files in a proposal was a challenge. Even a slight change/revision/ amendment resulted in a change in the entire formatting of the documents. Due to the high expectations of the management, the entire proposal needs to be in a well-presentable form. Because these documents include tables, text boxes, pictures, charts, and text, the business unit is to ensure proper formatting at all times.

The work-life balance of the corporate bankers was disturbed in large numbers at Meezan Bank since the entire process of making a proposal/ renewal was so cumbersome and burdening for an individual that it took a lot of late sittings to complete a proposal in time. Therefore, many employees started considering switching to banks with automated request systems so that they could leave work at a more reasonable time.

The work-from-home policy during the Pandemic further highlighted the cons of the previous manual paper-based system as an individual becomes handicapped with all the physical files being stored on the bank's premises. Furthermore, no approvals can be processed from home as it requires manual signatures over the proposal from different personnel.

The Credit Proposal

The typical credit proposal consists of several files and annexures, briefly discussed below.

Credit proposal (CP) – A credit proposal, in the form of a Word file, is a summary of the entire proposal, which includes financial analysis, industry analysis, relationship strategy, facility rationale, financial projections, and facility summary. Currently, the initially made credit proposal is routed to different line managers and heads for review, and if any change is highlighted during review by any line manager or head, the entire Word file has to be re-printed to cater to their requests. This cumbersome process is repeated several times whenever an amendment is suggested at any level of approval, and the same is manually approved by all those who have already approved.

Basic Information Report (BIR) – It is in the form of a Word File. It contains basic information about the company, including the company profile, shareholding pattern, capacity and utilization, other bank lines, and major buyers & suppliers. The manually prepared proposal, at times, takes months before getting finally approved. During the time duration when the proposal is under review and discussion, there might be any change in the company that relates to BIR. Therefore, the entire BIR needs to be revised and printed again.

Financial Snapshot (FS) – The FS, in the form of an Excel file, consists of annual audit accounts of the company for the last three years, latest quarterly management account, and a comparison among them in percentage change. Different ratios for all three years are also calculated in the same file. The numbers are incorporated, while some heads of the financials are calculated manually using Excel. Ratios are also calculated by using different formulas and linking the cells together. Quarterly accounts figures are proportionate accordingly as per the number of months. The entire file is highly error-prone, and any mistake or negligence may result in a false outlook of the company. The change in terms of percentage is also calculated by incorporating formulas over Excel, which may give a false overview if not calculated correctly.

Potential Regulation Checklist (PRC) – This checklist, in the form of a Word file, highlights all the potential regulations (As per State Bank of Pakistan) and confirms whether the specific company complies with the same or not. The PRC needs to correctly account for the company's and group's overall borrowing against Meezan Bank and their limit as per PRC. Any typo error of the wrong accumulated borrowing figure of the customer may lead to a discrepancy in the document.

Facility Risk Rating (FRR) – Excel File: FRR calculates risk rating separately for all the facilities that are provided to a customer. This internally developed model highlights a certain risk level associated with a facility. Different check boxes are marked for each facility as per the nature of the facility/product, and a formula is in place with the help of Excel to calculate the relative risk associated with the facility. A single wrong check box marked can completely alter the result. Therefore, the same must be done with close attention to minimizing any chances of error.

Obligator Risk Rating (ORR) – An ORR, in the form of an Excel file, calculates a company's risk rating based on different ratios, company history, industry view, ownership structure, and future outlook.ORR is calculated in the same way as FRR. However, the model enables the user to calculate the overall risk attached to the company. The issues highlighted in FRR are the same for ORR, but the importance of ORR is high as it is considered one of the basic elements in making decisions for any lending to the company.

Facility Appendix (FA) – An FA, in the form of a Word file, consists of the details of all the facilities and their respective security structure mentioned in the FA. That is one of the most important sections as all the facilities, their details, conditions, security, and rate that are mentioned on FA are written as it is on the Offer letter of the customer once the case is approved. Once the FA is approved, any error or amendment cannot be made to the FA.

Profitability Sheet (PS) – A PS, in the form of an Excel sheet, highlights all the income and their break-up (facility-wise) that the bank earns and calculates proposed income and yield for the next year. The profitability sheet also calculates the Company's hurdle rate based on net average assets, ORR, and external rating. Once Excel calculates the hurdle rate after incorporating certain information, the next step is calculating the yield by inputting the income earned during the year. Proposed yield and income for the next year are predicted based on facility offering in the renewal, rates proposed for the facilities, and relationship strategy for the coming year. The Excel sheet comprises different formulas and linked cells to calculate the figures as already discussed.

Meezan Bank History

The bank started as an Islamic Investment bank in 1997 and was then known as Al-Meezan Investment Bank. In 2002, the State Bank of Pakistan declared it the first Islamic Bank of Pakistan. In 2002, MBL acquired the Pakistan operations of Society General, and in 2014, MBL signed an agreement with HSBC Bank Middle East to acquire its operations in Pakistan. Founders of Meezan Bank are Riyadh S.A.A. Edrees, Habib Haidar and Muhammad Taqi Usman. Meezan Bank is renowned as a full-coverage Islamic bank that follows banking operations according to the Shariah of Islam, which includes multiple products such as debit cards, consumer/premium/business banking, and loans and savings. MBL mobile app is also the highest-rated app in Pakistan in 2021, with more than 123,000 encouraging reviews. Its headquarters is located in Karachi, famously known as Meezan House. The bank is part of the top 4 banks in Pakistan in terms of profitability, with a net profit of PKR 28.5 billion for the financial year 2021. The total assets acquired by the institute are PKR 1.9 trillion.

Meezan Bank is the first and largest Islamic bank in Pakistan. With over 900 branches in over 240 cities, it has the largest Islamic banking network in Pakistan. Meezan Bank has consistently been recognized as the Best Islamic Bank in Pakistan by numerous local and international institutions, including its recognition as the 'Best Bank of the Year 2020 – Large Size Banks' by the CFA Society of Pakistan, 'Best Bank – 2018' by Pakistan Banking Awards – the most prestigious award in the country's financial sector and by Islamic Finance News – Malaysia, Global Finance magazine – New York, Asset AAA – Hong Kong, Asiamoney – Hong Kong, The Banker – United Kingdom, South Asian Federation of Accountants, Islamic Finance Forum of South Asian Awards, – Dawn & IBP Pakistan, Employers Federation of Pakistan and CFA Association – Pakistan.

VIS Credit Rating Company Limited (Formerly JCR-VIS Credit Rating Company Limited), an affiliate of Japan Credit Rating Agency, Japan, has reaffirmed the Bank's long-term entity rating of AA+ (Double A Plus) and short-term rating at A1+ (A One Plus) with a stable outlook. The rating indicates sound performance indicators of the Bank.

History of Information Systems at Meezan Bank

Being a bank subject to regular audits by the regulator, that is, the State Bank of Pakistan (SBP), and prudential regulations that secure the deposits of the general public, there has been quite an emphasis on the importance of information systems and data management. But considering the year-on-year growth in both operations and core business model, which moves to *increase the footprint of Islamic banking* in Pakistan and expands the overall operations of the corporate finance, commercial department, and the stakeholders (Risk Management department, shariah compliance department, and Corporate Portfolio Management Unit etc.), the need for any online system was felt which has been addressed through the introduction of Brisk to streamline the workflow.

Exhibit 1 shows the entire workflow from the start of making a credit proposal until it gets approved and submitted to the Credit Administration department for disbursement of facilities.

Corporate Finance & Commercial Departments

Corporate finance departments govern and oversee their firms' financial activities and capital investment decisions. Such decisions include whether to pursue a proposed investment and pay for the investment with equity, debt, or both. Corporate finance deals with corporate-level customers and blue-chip companies requiring large bank lines. The Bank has different financial products offered to the corporate customer as per their need and requirements. Every product is specified with its terms & conditions, process flows, tenure, and profit calculation method. Meezan Bank has a corporate portfolio of approximately PKR 600 billion distributed in 3 regions: North, South, and Central, comprising 15 Relationship Associates, 15 Relationship Managers, 6 Team Leaders, and 3 Unit Heads. Corporate finance is also responsible for increasing the footprint in trade segment and capturing the trade market of their corporate customers to increase the no-funded income of the bank.

The commercial department mainly deals with the small sector business and personal landings to sole proprietors. They offer the same financial products as the corporate finance function, but the major difference is that their exposure size is smaller per customer than that of corporate finance. The Commercial department portfolio currently stands at PKR 300 billion and comprises ten relationship managers and 02 team leaders.

The prime objective of the Corporate Finance & Commercial department is to generate business through the below-mentioned means.

- Finance – Working capital, Long-term loans, and structured finance.

- Transaction Banking – Trade finance, Supply chain solutions, Remittances, Cash management, and Escrow services

- Investments – Term deposits, Mutual funds and structured instruments

- Treasury – Debt capital markets, Forex, and Derivatives

Many professionals stay in corporate banking for the long term because it offers an excellent work/life balance, reasonable advancement opportunities, and high-paying salaries.

Risk Department

Risk management in banking has been transformed over the past decade, largely in response to regulations that emerged from the global financial crisis and the fines levied. But important trends suggest risk management will experience even more sweeping changes in the next decade. The change expected in the risk function's operating model illustrates the magnitude of what lies ahead. Today, about 50 percent of the department's staff is dedicated to risk-related operational processes such as credit administration. The role of the risk department revolves around assessing the creditworthiness of an individual or company to determine the likelihood that they will honor their financial obligations. Credit analysts evaluate borrowers' past financial and credit history to determine their financial health and ability to repay credit advanced to them by a lender.

When evaluating a borrower's financial health, the credit analyst gathers important financial information and evaluates it using financial ratios. They can also compare the ratios with industry benchmarks to decide if a borrower's cash flow is sufficient to repay the loan. The credit analyst will then recommend the credit limit for a new customer based on the company's lending policies, but the final decision on whether to grant credit will be made by the underwriters, who rely on the analyst's intelligence to make their decision. At Meezan Bank, the risk department comprises approximately 100 people, including Analysts, Managers, and head of department who are looking after portfolios from all the regions of Pakistan.

System Selection

The time-consuming and pain stacking process of huge paper files, which were hard to maintain in records and delayed the approval process due to the constant changes required by different approving authorities, were under the noting of the top management. There had also been pressure from the regulator i.e. SBP, to strive the banking industry towards digitization whereby the maximum processes are automated, and usage of paper was at bare minimum.

The departmental heads also pursued top management to launch software that could cater to the approval process. Thus, a discussion took place with the Risk Management Department's head with the presence of the IT department as well. The Risk department was chosen for an initial discussion and subsequently for spearheading the development in liaison with the IT department because they were the competent authority in the bank who could contribute towards the building and implementation of the required software on the basis that they had more hands-on experience with the process of approval needed for overall banks various departments such as Corporate, Commercial, Car Ijarah, House financing, Consumer financing, etc. and were accustomed to the various types of requests which were processed in the bank. If the same task had been given to any other department, then they would have developed the software as per their requirements/nature of approval, which would have needed a high degree of changes upon usage by any other department.

In the meeting that took place between the top management consisting of the CEO, Deputy CEO, and CFO with heads of the Risk Management Department and IT, it was concluded that the Risk department would be the contact point for the IT department who will guide them about the requirements which had to be catered through the new software. The risk department would appoint one person who would be leading the project from their side along with the IT dept doing the same. The IT department would have a dedicated team (number to be decided by the head who would only look after the project's development). There was no such team for the Risk Management Department (RMG) department as they were to be more involved with requirements that shall be catered through the software and had an advising role. IT team would take quotations from different vendors after understanding current paper-based approvals and the requirements. There would be monthly briefings to the top management upon the project update. The same had to be implemented, and pilot run to be conducted before the year-end so the same could be highlighted in the annual report to the bank's shareholders, leaving just shy of 10 months for the involved departments to start and complete the massive task assigned to them.

The risk department then afterward had a meeting internally where their senior officials discussed the possible individuals who could be tasked with leading the project. The same was a difficult task as the selected individual would effectively be looking after the project development, which will cater to the financing approvals and was instrumental; thus, they would have to have a holistic view of the whole approval process, from start to end with regards to the requirements and the approving powers of various authorities, etc. Many names were put forward and debated; however, in the end, the name of Mr Asad Nauman was agreed upon by all the attendees.

Mr. Asad Nauman is an IBA graduate of the Class of 2005 (MBA) and started his professional career with Meezan Bank as Assistant Manager in the Risk Department. Through his dedication and tireless efforts, he rose through the ranks and got his latest promotion as a Senior Vice President in the organization in just 13 years and was young and energetic as regarded in the SVP ranks. He had served briefly in the Corporate Department as well during his early years in the capacity of Relationship Manager, which gave him an edge over his peer as he had also tended to a client dealing in the front office and processed financing requests, unlike the others who had only served in the back office and had only been on the receiving end of the Business Unit's Request.

At the IT department's end, the name of Mr. Saad Khilji was proposed and was accepted by the department. Mr. Saad's long-serving career at MBL proved to be a deciding factor as he had an accumulated experience of 9 years in the banking industry, 7 of which were at MBL and the initial two were at Habib Bank Limited as an IT officer, which meant that he had amassed the experience required for the implementation of the project. He was currently serving as an Assistant Vice President and was due for the big promotion to Vice President, which came with the sought-after perk of a 1000 CC company-maintained car and 150 liters of petrol from the bank. To achieve the same, he took on the project to prove his mantle. He was given ten dedicated resources that would assist him with the project.

M.r Asad met with Mr. Saad Khilji in a series of meetings over the coming days to discuss the financing proposal, the various types of requests, documents, etc. Mr. Asad briefed him about the issues currently faced by the incumbents and developed Mr. Saad's understanding of what was required to seek the same with the vendors. With the complete information, Mr. Saad was now well versed with and inquired in the market about possible, reliable vendors who were capable of providing the required digital solution. A total of 7 vendors were selected who came as reliant on background checks and whose names and work were worthy of being considered by Meezan Bank. They were approached by Mr. Saad, who briefed them about the requirements. Mr. Asad was also taken on the discussion where the vendor required greater understanding. All the vendors were asked to give their presentation along with the final proposal incorporating their quotations and the proposed software's salient features within four weeks. Upon receipt of all proposals and presentations, Mr. Saad and Mr. Asad reviewed them. They selected three vendors based on their quotation, past projects, a committed timeline for development and submission of the software, and market reviews.

Out of the 3, one of the vendors took their name out of the contention as they wanted to revise their quotation. However, this was not possible. After getting the relevant go-ahead from the IT and Risk Management Dept department head, the remaining two vendors were called for a final presentation with the top management for their approval. The top management took the presentations and finalized the vendor by the name of "Bench Matrix". The selection of the vendor was primarily made based on two driving factors. First and foremost, cost. Bench Matrix committed a lower cost than the other vendor and thus was already higher in the running. The second was the success story and positive feedback associated with the vendor. He had just developed and installed a similar software solution for the Soneri Bank and was riding on its success. A formal agreement was signed with the vendor, who started working right away.

Detail of Solution Implemented

Building on the experience from working on an earlier project in the same industry and capacity, the vendor proved to be instrumental as they could quickly derive a basic understanding of Meezan's operations. They had weekly meetings with Mr. Asad and Mr. Saad, updated them on the developments, and took advice and recommendations for incorporating the software. The same briefed the top management on any major developments in the software.

For this project, chocolate implementation was adhered to whereby the vendor. However, it had a similar product developed for Soneri Bank. Still, due to requirements that served to cater to the users more and make the software friendly, it took time to develop the software accordingly.

Bench Matrix gave software by the proposed name of "**BRisk**" within the next five months. The same was suggested by Mr. Asad and accepted by all the stakeholders and stood for Business Risk, which has many associated risks like Strategic, Compliance, Operational, and Reputational, which was appropriate in financing. Seven months had lapsed since the first meeting about the software.

Bench Matrix provided an end-to-end solution by developing customized software that included all the required information tabs for incorporating the data. The software ran on an intranet and provided security of the highest standard, as only the designated officials from the relevant departments, like Risk Management, Corporate, and Commercial, could access the software upon the allocation of rights by the IT department. The user interface (UI) was made friendly, with a clear division of viewing powers and approving rights. For better clarity, requests were to be initiated by the relationship team, namely the designated Assistant Relationship Manager and Relationship Manager who was tasked with the initiation of all the requests had separate rights such as attachment of documents and write-up of the request but not approving authority which was allowed to senior officials like Department Heads who shall approve or reject the request.

The system, at first glance, was perceived to be well thought out due to a number of reasons mentioned below:

1. First and foremost, all the required ratios (like Current Ratio, Interest Ratio, Debt Service ratio etc.), which are absolute necessities for gauging the financial health of a company regardless of its industry, were automatically calculated by the software as all the relevant formulas were already incorporated in the backend. They required only the punching of the audited accounts (Balance Sheet and Profit and loss Statement) in the software.

2. The cash flow statement was also automatically generated by the software and was accurate, which was time effective, unlike the old practice of inputting the complicated cash flow statement.

3. The software was capable of storing records for the previous three years, and the same shall be accessible by both users and auditors (external and internal) without any hassle of reviewing and shall maintain the audit trail.

4. Facility structure (type of financing product) along with relevant security could be added & tagged with each other. The same could be revised accordingly in the system. That was a significant relief in terms of efficiency as it would only be required to input once instead of multiple times, and any change would be updated in real-time.

5. Real-time updates and progress of the initiated request could be monitored as to where the request was currently under review with, i.e., with the Corporate Dept or with the Risk Department.

6. The old practice of manually printing huge stacks of paper, which were eventually discarded along with taking the whole file from one official to another, which was a tedious task, was finally poised to finish. If the same official requested a change in the proposed request, then the same was printed with the revised wording, and a sign-off was arranged by the officials again.

See Exhibit 7 for snaps of the system.

System Approval Process

After the initial version of the software was made available to the IT dept and Mr. Asad Nauman, they asked the vendor for some tweaks before portraying the same internally to their line managers. The updated version, which incorporated the proposed changes suggested by the Risk Management Department, one of the intended users of the program, was showcased to both the corporate and commercial departments for taking their feedback on the same.

The Heads of both the above departments, who were already aware of the changes, were then given a presentation by the IT dept and a live demonstration of the software with demo IDs. Both the heads stated that they would give their final go-ahead after looping their resources, who shall be the ones who are going to be using the system. The presentation was routed to both heads for sharing with their departments, and a live demonstration was also set for them in the coming days to give them a better idea of the software that was going to be implemented.

All the departments' resources reviewed the detailed presentation, and the same took the live demo as well. They proposed some minor changes in the software, which were considered by the IT department, which coordinated with the vendor to implement the same. After the proposed changes were incorporated, the department heads were again given a live demo with a description of changes incorporated in the software per the requests received. Both the departmental heads then provided their sign-off on the software.

The final concept and implementation process was available now that the main departments (Corporate, Commercial & Risk Department) had provided their concurrence on the software and an updated version addressing their needs and requirements. The software was then presented to the top management to accord their approval on the version. The training was given to all the users. The system went live with the old system of paper-based proposals made redundant within six weeks after all the previously routed requests were approved, with any fresh request to be routed using the Brisk software.

The Implementation Process

It was decided that overall, all the corporate and commercial department regions will be taken live on the software with only partial employees in the Risk Management department, i.e., those who were working with corporate and commercial. The approach to take software online region by region was also discussed, i.e., both the Corporate and Commercial comprise of several regions like North, South, Multan, etc., but the same was not finalized due to various reasons.

Firstly, it made more sense to take the whole department online at once since it would seem odd that some resources were working online and some were working on the old format. Secondly, it would have resulted in continuous training of the employees of various regions, which would have consumed more time. Lastly, the vision was to take the whole department online at once. Thus, the same was to be achieved.

It was acknowledged that the employees would take time to get used to the new system despite the training. There were already some requests which were under process and, due to the urgency of nature, will need to be processed on an immediate basis, so the parallel approach was decided to be implemented for the next two months after taking the system alive whereby the paper-based system will be made redundant after the time passes. There were also bound to be some issues and bugs that would hamper the processing of the requests like the system not recognizing the inputted facility or not allowing the request to move forward despite meeting all requirements, which necessitated the continuation of the paper-based approach for some time.

The IT department created the credentials and rights of the departmental workers in the system with the help of the vendor. Initially, the main request is that the Annual Renewal be taken live on the software with other requests like NOC, Security changes, deferrals, etc., to be taken alive after a few days of reviewing the progress of the annual renewals first.

The IT department gave the training to all the users, who took them through all the tabs of the software and taught them how to navigate the same. The training was specific to each set of users in line with the approving powers or processing requirements of the intended users; for example, the rights allocated to the Assistant Relationship Managers of the Corporate Department had different rights when compared to Credit Analysts of the Risk Department who had separate rights and were to use different tabs in the software.

The training was spread throughout a few sessions for the user sets, which allowed them to grasp the information and raise queries that were appropriately responded to by the IT dept. Any suggestions were also noted, and if the same was found relevant, then Mr. Saad Khilji would discuss the same with Mr. Asad and request the vendor to incorporate the same in the software. After the training was complete, the software went live for usage across the departments.

There were many implementation issues faced by the IT department, which they had to cater to.

First and foremost, the new software required a much higher intra-net connection than what was already used at MBL. Therefore, a new intra-net with enhanced speed was procured, which had its own costs and challenges. In addition to intra-net, the software was only compatible with Windows 10 and above; thus, the IT Department had to update the Windows operating system of many users who were using old, outdated versions of Windows. Furthermore, old personal computers, which were slow, also had to be replaced with their data copied to the new computers, which tested the IT department's scarce resources and were overburdened with work.

Another major challenge faced by the IT department team was educating the end users on the efficient use of the system as they were not used to such systems. The IT department had to develop special training for all the types of different users based on their usage of the system.

Approval processes and workflow used for routing requests had to be catered in the system, unlike in the paper-based format. For example, a relationship manager could not route the request directly to the departmental head, and the same had to go through all the approving authorities before going to the head.

Further, the implementation process was very lengthy as initially new system was made from scratch custom to MBL's requirements. There were many versions as various changes were highlighted that had to be incorporated. The system was the first of its kind in the MBL and took some getting used to by all the involved departments.

Further, upon the system going live, there were many issues that had to be tackled hands-on by the IT department. Many users could not access their accounts. Therefore, they were reallocated rights in the system. For the ones who still couldn't access it, old system rights were deleted, and new rights were incorporated and assigned. The system also crashed when the users were high, and the same had to be rectified by the IT department. There were many other glitches and bugs that were dealt with by the IT department.

The Way Forward

After the implementation of the BRisk software in the Corporate, Risk, and Commercial departments, the same is under development for other departments like Car Financing, Consumer financing, and House financing, etc., whereby the number of transactions is much higher as approval is sought for many different applicants daily and are raise mostly one. It shall have its pilot run in the last quarter of FY22. The bank is also advancing on other technological platforms, like its mobile app for payments. Conferences are also taking place on Zoom and Microsoft instead of physical meetings, which have always been the practice.

Exhibit 1
Process Flow For Approval From Departments

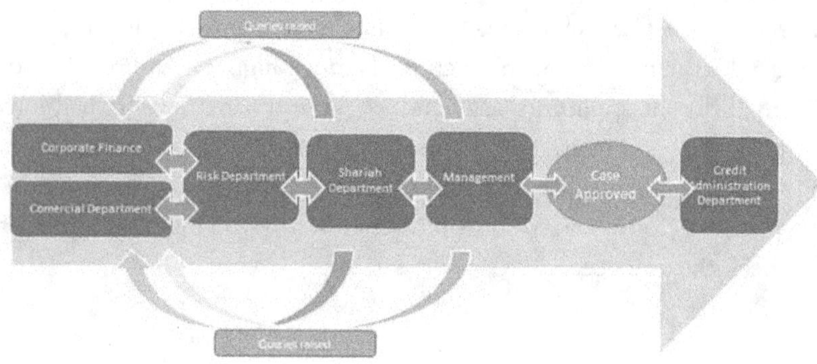

Exhibit 2
Meezan Bank's Key Indicators

Indicator – PKR Millions	Jun-19 Audited	Jun-20 Audited	Jun-21 Audited	Change %	HY 2022 Unaudited
Sales	4,394	5,234	6,064	16%	3,681
Gross Profit	265	348	485	39%	487
EBITDA	645	697	869	25%	678
EBITDA Margin (%)	15%	13%	14%	8%	18%
Operating Profit	318	401	508	27%	493
Other Income	53	53	22	-59%	5
Finance Cost	77	76	95	25%	44
Net Income/Loss	152	194	360	86%	378
Current Assets	1,436	1,842	2,332	27%	2,755
Total Assets	6,465	6,683	9,169	37%	9,838
Current Liabilities	1,297	1,444	1,898	31%	1,942
Total Bank Debt	782	528	900	71%	1,170
Short Term Debt	178	141	132	-6%	95
Long Term Debt	389	262	474	81%	736
CMLTD	215	125	294	135%	339
Total Liabilities	1,805	1,830	2,639	44%	2,929
Equity	4,660	4,854	6,530	35%	6,908
Surplus on Revaluation	3,210	3,192	4,467	40%	4,467
Subordinated Loan	-	-	-	0%	-
Current Ratio (x)	1.11	1.28	1.23	-4%	1.42
Leverage (x)	0.39	0.38	0.40	7%	0.42
Adjusted Leverage (x)	0.54	0.32	0.44	37%	0.48
DSCR (x)	2.21	3.47	2.24	-36%	1.77
ICR (x)	4.13	5.28	5.36	2%	11.30
Gross Margin (%)	6%	7%	8%	20%	13%
Operating Margin (%)	7%	8%	8%	9%	13%
Net Margin (%)	3%	4%	6%	60%	10%
Net Cash from Operating Activities	403	527	652	24%	343
Cash Conversion Cycle	(20)	3	3	-5%	14
Days Receivable	48	42	46	9%	87
Days Inventory	18	19	18	-3%	37
Days Payable	86	58	61	6%	110
Working Capital	139	398	434	9%	813

Exhibit 3
Prudential Regulation

Prudential Regulations Corporate and Commercial Check-Off List

PR	Customer Name: XYZ	xx-xxx-xxxx		
		Yes	No	NA
R-1	Total Exposure is not exceeding Rs. 37,325 Million	Yes		
	Total Fund-Based exposure is not exceeding Rs. 37,325 Million	Yes		
	Total Group Exposure is not exceeding Rs. 46,657 Million	Yes		
	Total Fund-Based Group exposure is not exceeding Rs. 46,657 Million	Yes		
	Single related party exposure limit is not exceeding Rs. 13,997 Million	Yes		
	Group related party exposure limit is not exceeding Rs. 27,994 Million	Yes		
R-2	Contingent liabilities of UBL shall not exceed 10 times of its equity. (Confirm from FINCON)	Yes		
R-3	CIB report is available.	Yes		
	Audited Financial Statements are available.	Yes		
	Borrower Basic Fact Sheet is available.	Yes		
R-4	Clean facility is upto Rs.2,000,000/-			NA
	TFCs rated 'A-' and 'BBB' are subject to minimum margin of 20%.			NA
	Shares are subject to minimum margin of 30%.			NA
	Minimum margin is kept on the security.	Yes		
R-5	Joint Inspection of pledged stocks has been conducted.			NA
R-6	Exposure against Shares/TFCs- Upto 5% of equity Rs _________ Million			NA
R-7	All LGs are fully secured.	Yes		

115

Exhibit 4

Sample FRR Model

BG – FRR Model – Ziauddin University

o.	Factors	Weightage	
	Facility -40%		
1	**Nature of Loan**	10%	
	Self Liquidating Short Term/LC Sight	10	
	Short Term/ LG	6	6
	Long Term	3	
2	**any**	4%	
	0	4	4
	0-6 Months	3	
	>6-1 year	2	
	>1 year – 2 Years	1	
	>2 Years	0	
3	**Repayment Structure**	8%	
	Monthly repayments/ Short Term	8	
	Quarterly repayments	5	
	Half Yearly repayments	3	
	Yearly Repayment	1	
	Bullet repayment	0	0
4	**Purpose of Loan**	10%	
	Working capital requirement/ LC/LG < 6 Months	10	10
	LG>=6 & < 1 Year	8	
	Addition/ improvement in fixed assets/BMR/LG >1 Year	7	
	Expansion	5	
	Greenfield	2	
	Rescheduling/ Restructuring of Loans	0	

5	**Loan Structure/Product Type**	**8%**	
	Non – Funded/ Sight LCs	8	
	Non – Funded/ DA LCs/LG	5	5
	Funded/ Local LCs	2	
	Collateral – 60%		
6	**Degree of collateralization**	**6%**	
	Security Indicator A/ Y	6	
	Security Indicator B	5	
	Security Indicator C	4	
	Security Indicator D	3	
	Security Indicator E	2	
	Security Indicator F	1	
	Security Indicator G	-2	-2
7	**Composition of collateral**	**10%**	
	100% readily realizable	10	
	<100% - 80% readily realizable	8	8
	<80% - 60% readily realizable	6	
	<60% - 40% readily realizable	4	
	<40% - 20% readily realizable	2	
	<20% readily realizable	-2	
8	**Liquid nature of collateral**	**11%**	
	Security Class I	11	
	Security Class II	10	
	Security Class III	9	
	Security Class IV	8	
	Security Class V	7	
	Security Class VI	-3	-3

#		Weight	Score	Value
9	**Perishablity of the collateral**	2%		
	Non Perishable		2	2
	Perishable		0	
10	**collateral**	2%		
	Insured against all risk		2	2
	Insured against selective risk		1	
	Uninsured		0	
11	**Type of charge**	8%		
	Lien on securities (Security classes 1-IV)		8	
	Lien on documents/Securities, Pledge on goods, Full Registered Mortgage		6	
	Token Registered Mortgage		5	
	Exclusive Charge on Fixed Assets (FA)		4	
	Pari Passu Charge on FA/ Joint Pari Passu Charge on FA		3	
	Ranking charge, Equitable Mortgage		2	
	Charge on current assets		-2	-2
12	**Legal enforceability –Realizability**	7%		
	Without legal recourse		7	
	With legal recourse		1	1
13	**Legal Status of rights**	6%		
	No document deferred		6	6
	Collateral related Non-Crucial documents deferred		4	
	Collateral related Semi-Crucial documents deferred		2	
	Collateral related Crucial documents deferred		0	
14	**Time required to dispose off**	8%		
	Upto 1 Month		8	
	>1 to 6 Months		5	
	>6 Months to 1 Yr		4	4
	>1 Yr to 2 Yrs		2	
	>2 Yrs to 5 Yrs		1	
	>5 Yrs		0	
	Total	100%		41
	Grade			D

FRR Model	
A	0%
B	Up to 20%
C	21% to 40%
D	**41% to 60%**
E	61% to 80%
F	81% to 100%

Grade	D
Total Score	41.00
FRR Score	59.00

Exhibit 5
Obligor Risk Rating Model

Obligor Risk Rating Model - Corporate/Commercial

				Insert "X" in correct box. Do not tamper with the formulae	Weightage	Scores
COMPANY:	XYZ		ORR 5			
Segment / Sector:	Corporate Banking	Corporate				
Date of Rating:	xxx					
				Insert X in box		

1 Condition of Industry — 7%

	Insert X	Weightage	Scores
Expanding - Grow, as per industry concentration limits	x	7%	7.0%
Stable - Hold, as per industry concentration limits		3%	
Recessionary - Reduce, as per industry concentration limits		0%	

2 Firm's Position in the Industry — 5%

	Insert X	Weightage	Scores
Top 0-10% in terms of market share		5%	
Top 11-30% in terms of market share	x	4%	4.0%
Top 31-50% in terms of market share		3%	
51-80% in terms of market share		1%	
Bottom 20% in terms of market share		0%	

Data is available for documented industries.
For undocumented industries, use

3 Borrowing/Equity — 5%

Fund-Based Exposure is

	Insert X	Weightage	Scores
Less than 1 time of Equity	x	5%	5.0%
Between 1 to 2 times of Equity		4%	
Between 2 to 3 times of Equity		3%	
Between 3 to 4 times of Equity		2%	
*Greater than 4 times of Equity		0%	

OR

For Seasonal Financing (Sugar & Textile sector only)

	Insert X	Weightage
Less than 2 times of Equity		5%

For Seasonal Financing (Sugar & Textile sector only)

	Insert X	Weightage
Less than 2 times of Equity		5%
Between 2 to 4 times Equity		4%
Between 4 to 6 times Equity		3%
Between 6 to 7 times Equity		2%
Between 7 to 8 times Equity		1%
*Greater than 8 times of Equity		0%

4 Management Quality — 10%

Insert X in relevant boxes

	2.5 Outstanding	2 Strong	1.5 Acceptable	1 Weak	0 Very Weak	Weightage	Scores
Data Sharing with UBL			x				
Presence of Second Line Management / Succession			x				
Technical & Market know how			x				
Automated MIS			x				
TOTAL:	0.0	0.0	6.0	0.0	0.0	6.0%	6.0%

5 Ownership Structure — 10%

	Insert X	Weightage	Scores
Majority owned by an MNC (rating - investment grade or better) or GOP		10%	
Minority owned by an MNC (rating - investment grade or better) or GOP - Not less than 25%		8%	
Public Limited Company (Listed)		7%	
Public Limited Company (UnListed)		6%	
Private Limited Company	x	4%	4.0%
Registered Partnership		2%	
Unregistered Partnership/ Sole Proprietorship		0%	

6 Relationship with UBL — 5%

	Insert X	Weightage	Scores
Client 7 years & over	x	5%	5.0%
Client 4 years & over		4%	
Client 3 years & over		3%	
Client 1-3 years		2%	
New Client		0%	

* Account to be marked "Debit Block" unless SBP clearance is obtained.

7 Past Repayment/ Relationship History — 14%

CIB Report

	Insert X	Weightage	Scores
Clean with no DUB	x	5%	5.0%

Criteria	Check	Weight	Score	Weight %	Score %
Clean with no R/R	x		5%	5.0%
Clean with one R/R			3%	
Clean with more than one R/R/Overdues / Defaults			0%	
Default History with UBL		For Existing Obligors Only		
No default / delay in payment of principal beyond 30 days and Cleanup requirement is m	x		5%	5.0%
No default / delay in payment of principal beyond 30 days or Cleanup requirement is met (For NICF etc.) (one condition is met)			2%	
Incidence of default / delay more than 30 days/Cleanup requirement is not met (For NICF etc.)			0%	
Markup Servicing*:				
Average Payment within 15 days	x		4%	4.0%
Average Payment within 30 days			2%	
Average Payment exceeding 30 days			0%	

OR

Criteria	Check	Weight	Score	Weight %	Score %
No. of years in Business		For New Obligors only		
Above 15 years			9%	
>/= 9 Years			7%	
>/= 3 Years			3%	
< 3 years			0%	

8 Deferrals in Documentation — 5%

No Deferrals	x		5%	5.0%
Deferral (s)/ Ranking charge on current/fixed assets			0%	

9 Quality of Audited Statements** — 9%

Financials Statements   (Audited last Financial year)

Audited and Unqualified	x		4%	4.0%
Unaudited / Audited but qualified			0%	

Quality of Firm's Auditors   (According to SBP Category of Audit Firm)

Category A	x		5%	5.0%
Category B			2%	
Category C			1%	
Category C			1%	
Other			0%	

**10 Financial Performance
[As per audited financials]** — 30%

Sales Trend

Increasing sales trend (over past two years)	x		2%	2.0%
Stable sales trend			1%	
Decreasing sales trend (over past two years)			0%	

Net Profit Trend

Increase in each of previous two years	x		2%	2.0%
Increase in past year only			1%	
Other			0%	

Gross Profit Margin

GP Margin greater than 15%			2%	
GP Margin less than 15%	x		0%	0.0%

* 6 month average
** Overall Judgemental ORR will be assigned if latest audited financials are not used.

Net Profit Margin

NP Margin greater than 2%	x		4%	4.0%
NP Margin less than 2%			2%	
NP Margin less than 0%			0%	

Net Operating cash generation

Positive cash flow in consecutive last 3 years	x		4%	4.0%
Positive cash flow in 2 years out of last 3 years			2%	
Positive cash flow in 1 year out of last 3 years			0%	

Current Ratio

Equal to or Greater than 1:1	x		3%	3.0%
Equal to or Greater than 0.80:1			2%	
Equal to or Greater than 0.65:1			1%	
Less than 0.80:1			0%	

Leverage [Total Liabilities to Equity (w/o surplus)]

Less than 1 times	x		5%	5.0%
Less than 2 times (greater than 1)			4%	

Less than 1 times | x | 5% | 5.0%
Less than 2 times (greater than 1) | | 4% |
Less than 3 times (greater than 2) | | 3% |
Less than 4 times (greater than 3) | | 2% |
Greater than 4 times | | 0% |

Debt Service Coverage Ratio
Greater than / equals to 2.0 times | x | 3% | 3.0%
Greater than 1.5 times (less than 2.0 times) | | 2% |
Greater than 1.25 times (less than 1.5) | | 1% |
Less than 1.25 times | | 0% |

Interest Coverage Ratio
Greater than / equals to 1.5 times | x | 3% | 3.0%
Greater than 1.25 times (less than 1.5 times) | | 2% |
Greater than 1.0 times (less than 1.25) | | 1% |
Less than 1 time | | 0% |

Net Cash Cycle
Less than 90 days | x | 2% | 2.0%
Less than 180 days | | 1% |
More than 180 days | | 0% |

100%   Total Score   87%

Total Scores	Risk Rating
≥ 90	1
82 ≤ x < 90	2
74 ≤ x < 82	3
66 ≤ x < 74	4
58 ≤ x < 66	5
50 ≤ x < 58	6
42 ≤ x < 50	7
34 ≤ x < 42	8
26 ≤ x < 34	9
15 ≤ x < 26	10*
8 ≤ x < 15	11*
0 ≤ x < 8	12*

X

ORR Summary	Obtained	Total
Condition of Industry	7%	7
Firm's Position in industry	4%	5
Borrowing/Equity	5%	5
Management Quality	6%	10
Ownership Structure	4%	10
Relationship with UBL	5%	5
Past Repayment/ Relationship History	14%	14
Deferrals in Documentation	5%	5
Quality of Audited Statements	9%	9
Financial Performance	28%	30
Total	**87.0%**	**100%**

Total Scores 87%
Risk Rating 5

ORR is being upgraded from 6 to 5 based on the growing business and stable financial position of the company. The ORR is classified as 5 despite

subjectively classified as ORR 5

>90 days Substandard
>180 days Doubtful
>1 Year Loss

Exhibit 6
Return on Risk Weighted Assets

Return On Risk Weighted Assets

Name **XYZ**

Amount in Rs "000"

	Income component	2021 Actual	2022 Projected
1.			
1(a)	Net Interest Income (NII)	6,460	10,835
1(b)	Trade Commission (TC)	870	957
1(c)	Fx-Income (FI)	157	173
1(d)	Income from Cash Management (ICM)	0	0
1(e)	Corporate Finance Income (CFI)	1,000	1,000
1(f)	Retail Income (RI)	0	0
1(g)	Others	0	0
	Total Income	8,487	12,965
2.			
2(a)	Average Funded Utilization	162,427	370,000
2(b)	ORR	5	5
2(c)	External Rating	Unrated	Unrated
2(d)	Client Type	Corporate	Corporate
	Risk Weight (RW)	100%	100%
	Risk Weighted Assets	162,427	370,000
	Expected Loss	367	835
	Annualized Yield	5.23%	3.50%
	Minimum required Yield (Hurdle)	1.92%	1.92%
	Surplus / Deficit in Yield	3.31%	1.59%

1. (a-g)
Actual 2016: Only TeraData output to be used and screenshot / printout to be attached.
Projected 2017: Detailed analysis and justification of projected numbers / ratings to be provided below in "Justification of Projection" cell.

2(a)
Funded Exposure Net of any Liquid collateral (i.e. Cash, GOP Securities, GOP Guaranty) and consider 50% of exposure which are guaranteed by Bank.

2 (b)
Select ORR from Drop-Box from 1-6.

2 (c)
Select External Rating from Drop-Box; Unrated2 is for Large unrated Corporate where client having industry exposure > 3 Billion.

2 (d)
Type of counterparty to be selected i.e. Corporate, PSE (Public Limited Companies)

122

Exhibit 7
Brisk Tabs

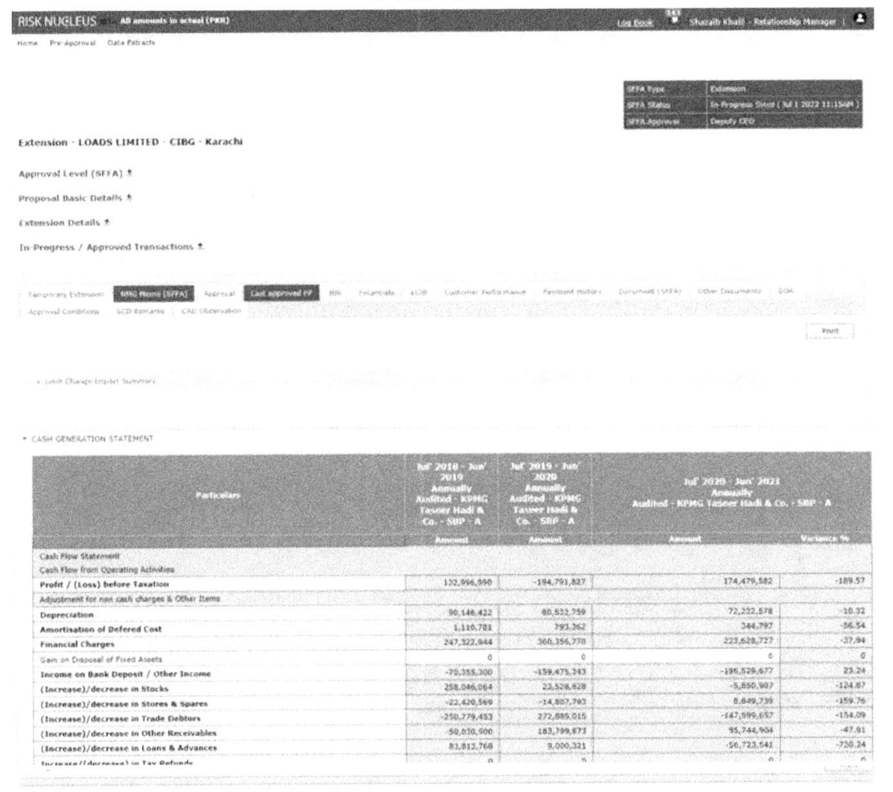

Particulars	Jul' 2018 - Jun' 2019 Annually Audited - KPMG Taseer Hadi & Co. - SBP - A	Jul' 2019 - Jun' 2020 Annually Audited - KPMG Taseer Hadi & Co. - SBP - A	Jul' 2020 - Jun' 2021 Annually Audited - KPMG Taseer Hadi & Co. - SBP - A	
	Amount	Amount	Amount	Variance %
Cash Flow Statement				
Cash Flow from Operating Activities				
Profit / (Loss) before Taxation	132,996,990	-194,791,827	174,479,582	-189.57
Adjustment for non cash charges & Other Items				
Depreciation	90,146,422	80,532,759	72,232,578	-10.32
Amortisation of Defered Cost	1,110,781	793,262	344,797	-56.54
Financial Charges	247,322,944	360,356,778	223,628,727	-37.94
Gain on Disposal of Fixed Assets	0	0	0	0
Income on Bank Deposit / Other Income	-70,355,300	-159,475,343	-196,529,677	23.24
(Increase)/decrease in Stocks	258,046,064	23,528,428	-5,850,907	-124.87
(Increase)/decrease in Stores & Spares	-22,420,569	-14,887,793	8,849,739	-159.76
(Increase)/decrease in Trade Debtors	-250,779,453	272,885,015	-147,999,657	-154.09
(Increase)/decrease in Other Receivables	-50,030,900	183,399,873	95,744,904	-47.91
(Increase)/decrease in Loans & Advances	83,813,768	9,000,321	-56,723,541	-730.24
Increase/(decrease) in Tax Refunds	0	0	0	0

Obligor Group	Trest Group
Obligor Name	LOADS LIMITED
SBP Industry	Manufacture Of Other Transport Equipment
MBL Industry	Auto and Allied Products

SBP Industry Segment	Manufacture of other transport equipment n.e.c.
MBL Industry Segment	Spare-parts and Accessories - (Both Automobile and Motorcycles)

Business Profile: Established in 1979, Loads Ltd manufactures Radiator (produced from Copper and Brass), Mufflers/Exhaust Systems (produced from Stainless Steel, Aluminized Steel and Galvanized Iron) as well as Sheet Metal Components of various kinds. Major buyers include Indus Motors, Pak Suzuki, Millat Tractors, Atlas Honda and Hino Pak Motors.

Main Purpose of Financing Proposal

Main Facility Summary

Facility No	Type of Facility	Existing Limit	Proposed Limits	Net Change PL - EL	Risk Weighted Asset (Limit)	O/S	Overdue Amount	Overdue Days	Utilization Max	Utilization Min	Utilization Average
1	Istisna	200,000,000	200,000,000	0	40,000,000	0	0	0	0	0	0
N/A	Fund Based	200,000,000	200,000,000	0	40,000,000	42,728,431	0	0	0	0	0
N/A	Non-Fund Based	202,500,000	202,500,000	0	8,230,000	1,876,713	0	0	51,739,000	0	0
N/A	Total Fund Based and Non-Fund Based	200,000,000	200,000,000	0	40,000,000	44,605,141	0	0	51,739,000	0	0
N/A	Bank Risk Line & Forward Cover	0	0	0	0	0	0	0	0	0	0

Customer Outstanding Detail

1. FINANCIAL ANALYSIS

Particulars	Jul' 2019 - Jun' 2020 Annually Audited - KPMG Taseer Hadi & Co. - SBP - A	Jul' 2020 - Jun' 2021 Annually Audited - KPMG Taseer Hadi & Co. - SBP - A		Reason To Change Justification to be Provided for Variance of +/- 15%
	Amount	Amount	Variance %	
Income Statement				
Local	2,778,630,637	4,717,228,398	69.77	Sales of the company increased by 58% mainly due to growth of automobiles industry in the light of fiscal measures taken by the Government for recovery of economy. Breakup of sales is as follows: 1) Exhaust systems amounting to PKR 3,628 Mn (FY20; 1,646 Mn), 2) Sheet Metal Components amounting to PKR 1,055 Mn (FY20; 273 Mn) and 3) Radiators amounting to PKR 632 Mn (FY20; 152 Mn).
Export	0	0	0	
Net Sales	2,778,630,637	4,717,228,398	69.77	As discussed above
Gross Profit	272,103,414	464,026,638	70.53	Increase in GPм in line with the increase in sales mentioned above. Overall demand increased for automobiles in FY21 which has translated to higher sales for the company.
Gross Profit Margin %	9.79	9.84	0.48	
EBITDA	102,807,479	286,241,424	178.42	Improvement in EBITDA is on account of increase in topline figure of the company. Other income comprises of 1) Income from financial assets and 2) Income from assets other than financial assets. Other Income from financial assets, Exchange gain amounting PKR 32 Mn (FY20; nil) and Deferred grant amounting PKR 6.7 Mn (FY20; PKR 0.2 Mn) have been posted.
Other Income	159,475,343	196,529,677	23.24	
EBIT	165,564,943	398,108,309	140.45	Increase in EBIT is attributed to improved topline figure and cost management.
Financial Charges	360,356,770	223,628,727	-37.94	Decrease in financial charges is mainly on account of lower discount rate during the review period.

Proposed Facilities

1-Istisna -Limit:200,000,000.00-(Regular - Renewal) (0/0)

1.1-Istisna FE-25-Limit:0.00-(Regular - Limit Cancellation Requested) (0/0)

1.2-Tijarah -Limit:200,000,000.00-(Regular - Renewal) (0/0)

1.3-Tijarah FE-25-Limit:0.00-(Regular - Limit Cancellation Requested) (0/0)

1.4-Letter of Guarantee-Limit:2,500,000.00-(Regular - Renewal) (0/0)

1.5-Sight LC under MSFA-Limit:200,000,000.00-(Regular - Renewal) (0/0)

1.5.1-Sight LC without MSFA-Limit:200,000,000.00-(Regular - Renewal) (0/0)

1.5.2-Usance LC without MSFA -Limit:200,000,000.00-(Regular - Renewal) (0/0)

1.6-Muswammah (Local-Imports) -Limit:200,000,000.00-(Regular - Renewal) (0/0)

1.7-Muswammah Spot-Limit:0.00-(Regular - Limit Cancellation Requested) (0/0)

1.8-Muswammah Local Pledge-Limit:0.00-(Regular - Limit Cancellation Requested) (0/0)

Offered Collaterals

Accepted Bill of Exchange and Trust Receipt-Value:200,000,000.00 (0/0)

Lien over Import Documents-Value:200,000,000.00 (0/0)

Plant and Machinery-Value:83,000,000.00 (0/0)

Stocks and Receivables-Value:317,000,000.00 (0/0)

Proposal Basic Details

Rating by External Agency

Financing Proposal | Purpose Of Financing | RMG Memo | Approval | BIR | Financials | Financing Memo | eCIB | ICRR | Facility & Collateral | Customer Performance | Payment History | Documents | Exceptions | PR Compliance | DOA | Approval Conditions | SCD Remarks | Audit | Comments | Sanction Advise

Delegation Of Authority

- Level 09 Approver (C.C).

Is Non-Approver?	Level 09 Approver (C.C).
Yes	L9: Delegation of Authority; Level 09 Approver.

☐ I have reviewed all the above Level 09 Approver (C.C).

- Level 08 Approver (DCEO & CEO).
- Level 07 Approver (CRO & DCEO).
- Level 06 Approver (Group Head SME/Commercial/Corporate & CRO).
- Level 05 Approver (Head Credit SME/Commercial/RGM/GM/RCH & SRO1).
- Level 04 Approver (RGM/GM/RCH & SRO2).
- Level 03 Approver (GM/RCH & RO1).

Proposal Basic Details

Rating by External Agency

Financing Proposal | Purpose Of Financing | RMG Memo | Approval | BIR | Financials | Financing Memo | eCIB | ICRR | Facility & Collateral | Customer Performance | Payment History | Documents | Exceptions | PR Compliance | DOA | Approval Conditions | SCD Remarks | Audit | Comments | Sanction Advise

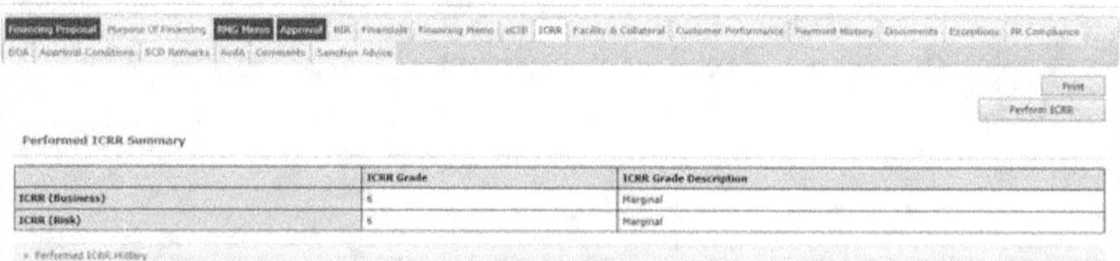

Print

Perform ICRR

Performed ICRR Summary

	ICRR Grade	ICRR Grade Description
ICRR (Business)	6	Marginal
ICRR (Risk)	6	Marginal

- Performed ICRR History

SHORT FORM FINANCING APPLICATION (SFFA)

Customer Status	Regular	Customer Name	LOADS LIMITED	e-CIB	N/A
Group Name	Treet Group	Branch	PNSC Branch	Risk Rating	6-Marginal
Existing Expiry		Proposed Expiry	30 Jun 2022	Activity Initiated On	
Segment	CIBG - Karachi	Approver Level	N/A	Relationship Manager	Shazaib Khalil

Approval Activity Taken	Current Authority	Initiated By	Initiated On	Status
Extension	CRO & GH - RMG	Shazaib Khalil	01 Jul 2022	In-Progress
Extension		Shazaib Khalil	19 May 2022	Approved
NOC	Credit Risk Analyst	Shazaib Khalil	11 May 2022	In-Progress
Extension		Shazaib Khalil	29 Mar 2022	Not Supported
Extension		Shazaib Khalil	23 Feb 2022	Approved
Renewal	Credit Risk Analyst	Shazaib Khalil	11 Jan 2022	In-Progress
Deferral/Waiver		Ayesha Khan	18 Nov 2021	Approved
Review of ICRR		Ayesha Khan	15 Nov 2021	Approved
Extension		Ayesha Khan	30 Jul 2021	Approved

Obligor Group   Obligor Search   Obligor Profile   **Archival Activities**   Business Segment Shuffle

Archival Report

Back to Portfolio

Activity Step(s)	Customer Key	Customer Name	Archival Date	Case	
	FEB-2018/78	LOADS LIMITED	Aug 29 2018 10:25AM	Fresh Case Approved (Approved)	Generate PDF
	FEB-2018/78	LOADS LIMITED	Jul 18 2019 1:10PM	Renewal Approved (Approved)	Generate PDF
	FEB-2018/78	LOADS LIMITED	Oct 23 2020 1:36PM	Renewal Approved (Approved)	Generate PDF
	FEB-2018/78	LOADS LIMITED	Aug 31 2021 10:15AM	Renewal Approved (Approved)	Generate PDF
	FEB-2018/78	LOADS LIMITED	Jan 11 2022 5:53PM	Renewal In Progress (In-Progress)	Generate PDF

This page was intentionally left blank.

PAKISTAN STATE OIL'S AUTOMATED QUEUE MANAGEMENT SYSTEM (AQMS)

Marium Ali, Owais Ahmed, and Syed Gulraiz Haider of Karachi School for Business and Leadership (KSBL) prepared this case under the supervision of Dr. Amir Manzoor. The case was prepared solely to provide material for class discussion. The authors do not intend to illustrate either effective or ineffective handling of a managerial situation. Certain names and other identifying information have been disguised to protect confidentiality.

Company's History

Pakistan State Oil Company Limited (PSOCL) is the largest oil marketing company in Pakistan, with a widespread network comprising 3,500+ retail outlets, nine installations, 23 depots, refueling facilities at ten airports, with two state-of-the-art lubricant manufacturing facilities, and LPG storage & bottling facilities. The company has been actively involved in enriching the lives of people since its inception in 1976. PSO has a vast history of shaping the industry and bringing innovative fueling products and services to serve the nation effectively. The company takes pride in fueling the journeys across air, land, and sea for over four decades and becoming the nation's choice. During FY21, the company continued its journey of leading the oil marketing segment by closing the year with a market share of 46.3%.

The company's business activities involve sourcing (imports and local), storage and marketing of petroleum products, and importing Re-gasified Liquefied Natural Gas (RLNG). Moreover, the non-liquid fuel businesses, such as non-fuel retail, cards, lubricants, and gaseous fuels, assist the company in adding value to the bottom line. Additionally, shareholding in various subsidiaries and associates such as Pakistan Refinery Limited, Asia Petroleum Limited, Pak Grease Manufacturing, Eastern Joint Hydrant, Joint Installation of Marketing Companies (JIMCO), Pak Arab Pipeline Company, and New Islamabad International Airport assists the company in strengthening its value chain.

As the nation's own company, PSO strives to conserve the environment through its offerings, including Hi-Octane 97 Euro 5, Premier Euro 5, and Hi-Cetane Diesel Euro 5 fuels. Moreover, the company is taking strides in the electrical vehicle charging business, wherein a charging unit with the brand name "Electro" has already been installed in Islamabad, while several units are in the advanced stages of implementation.

The company ensures that a congenial working environment is provided to its people wherein several initiatives are being rolled out. Recently, the company completed vaccine inoculation for its staff, exhibiting the care and value it holds towards the people. Additionally, increasing shareholders' income through profitability has been the company's prime focus since its inception. A focused approach is being exerted toward ensuring profitability prospects at all times.

The PSO is striving to add value to society by participating in several community development, healthcare, and educational projects through PSO's CSR trust. During the period under review, the company committed PKR 102 million towards these projects. The company considers its customers as the nucleus of its business by placing the utmost value on receiving customer feedback, resolving queries, and increasing customer satisfaction, while a dedicated customer services center and helpline are in place. Additionally, several customer care days are being arranged wherein the company's top management directly interacts with the customers at the forecourt.

PSO is Pakistan's largest and most dynamic energy company with a long and proud history of fueling every sector of the country's economy and, for over four decades, touching lives and enabling journeys across Air, Land, and Sea. As the market leader, PSO enjoys the lion's share of Pakistan's downstream oil sector, with primary businesses being Sourcing (Imports and Local), Storage, and Marketing of Petroleum Products along with the import of liquid natural Gas. The company also had ancillary business in Non-Fuel Retail and Cards, with a turnover of over PKR 1.4 Trillion (USD 8 Billion) and a market capitalization of more than PKR 90 Billion (USD 500 Million).

PSO had the largest reach and infrastructure amongst all oil marketing companies (OMCs) in Pakistan. It is comprised of more than 3500 retail outlets, 23 depots, nine installations, and refueling facilities at ten airports with a market share of 95% in aviation. They also have 10 LPG storage and bottling facilities, 200 CNG stations, a fleet of more than 10,000 tank Lorries, and two state-of-the-art lubricant manufacturing facilities which produce over 70,000 metric tons of top-quality lubricants every year for cars, motorcycles, buses, trucks, and industrial equipment.

PSO held a total storage capacity of approximately 1 million tons, which accounts for 40% of the total storage in Pakistan. Serving more than 3 million consumers every day, PSO has a sales volume of around 10 million tons and a 46.3% market share. PSO contributes to 70% of all energy produced through furnace oil while maintaining approximately 55% of LNG supplies. In the fiscal year 2020-2021, PSO managed the import, berthing, and discharge of 117 cargo ships with 5.5 million tons of motor gasoline, high-speed diesel, jet fuel, and furnace oil. In addition to imports, the company also uplifted 4 million tons of product from local refineries. PSO is Pakistan's major LNG importer, with volumes exceeding 5.6 million tons annually.

PSO's commitment to environmentally friendly energy was long-standing as the company accelerated the adoption of cleaner energy alternatives consistent with the company's climate goals. PSO became the first energy company for upgrading Pakistan's fuel standards from Euro 2 to Euro 5 for both motor gasoline and high-speed diesel, along with being one of the first companies to introduce an Electric Vehicle Charging facility in Pakistan. Pioneering Pakistan's technology and cards business, PSO currently has a cards base of 200,000 in fleet and corporate and approximately 190,000 B2C DigiCash cards for cashless transactions.

PSO has several strategic Investments, which include a 66.3% share in Pakistan Refinery Limited, 62% in Joint Installation of Marketing Companies, 50% in the new Islamabad International Airport, 49% in Asia Petroleum Limited, 44% in Eastern Joint Hydrant Depot, 22% in Pak Grease Manufacturing Company Ltd and 12% in Pak Arab Pipeline Company. PSO is investing in technology and exploring new ways to serve our customers by building our digital capability, creating efficiencies, and reducing human intervention through automation.

The Group comprises Pakistan State Oil Company Limited (the Holding Company) and Pakistan Refinery Limited (the Subsidiary Company). PRL became PSO's subsidiary on December 1, 2018, due to an increase in the shareholding of PSO in PRL from 24.11% to 52.68%. During the year ended June 30, 2020, PSO acquired a further shareholding in PRL, thereby increasing its stake in PRL to 60%, which was further increased to 63.6% in FY21.

Value Chain of the Oil Industry

The oil industry value chain is segregated into three distinct tiers, i.e., upstream, midstream, and downstream. PSO holds a position in both the mid and downstream of the value chain owing to its strong presence in the oil marketing segment and shareholding in PRL. Additionally, PSO is amongst the major shareholders of PAPCO, a cross-country white oil pipeline company. PSO is also the largest importer of POL products, with storage facilities and retail outlets in almost every part of the country. Based on its product range and footprint, PSO touches the lives of over 3 million Pakistanis every day.

Business Model and Strategies of PSO

Pakistan's downstream segment is witnessing a transition wherein a fast-paced influx of competition and disruptive technologies have necessitated a shift in business objectives and strategies. The company has also undertaken several initiatives oriented toward the recently realigned vision, mission, and values. The objectives and strategies aim to add value for the shareholders from existing product lines with the diversification of the portfolio for sustainability, increased market participation through key products, enhanced focus towards automation and business process optimization, and added value to society. All of these objectives are devised with a long-term perspective of bringing enhanced sustainability to the business.

The following are among the significant plans and decisions that the company intends to pursue in the future:

- Increase market share in MoGas and HSD.
- Reduction in receivables over last year.
- Adding new electric vehicle charging facilities.
- Timely completion of infrastructural projects to increase capacity and availability.
- Automation of key business processes.
- Taking strides in the renewable energy business

Logistics

Robust inventory movement plans enabled PSO to transport 9.3 million tons of white oil during the period through road, rail & pipelines, marking a growth of 18% over last year and achieving highest ever MoGas dispatches to upcountry locations from Karachi (over 286 thousand tons) in a single month, i.e., July 2020.

In line with the company's commitment to ensuring the safe transportation of hazardous petroleum products by road, PSO has a fleet of over 2,900 state-of-the-art tank lorries that are fully compliant with OGRA's notified technical standards as well as the requirements specified by National Highways Authority (NHA). These compliant tank lorries are equipped with international standard gauges and rollover prevention mechanisms to minimize the chances of accidents and rollovers. Promoting secondary transportation to retail and industrial customers through OGRA and NHA-compliant tank lorries, the scope of the Fleet Management Tank Lorries (FMTL) mechanism has been augmented. A new FMTL contract was executed for Bahawalpur & Hyderabad divisions at competitive rates during the year.

PSO has joined hands with Automobile Track Services Pakistan (ATS) to ensure the provision of roadside emergency and other allied services to PSO tank lorries. With the joint efforts of the National Highway & Motorway Police (NH&MP), M/S ATS, and in-house HSE trainers, regular drivers training/awareness and HSE refresher sessions were conducted at logistics locations throughout Pakistan. More than 3,000 tank lorry drivers were trained with safe/defensive driving techniques to minimize the risk of road accidents and emergency response in case of accidents.

PSO and ATS have also initiated a medical assessment campaign to ensure the deployment of trained and medically fit drivers in PSO's fleet. Tank lorry drivers were medically assessed for blood pressure, Hepatitis B & C, blood sugar, and eyesight. The most anticipated automated tank lorries queue & scheduling system project was successfully initiated. This new project has enabled PSO to manage tank lorries queue and schedule their next loads based on real-time geofencing data received through tracking vendors via technological integration. The automated scheduling /allocation of load will bring more transparency and ensure the provision of equal business opportunities to all haulers. As a result of this end-to-end automation, multiple deliveries and loads will be allocated to tank lorries with a single click.

Restructuring & Automation

The company has gone through a restructuring process, reallocating its resources to enhance administration and profitability. A new department, BPR&PMO, has been set up to automate the company's operations and to bring innovative solutions to digitize the company further.

Old Business Model and the Need for Automation

The daily tasks that are being performed at PSO have so much significance that even slight miscalculations or even slight delays in procedures and operations (due to human error or human negligence) can lead to a domino effect inside the organization as all the tasks are interrelated with each other the timely flow of information is very important for operations and delays can prove to be very detrimental for ongoing processes and operations of PSO. The organization has to process large pieces of information which is just related to the amount of tank Lorries that have been filled and sent to different locations for delivery of its products and the number of tank Lorries left that are yet to be filled up and then dispatched to different locations. Among this busy scheduling, PSO must ensure that it maintains equal opportunity for all of its fleet partners so that its logistics flow is not disturbed and the organization can achieve efficiency in its daily operations and tasks, achieving its long-term strategic goals and expanding its market presence.

APOTOA, being the owner of the tank Lorries, has a history of conflicts and resolves with the company (PSO) and used to create supply disruptions for different reasons, putting PSO in a weak position. These cartages did not spend a lot of resources in training the drivers as training was very important to ensure that the driver knew how to handle the Tank Lorry that contained a huge load of combustible products. If that is not handled with caution, it leads to leakage of petroleum products on road which can even lead to a terrible accident or catastrophic event. Drivers must be aware that it is not like driving a normal truck but also ensuring the safety of the environment and the safety of human life and public infrastructure. But many lorry owners were not convinced that attention was required in this area and consequently did not train the drivers a lot.

Many tank Lorry owners have a history of disputes with PSO as they wanted to be less compliant with PSO regulations and demanded more business opportunities from PSO to recover their costs. PSO faced tremendous pressure from tank Lorry owners demanding that more orders should be given to specific groups. PSO wanted to have all its business partners' onboard, ensuring equal opportunity for all its partners and maintaining its work ethics and principles that are valued at PSO. Some tank Lorry owners tried to contact the different individuals in management, hoping to get some leverage in their orders. One manager also reported to top management that he was offered a commission if he could get more refilling orders for a specific tank Lorry owner. This outreach also raised concerns in the mind of top management that these practices will lead to some unethical, corrupt, and unprofessional activities where some people in management may place their own self-interests above the business practices of PSO, and PSO has made its efforts to make sure that its ethics and values are well engrained in the organizational culture.

PSO relies heavily upon its tank Lorry owners to deliver its petroleum goods to different locations; without them, the business of PSO will suffer many losses and inconveniences. The top management at PSO was concerned about the rising possibility that these sub-contractors may even form cartels based on common interests and demand higher margins from PSO to ensure the movement of its products from one place to another or may even threaten to refuse to work with PSO until their demands were met this could potentially halt the supply line and movement of petroleum goods causing huge losses for the organization. In a meeting among some of the top-level executives, problems arising with tank Lorry owners were discussed. The top-level executives were well aware of the tactics that tank Lorry owners may use to get the upper hand in negotiations.

One executive specifically mentioned his concerns in a meeting with the top management,

> *"What will we do if these tank Lorry owners and their drivers call a strike? Freeze our entire logistics system and business processes that can only be resumed if their demands of more load orders and higher profit margins are met? Making huge demands that put our company and business at risk of losing their negotiating power and ultimately damaging our credibility. What will remain of our image in the industry when we cannot fulfill our commitments and cannot keep our word? Should we allow tank Lorry owners*

to bring us down to our knees? Should we maintain the status quo and remain vulnerable to these growing threats, or should we take control of matters so that we cannot be forced to make decisions that are against the long-term interests of our organization and its committed employees? We need to make sure that we fix the problems with the most appropriate solutions; otherwise, things will be beyond fixing, and when we are held hostage at gunpoint, we will be fulfilling the demands of people who work in our organization for their own self-interests, demolishing what was built after many years of pure dedication and hard work from many individuals".

For PSO, the automation of its tank Lorry system and related business tasks has become absolutely crucial and inevitable so that it can maintain transparency within its organizational culture, process, and operations while also maintaining efficiency to ensure the timely completion of delegated responsibilities. Automation is deemed to be the only way in which they can tackle the rising problems and demands of tank Lorry owners and maintain control over the mainstream business process and logistics system. PSO is determined to make sure that the business of one of its partners in tank Lorry contracts does not happen at the expense of others. Many types of manual forms and documentation are required in the older system where different individuals have to manually check the number of a specific tank Lorry in the queue and cross-check it with the record that tells when this specific lorry was filled last time. In such conditions, it was very easy for tank Lorry owners to offer bribes to people working in the queue management system as this information would circulate in a specific set of hands, and top managers could be kept in the dark about what really was happening in the loading stations, from reporting to accountability everything was at risk as no one really knew that what exactly was happening at the ground level.

To better understand the management concerns and magnitude of the issue at hand, suppose only 10 Lorries are operating in PSO that are filled and sent to deliver petroleum goods to different locations. After a documentation check and verification, a lorry would be filled and sent to its destination, but it is not checked if the lorry had skipped the queue and the load of the 4th Lorry waiting in queue for loading and delivery, remember the loading and delivery is a way for lorry owners to recover the heavy investments that they have made in PSO infrastructure. By the time it was checked and recognized that if the same Lorry was taking the load of the 4th lorry, it was too late as that lorry was already on its way to deliver the loaded goods and another lorry 5th and 6th and 7th lorry were concerned if this could happen with their specific load as well. In this case, who is supposed to be held responsible for the loss of one lorry owner, and where are they supposed to go with their grievances, and how will the dispute be resolved, preventing this from happening again in the future?

In addition to these problems, PSO management was able to identify that it takes a lot of time to check all the documentation and manage the queue system, which relied heavily on some specific individuals who knew how the tasks were performed relating to loading and management of queue. PSO wanted to make sure that top managers had full access to information related to all these activities and could check the ongoing activities easily and quickly to make strategic decisions in the long run and also enable the managers to keep a check on which lorry owners were performing well, meeting the requirements of the organization and which were not, this will enable the organization to make better decisions in the future. Upon conducting some interviews, management also found that they also need to make a training environment ensuring that both lorry owners and drivers know the job's technicalities and are equipped to deal with a problem or accident that may endanger others.

Without an automation system, the operations and smooth flow of goods are at risk of high delays and disturbances. The organizational values of devotion and honesty are also at risk and need to be kept intact from the rising unethical practices. PSO faced resistance when it wanted to change things in the system and keep equal business opportunities alive for all its partners. PSO could not afford disruptions and delays, so it evolved its business model, and PSO strengthened the contractors by negotiating with them and asking them to bring their own fleet of tank Lorries, reducing the bargaining power of APOTOA over PSO. Over time, both parties agreed and signed the contract, giving them control of the logistics system.

With this contract between PSO and tank lorry contractors, it was the contractor's main responsibility to make sure that the supply and movement of PSO products were not disrupted at any cost. Along came the OGRA-compliant tank Lorries, fully equipped and updated with the latest geo fencing and geo-tracking features. Additionally, the drivers were chosen carefully on high criteria of (after training) ability to use high-end technological gadgets, effective communication, and knowledge of associated technicalities with their job. After hours of training on technicalities and responsibilities related to their job, they were further examined if they were equipped with skills and knowledge required to deal with an emergency or an accident.

Automated Queue Management System (AQMS)

PSO has successfully developed a homegrown solution-based smart algorithm that provides equal opportunity to all Tank Lorries for business. AQMS is developed in SAP and is integrated with the tracking companies' alert system on a real-time basis. With AQMS, the Tank Lorries' trip/load assignment process is completely automated and streamlined over a digital platform. This system has drastically improved the operation of the Logistics department and provides functional efficiencies.

AQMS-Transshipment is the first fleet queue management system developed and implemented by PSO at the country's major transshipment hub, Karachi. PSO locations are geo-fenced, and the system picks up T/L status through geo coordinates. It computes product loads on a FIFO basis and system-triggered logic for the type of load (haul selection) that a T/L should be assigned for, creating an equal playing ground for all cartage contractors/T/L operators. The AQMS is the first of its kind in the industry, a fully automated system that functions based on completely system-based business parameters and scenarios for generating a transparent system-based and unbiased output based upon complex system algorithms and deriving data from multiple systems for decision making.

The system was developed on the SAP platform. The execution of the automated process is SAP T-code based, which executes multiple SAP transactions in an automated fashion, utilizing data from tracker systems for determining availability and geographical positioning through the use of real-time alerts based upon PSO Geo fenced locations, as well as deriving Tank Lorry related data from SAP as per an algorithm based criteria in order to determine eligibility for transshipment load selection. Further, the system also, in an automated manner, derives the previously carried loads of tank lorries from determining the next system-based suggested load using a system-based algorithm that ensures transparency and an equal opportunity for business for all tank lorries alike.

Lastly, as per the location-wise business demand of product quantity required to be moved via transshipment, the system calculates the number of tank lorries required, identifies available and eligible pools of tank lorries, establishes the tank lorry queue/priority number on a FIFO basis and creates the SAP Outbound Delivery and Shipments for all selected tank lorries all through automated processes, thereby not allowing any human biases or interference to take place within the process while also vastly reducing the turn-around time for the process, shortening the TAT from entire days to a matter of minutes. (previously, every single document was created by manual operation of multiple SAP T-Codes resulting in a vast manual effort that would span entire days of activity)

The system also creates User ID-based audit trails/log entries for automated T-Code executions and centralizes the resultant data of transshipment executions within SAP for future reference and trend analysis, also exporting soft copies of the record externally to SAP for reporting and query resolution purposes.

Adaptation & Benefits of Automated Queue Management System (AQMS)

PSO had to devise an approach where they did not have to shut down the entire system to shift the business-related data to the new system. A meeting among the top management was called, and the approach was discussed. Clearly, this could not be achieved overnight as the new system needed information to be fed into it and checked for bugs and shortcomings. The new system was tested on technical parameters, mainly its ability to hold the information, process it, and present large chunks of data quickly and timely upon frequent requests. Also, the system must be able to generate the required reports and allow many users to access this information easily and quickly for decision-making and process improvements.

Hence the parallel approach was the most feasible option as it would allow the organization to continue performing its daily tasks and operational activities and consistently keep on putting the information in the new system after making sure that the information is based on accuracy, is less prone to human errors and will not raise concerns about the data integrity problems as witnessed in the past this was the cause of many problems that were linked with departments of the organization. As the new system was tested many times and proved its functionality, PSO was also able to achieve a high level of automation for its basic business process and related activities and daily operations, making things more controllable and manageable according to the organization's needs. This led to higher organizational automation and less dependency on the people who were scattered throughout the organization on different levels responsible for performing their job-designated tasks in different departments. Internally, employees would keep things to themselves in order to protect their own self-interests and ensure their position in the organization, especially if they are less productive than the requirements of their organization or it was relatively easier to escape from accepting the responsibility for missed targets and high-costing failures. Such practices were eliminated as now a system was in place to determine who was supposed to do what and clearly mention the associated responsibilities needed to be performed by specific individuals in a given period of time, meeting the targets assigned by the higher management. Accountability and responsibility were raised within the culture of PSO as the new system cannot be manipulated to keep one's own self-interests, and unethical practices are hidden from the top management of PSO. This improved the worth of dedication and hard work in the employees of PSO as now if they outperformed the rest, they will be encouraged and rewarded accordingly.

The only solution to bring transparency to the system and ensure long-term success was for PSO to take hold of the queue management system so that the company should be the one to decide who would get how much business (the ones who have invested in OGRA-compliant vehicles, is beneficial for the company in times of crisis, instead of those who have ditched the company). Moreover, PSO currently lacks a system that would generate quick reports and allow its management to make timely decisions based on this information. They also lack a system for checks and balances as there is no benchmark for the measurement of the performance of drivers and lorry owners, as they are the ones who have to ensure that PSO would not face problems in the movement of its petroleum goods. Tracker devices were incorporated into the system and are now installed in the entire OGRA-compliant fleet. Geo-fencing was implemented in all depots, including parking areas. With geo-fencing, until a tank lorry enters a particular geo-fencing area, it will not be considered available. The system was assigned criteria to ensure the prerequisites of the load.

The prerequisites were the following:

- If the tracker is installed and active
- If the tracker is valid
- If the calibration is valid
- If the vehicle has previously made an offense
- If the previous load of the vehicle has been delivered.
- If the vehicle is available in an XY geo-fencing area.

After the fulfillment of these prerequisites/criteria, the automated queue management system will show the vehicle available in the queue. Now let's say there are two vehicles meeting the criteria; who would decide which tank lorry will be loaded first? The role of tracker data is vital here. If a vehicle is detected even 10 seconds earlier than the second vehicle, it will be loaded first. The system now maintains the queue date and time. A report is generated showing a number of available tank lorries that have fulfilled the prerequisites and are now ready for the upliftment of the load. Now, in another report, the system shows the suggestive loads based on the previous two upliftments on the screens. If there is no unusual demand, the management takes the suggestions from the system as it is; otherwise, if the product is already in sufficient quantity at a depot, then this tank lorry will be put on waiting for today and will be sent the next day. Therefore, there are a few exceptions. In case a vehicle is available but still not receiving the load, the system also shows a reason board stating that it is because the tracker on the tank lorry is about to expire. This brought transparency. When the prerequisite is fully met, the system will also show which specific prerequisite has now been rectified on the basis of which the tank lorry can now be loaded. Previously, these loads were suggested by OTCA representation manually, which involved favoritism and lack of accountability. Also, shipments used to be manual in the past. 2 to 3 assistants used to spend 3 to 4 hours performing these activities, which are, in reality, nonproductive activities. With automation, the same set of activities can now be performed with a single click. As soon as the system shows the availability of a vehicle, the system generates the token and shipment itself and allocates the vehicle. This resulted in reduced man working hours and reduced man count.

With the new system's ability to generate reports quickly and store them from where information was easy to access, AQMS enabled these reports to be accessed by managers in minutes with a click for in-depth analysis and decision-making that would benefit the organization. Now, managers could check if the truck Lorries that were filled yesterday and that have left the filling station have reached their assigned destination and how long it takes them to reach the said destination. The availability of information at a click enables management to perform analysis and recognize the areas that are still causing delays in the system. These areas can be improved with techniques outlined in process management, and continuous improvement practices can be deployed with ease in specifically problematic areas that cause a delay so that the organization can achieve its goals and maintain its operational efficiency in the future as well.

The new system also enabled the organization to have a leaner and flatter organizational hierarchy than before to pass information to the top level it was required that the data was collected, and then reports were generated separately and manually. The manual input was highly prone to errors, and even slight miscalculations could leave a big gap in what the managers think they have achieved compared to what they actually have been able to achieve. This entire process took a lot of time, and data integrity problems raised significant questions about previously made decisions by management. Now, with the new system, data was more reliable, and decisions were based on findings that were less prone to errors or miscalculations, leading to more accurate forecasting and timely decisions.

The flow of information was now much faster as it was not bound to come from some other management team. Everything that was happening regarding the processes and operations of the business was recorded automatically in the system, generating reports allowing analysis and measurement of the effectiveness of processes performed on a daily basis. This information was available at all times through easy access by any member of the management who has been given access to this data, and timely decisions could be made without many delays.

The automated system also ensured that unethical conduct could not be practiced as now it was impossible for a Tank lorry owner to offer anything to staff at loading stations to try to cheat the system and gain extra business. Now due to the new system, everything was running according to schedule, and it was not possible to make big changes or favors to any specific group of individuals without it being noticed by the top management as such a favor or unethical conduct is deemed to be punished because the system will easily identify the individual who is trying to make changes without authorization or a sound reason to do so and will have to face the consequences for their actions, earlier it was very hard to catch the individuals violating the organizational code of conduct. In addition, the new system also placed direct responsibility on individuals responsible for performing different assigned tasks on time. If delays were caused now, it would be easier to identify who is to be held responsible for this delay and questioned accordingly for the delay in operations.

Perhaps the biggest achievement of the automated queue management system has been that this system has reduced the risks of bias in business practices. Now that when everything is recorded and maintained in the system on a daily basis, it is highly unlikely that tank lorry number 3 will even mistakenly take a load of tank lorry number 4 as the driver was not there or was late in arriving at the station, this is unlikely to happen as the traffic can be managed easily by the features of geo fencing and geo-tracking. On the system, it could tracked live that a specific tank lorry is carrying a load that it has picked on time or not, where it is supposed to be delivered, and even the estimated time it would take to reach the predetermined destination of that load and the process of documentation that comes after reaching the destination can be performed and approved from far away quickly. This has also raised the level of trust that lorry owners and other partners have in PSO that there are no unfair biases in distributing equal business opportunities among its partners.

Now, they are well aware that it is easier for PSO to track the deliverables of associated partners looking for business growth and opportunities with PSO. If they fail to deliver on the standards of PSO, they will not have a business opportunity with the industry giant. PSO has been able to communicate with clarity the requirements that must be fulfilled as stipulated by OGRA. These include the latest technological upgrades that are to be adopted and aligned with the organization's strategic goals, operational staff training, and innovations to protect damages made to the environment in the name of business expansion and market opportunities. Of course, the need has risen for continuous checks of the system based on human inspections and audits in order to ensure that the trackers are working, the OGRA-compliant fleet is maintained in the required condition where it is fully functional and suffering any damages in the mode of transportation. All of this has to be checked by a separately trained staff as PSO now relies heavily on the new system's effectiveness. For its quick decision-making, PSO has to make sure that the presented information is up-to-date and reliable and that the system will not be compromised due to negligence or late maintenance activities.

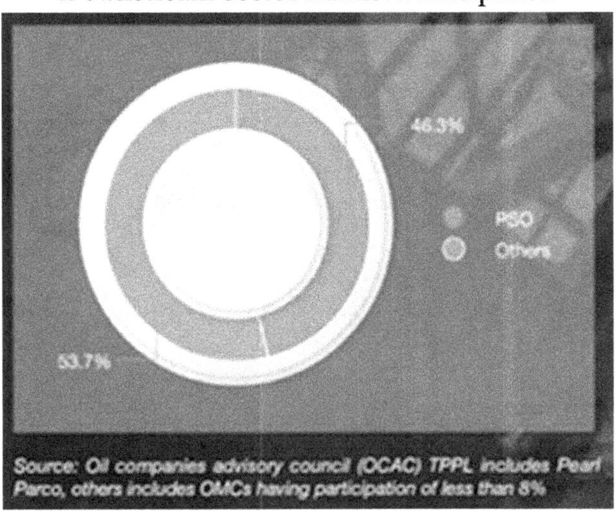

Exhibit 2
Markets Served and Product lines

Brand	Product	Usage/Customer Base
Hi-Octane	HOBC	Automobile
Premier	PMG	Automobile
Hi-Cetane	HSD	Motorist, Industrial & Power Sector
JP1	Jet Fuel	Aviation Sector
Furnace Oil	Furnace Oil	Power, Industrial and Marine Sector
SKO	Kerosene Oil	Industrial, Domestic
LDO	Light Diesel Oil	Agriculture
LPG	LPG	Domestic, Industrial
LNG	LNG	Power, Domestic and Industrial
Electron	Electric Vehicle Charger	Electric Vehicle
CARIENT / DEO	Lubricants	Automobile / Motorist / Diesel Engines
Cards	Cards	Automobile & Motorist
SHOP	Retail Outlet	Retail

Exhibit 3
PSO Business Model

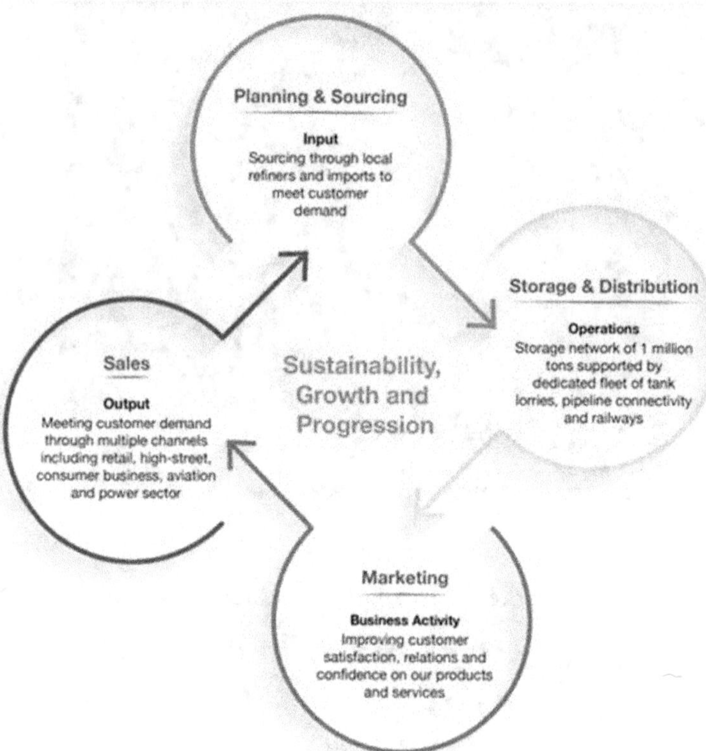

Exhibit 4
PSO Business Objectives & Strategies

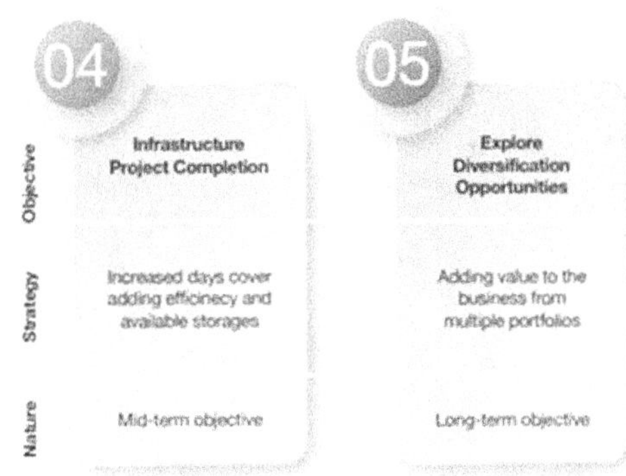

Exhibit 5
PSO SWOT Analysis

Strengths

- Largest network of retail outlets
- Largest storage capacity
- Leading player in petroleum products segment
- Strong brand recognition

Weaknesses

- Strong negotiating power of cartage contractors
- Focus only on core business
- Adherence to stringent rules and regulations like PPRA rules
- Substantial level of outstanding receivables with low receivalbe turnover ratio

Opportunities

- Ventures in renewable energy
- Diversification in tech business
- Business intergration through investment in energy trading business

Threats

- New entrants in market
- Introduction of electric vehicles
- Influx of alternates

Exhibit 6
Organizational Structure

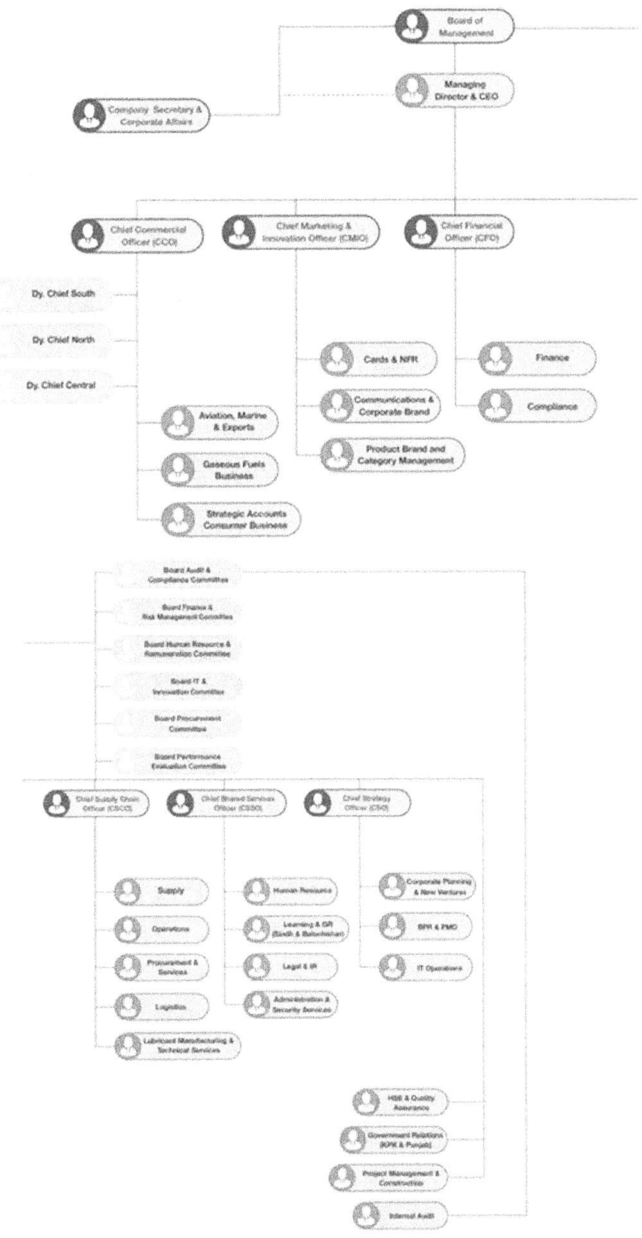

PSO Logistics Business Overview

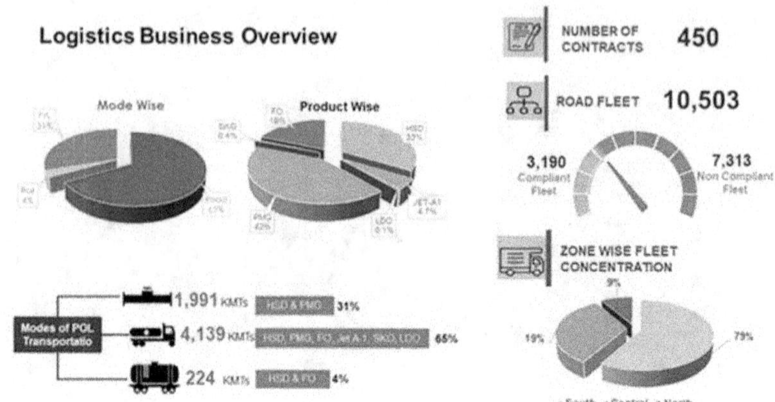

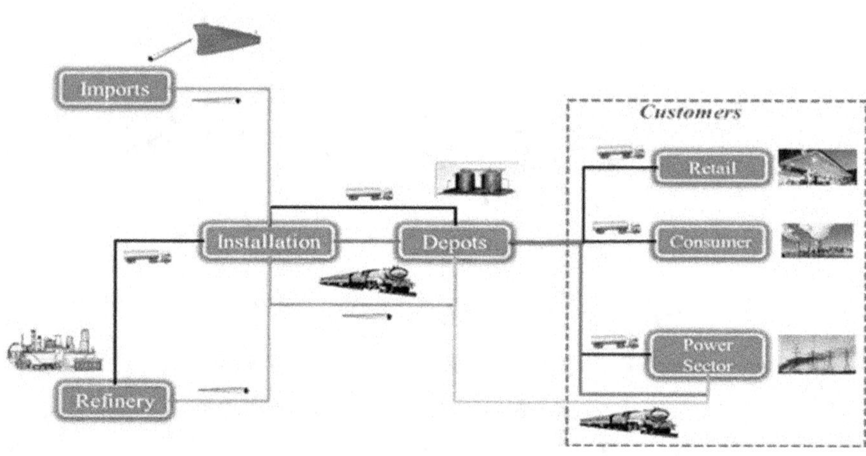

Exhibit 8
AQMS Highlights

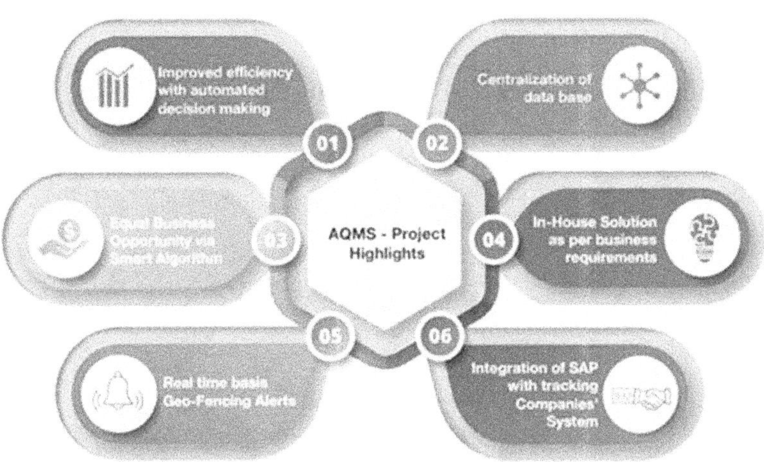

Exhibit 9
PSO Logistics Operations

Before AQMS Implementation

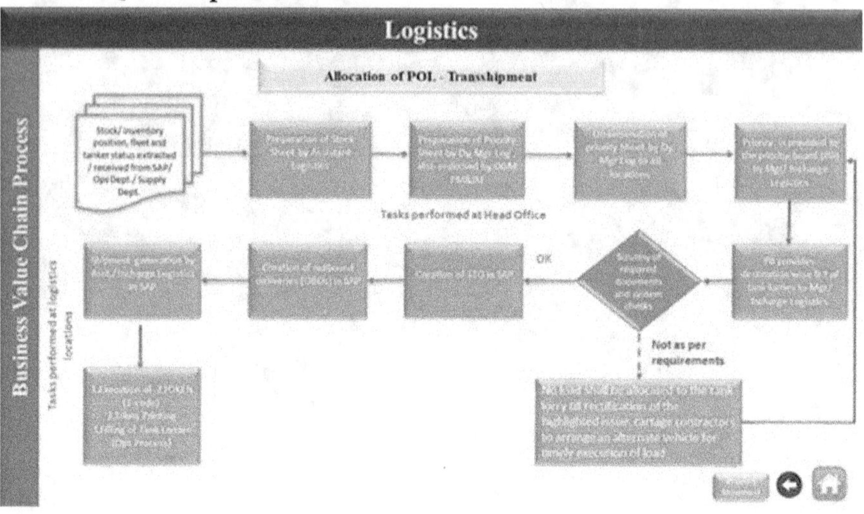

After AQMS Implementation

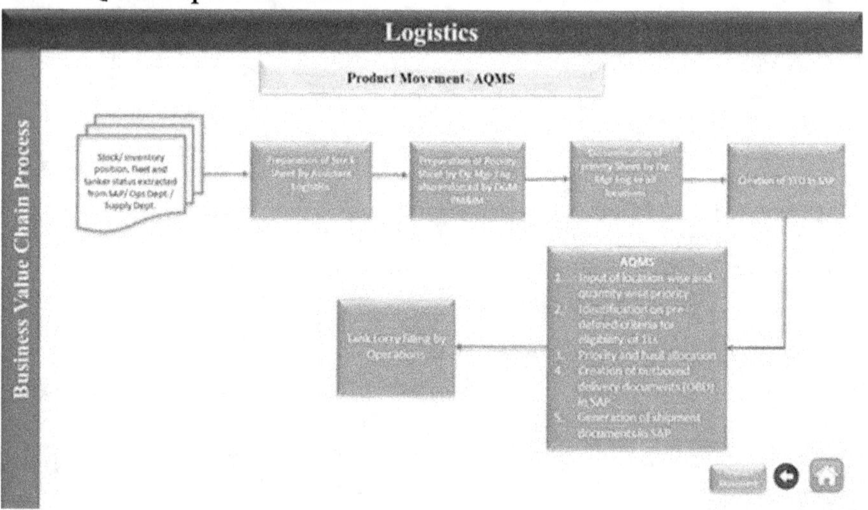

AA ENERGY: IMPLEMENTATION OF ENTERPRISE RESOURCE PLANNING SYSTEM

Shankar Talreja and Jahanzeb Qadeer of Karachi School for Business and Leadership (KSBL) prepared this case under the supervision of Dr. Amir Manzoor. The case was prepared solely to provide material for class discussion. The authors do not intend to illustrate either effective or ineffective handling of a managerial situation. Certain names and other identifying information have been disguised to protect confidentiality.

Since 2018, the company has been in financial trouble. The revenues have dropped, losses mounted, and loans have risen, sending its share price down from over Rs. 300 three years ago to just Rs. 11. A significant shift occurred in the overall market positioning of AA Energy Limited ("AA Energy" or "the Company"). The market share of petrol and diesel fell to 7.6% and 7.2%, respectively, in Dec 2018. In May 2022, market share on the same commodities has fallen to 0.7% and 0.3%, respectively – almost non-existent. Further, the regulatory actions against the Company in Khyber Pakhtunkhwa for unauthorized storage and selling petroleum products also marred its reputation last year. The company has lately been in the news for abrupt resignations by auditors, members of its board, and senior management.

AA Energy's growth trajectory over the years remains a complete case study for other OMCs like Attock Petroleum (APL), Shell Petroleum (SPL), and Pakistan State Oil (PSO). The Company's market share in petrol sales during October 2013 was 2.2%, reaching 5.3% in April 2014. Gradually, it rose to 6.2% in January 2015, 8.4% in December 2015, 9.5% in December 2016, and 12.1% in December 2017. Similarly, on diesel sales, in October 2013, the market share was 2.3%, 4.3% in April 2014, 5.5% in January 2015, 8.0% in December 2015, 12.1% in December 2016, and 13.1% in December 2017.

According to news flows and material notices shared with Pakistan Stock Exchange, the Company was involved in accounting misrepresentation whereby invoices were overpriced and sales numbers were fudged. Also, significant misuse of capital received from lenders was unearthed in a Federal Investigation Authority (FIA) inquiry. In total, claims of Rs. 60 billion are under scrutiny. The Company's financial results have been presented in Exhibit 3 for the years from 2011 to 2020.

Based on management, forward hedging of oil prices caused huge losses in adverse FX and oil price fluctuations., The company's insiders claimed that fake sales of ~Rs. 14 billion were generated against which parties never existed. This all happened because of no defined SOPs of workflows related to payments and invoices. Orders were not being generated via the system, and in some cases, system entries were being manipulated. When shareholders approached lenders for financial restructuring, the National Bank of Pakistan (NBP), representing a consortium of banks, immediately resolved to implement SAP HANA through a consulting firm 'Systems Limited.'

In response to these claims, previous auditors resigned, and every newly appointed auditor also resigned. This was not the case only – even CFOs resigned back to back. Not only did CFOs resign, but alongside this, many CEOs and directors were changed or resigned. A few of these movements are captured in Exhibit 1.

On April 29, 2019, at 12:37 pm, the Company announced financial results for the March quarter of 2019, wherein the Company posted earnings of Rs. 674mn or Rs. 3.73 per outstanding share, down 7% year-on-year. This was the catching performance of the company as the market leader in oil marketing. Pakistan State Oil (PSO) posted a 67% decline in its earnings for the same quarter. Other companies like Attock Petroleum posted an earnings decline of 80%, and Shell Petroleum posted an 81% decline. Table 1 summarises the results of these companies.

Table 1: Results of Companies

Company	March 2019 quarter earnings growth/decline
AA Energy	7%
Pakistan State Oil	67%
Attock Petroleum	80%
Shell Petroleum	81%

Still, analysts in the market were not surprised as AA Energy, based on past experience, was always ahead in giving surprises to the market. Things moved adversely in the June quarter when the Company posted six six-month losses of Rs. 11 bn and also restated the March quarter profit of Rs. 674mn to Rs. 6bn loss. From here, the journey of the company started with losses. The company's trend of profit/loss has been shown in Exhibit 4.

Continuous loss-making position of the Company and that too without explaining any reason to investors, raised eyebrows of all the lenders. After that, changes in key management happened with Vitol, and shareholders in AA Energy acquired majority stake in the company and controlled the board. After that, decisions for change in the information management system by one of the top lenders came on the surface, and after thorough research, SAP S4 Hanna was idealized and finalized.

Important Issues

There were multiple issues being faced by AA Energy. These were not just part of information management but also a management failure. According to an ex-employee, there wasn't a properly defined mechanism of segregation of duties and chain of command in AA Energy, which resulted in the delegation of high authority to some individuals.

Following are some of the important issues identified at AA Energy:

1. Misrepresentation of financial accounts

2. Change of top management frequently

3. Fake invoicing

4. Exposing themselves to the international market by hedging

Company History

AA Energy is a Pakistani oil marketing company that is active in the downstream sector. It is based in Karachi, Pakistan. The company has distribution rights for German lubricating oil Fuchs in Pakistan. The company was founded in 2001 under the Companies Ordinance 1984 and was granted an oil marketing license by the Government of Pakistan in February 2005. The Company made its initial public offering in 2007. In 2014, the company was listed on the Karachi Stock Exchange. In 2017, the company announced it was investing US$20 million, in collaboration with Fuchs, to set up a new plant in Bin Qasim, Karachi. In the same year, it became the second-largest oil marketing company in the country.

The Company's mission is:

"To gain recognition and leadership in the hydrocarbon and energy sectors by maximizing customer satisfaction and shareholder value through continuous improvement, high-quality human capital, appropriate technology, and by adhering to the Company's Core Values."

The Company's vision is:

"To become the leading energy marketing company in Pakistan through operational excellence, talent management, business diversification, and sustainable expansion."

Vitol BV Netherland ("Vitol"), a Dutch energy giant and one of the world's largest conglomerates, acquired 15 percent shares in AA Energy between 2015 and 2016 and bought another 10% in 2016 to become the largest shareholder in the Company. The market share of the company increased to 12%, and the Company became the third largest OMC after PSO and Shell. By 2017, AA Energy became the country's second-largest oil marketing company.

154

Company's Products

AA Energy is engaged in the purchase, storage, and sale of petroleum products such as the following:

- High-Speed Diesel
- Gasoline
- Fuel Oil
- FUCHS lubricants

AA Energy also markets LPG, and currently, there are 15 AutoMax LPG stations across Pakistan in various stages of approval with the Government of Pakistan.

Figure 1: Company Products

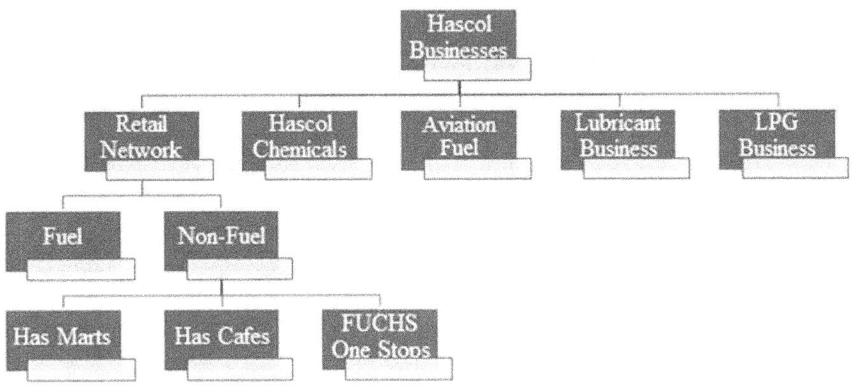

Retail Network

AA Energy is a fast-growing oil retail business in Pakistan. AA Energy prides itself on supplying customers with the best quality and strives to fulfill the requirements of customers by providing superior quality, energy-efficient fuels.

Fuel Retail: The Company operates over 500 retail outlets in all four provinces of Pakistan. The Company not only operates these fuel stations in the heart of a city but also in some of the country's remotest areas and covers almost all areas of the country with its wide network.

Non-Fuel Retail: AA Energy Petroleum also operates non-fuel retail stores/shops, which play an important role in the Company's business. These non-fuel retail initiatives offer a wide range of services, from One-Stop lubricant solutions to Hasmarts and Hascafes.

Hasmarts: At the heart of a retail forecourt, the Company operates Hasmarts retail stores for the convenience of customers. AA Energy operates a chain of these convenience stores on its forecourts under the brand name of 'Hasmarts' all over Pakistan. These stores provide a competitive advantage to the Company since they have relatively longer operating hours, are located in strategic prime locations, have shorter cashier lines, and are well stocked all the time. Currently, 62 active Hasmarts are operating all over Pakistan.

Hascafes: AA Energy also operates Hascafes aimed at providing customers with a cozy milieu for a quick pit stop. These cafes serve coffee, cold beverages, and confectioneries, encompassing a classy ambiance and a comfortable place to enjoy the time.

Fuchs One-Stops: The Company also operates Fuchs One-Stops to provide a complete solution for all automobile needs. These stores provide various services like wheel alignment, oil change, mechanical services, etc.

AA Energy Chemicals: AA Energy is engaged in bulk import, storage, and sales of chemicals. AA Energy has a storage facility in Karachi as well as Northern Pakistan.

Aviation Fuel Business: AA Energy also operates in the aviation business in Pakistan under a joint venture with Vitol, where Vitol provides core and technical support services to the Company to cater to the demand for jet fuels by the aviation industry in Pakistan at selected airfields. AA Energy has a joint venture with Vitol Dubai (a subsidiary of Vitol Aviation B.V) for developing and operating a 200,000 metric ton oil storage / terminal facility at Port Qasim Authority. Vitol Aviation is a leading provider of jet fuel worldwide as it supplies 5.7 million tons of jet fuel annually into wings at over 60 airports across the four continents. Vitol handles over 13 million tons of jet fuel annually in Europe, North America, and Africa.

Lubricant Business: AA Energy operates in the lubricant business by providing various engine oils and other lubricants through its One-Stop shops. The Company sells lubricants products from FUCHS, a German lubricants brand of 'Fuchs Petrolub SE Germany.' Fuchs Petrolub SE Germany Company is one of the leading global brands involved in researching, developing, producing, and distributing lubricants and related specialties. The company has a worldwide marketing and sales network operated through its licensees and partner companies. FUCHS lubricants have more than a million customers worldwide, covering most diversified segments, including automotive, commercial passenger vehicles, mining and exploration, engineering, metalworking, agriculture and forestry, aerospace, power generation, construction, steel, cement, food, glass, and miscellaneous Industries.

LPG Business: The Company operates in LPG (Liquefied Petroleum Gas) business under the brand '*Auto Max LPG.*' LPG is considered an economical, safe, and environmentally friendly alternative to CNG (Compressed Natural Gas), petrol, and diesel.

History of Information Systems

Before 2012, the Company was using local software to manage day-to-day operations. However, in 2013, the company successfully implemented 'Oracle JD Edwards' ERP software (JDE) which was comprised of six modules:

1. Financial
2. Procure to Pay
3. Order to cash
4. Inventory Management
5. Transportation

6. Advance pricing

With the implementation of this software, all AA Energy installations, depots, and storage houses were connected with the central office (Head office). This enabled real-time movement of data and controlled all business processes efficiently. Alongside this, the Company had its own state-of-the-art data center for safe storage of the Company's data with proper firewalls to ensure data security.

Oracle JD Edwards

"Owned by Oracle, JD Edwards ERP software is used by more than 7,000 organizations worldwide. JDE is unique in that organizations running their business processes through the software have a choice of database and deployment options." JD Edwards has more than 80 ERP modules with the capability of end-user reporting and robust industry functionality. JD Edwards was founded in 1977, and initially, it used to run on IBM hardware. Originally, this was an accounting-based software and was used by mid-sized businesses. After that, Oracle acquired JD Edwards in 2005, and it came under the umbrella products of Oracle.

Selection of System

The growth of the Company was visible to everyone. Each year, the Company adds 100 fuel stations and touches a total of over 700. Managing a network of 700 fuel stations, four depots, and inventory storage of over 300,000 tons of fuel required implementation of a wider Enterprise Resource Planning (ERP) network companywide to make decisions easier.

Considering these needs, the Company was in the process of selecting a new ERP, and based on the following points, SAP S4 HANA was selected.

1. 66% lower IT infrastructure cost
2. Database and data management cloud-based
3. Analytics
4. Application development
5. Integration

6. Intelligent technologies

Detail of Solution Implemented

SAP HANA (High-performance Analytic Appliance) is a multi-model database that stores data in its memory instead of keeping it on a disk. This results in data processing magnitudes faster than disk-based data systems, allowing for advanced, real-time analytics.

The key distinctions between HANA and previous generation SAP systems are that it is a column-oriented, in-memory database that combines online analytical processing (OLAP) and online transaction processing (OLTP) operations into a single system; thus, in general, SAP HANA is an OLTAP system. Storing data in main memory rather than on disk provides faster data access and, by extension, faster querying and processing.

System Approval

Due to the business's worst dynamics, market share was declining every passing day, and storage capacities were sitting idle due to weakening work capital availability. Amidst losses in 2019 and 2020, whole equity was eroded, and essentially, now the Company was being funded by lenders like the National Bank of Pakistan. In this chaos, lenders, in their high-level restructuring meetings, evaluated different possibilities to set the record straight. After thorough analysis, it was decided to implement SAP HANA.

Implementation Process

Implementing SAP S4 HANA was a challenging task for the Company, and in fact, implementing any ERP system requires considerable thought and process. However, the leadership at AA Energy accepted this challenge. Since the Company had already implemented ERP JD Edwards in 2013, the Company already possessed some level of experience with respect to implementation.

The implementation process was performed in five different steps. The followings are the steps and tasks performed during each step by the implementation team.

Step	Process	Details
1	Project Preparation and basic planning	<ul><li>Identification of business needs and requirement</li><li>Gap analysis between current operations and proposed system-based operations</li><li>Cost-benefit analysis</li><li>Shortlisting and Selection of vendors/alternatives</li><li>How will this be implemented?</li><li>Which departments will be affected?</li><li>Resource planning</li><li>Setting up deadlines and Gantt chart</li><li>Backup plan</li></ul>
2	Business Blue Print	This was a detailed document of the requirements gathered during different sessions held with customers, suppliers, employees, and other stakeholders. To create an atmosphere in the paper that reflects satisfactory completion of the requirements of all stakeholders.
3	Realization	Step-by-step completion of all the goals set in the business blueprint Time to time testing of data or process already migrated to the system to check its efficiency and efficacy
4	Final preparation	<ul><li>Testing of the whole software</li><li>Training of employees and all other stakeholders</li><li>Defining cutover activities</li><li>Division of chain of command</li><li>Identification of critical issues in soft launch (pilot launch)</li></ul>
5	Go live and support.	The aim is to migrate or transition to the system officially after declaring it error-free or rectified from the final preparation phase.

The Way Forward

The implementation team was doing a commendable job throughout the process. However, challenges were continuously faced at each and every step of the project plan. The team was determined to land this flight successfully. How does the new system perform? Will it generate the desired outcomes? Was it a good decision to move to a very high-end ERP system at this stage? Will the Company be able to resolve the problems faced with respect to fraud and misrepresentation with the help of the new ERP solution? These were all the questions to be answered with implementing the new system in the coming days.

Exhibit 1

Comparison of ERP solutions

Microsoft dynamics	Oracle E-Business Suite	SAP S/4HANA
Sales	Financial	Supply Chain and Logistics
Finance	Manufacturing	Manufacturing and Production
Customer Service	Order Management	Asset management
Field Service	Supply Chain	Finance and Accounting
Retail	Procurement	R&D
Human Capital Management	Transportation Management	Service and Contracts
	Human Capital Management	Sales and Order Management Human Capital Management

PAKISTAN BEVERAGE LIMITED: IMPLEMENTING BUSINESS PROCESS AUTOMATION

Aatika Sohail, Ilsa Abdullah, and Muhammad Rehan of Karachi School for Business and Leadership (KSBL) prepared this case under the supervision of Dr. Amir Manzoor. The case was prepared solely to provide material for class discussion. The authors do not intend to illustrate either effective or ineffective handling of a managerial situation. Certain names and other identifying information have been disguised to protect confidentiality.

It was day end on a Friday, and after a long day, Pakistan Beverage's Chief Information Officer (CIO), Mr. Asif, was packing his bag to go home. On his way out, he stopped upon seeing a long line of salespeople standing outside the finance office for their turn. He also saw one of his friends standing in the line, so he called him to his side and started talking to him.

"It is late. How come you are standing here? Instead of going home to your wife and kids?"

"I need to get the cash amount for this receipt for the order that I took today from a distributor, and since the weekend is coming, it'll be too late to get this cleared after."

"According to what you told me, you were allocated delivery in the morning in the hopes that you will be able to make it home in time to spend time with your family."

"Yes, I was allocated delivery time for early in the morning but had three sets of deliveries scheduled to make, for which all the order entry processes and getting cash for those receipts took around two hours for each location. Then, when I went for delivery to the next location, I was faced with heavy traffic at peak times, which could have been avoided and further caused my schedule delays. On top of that, sometimes, like today, the order was incomplete since we didn't take sufficient supplies, so then I had to come back and then go back to that location with the complete order."

"But the process of order taking is standard and straightforward, so why is it taking around 2 to 3 hours to process the order?"

"It usually takes approximately 1 hour in the morning as the details need to be manually entered in the system, but as the day goes on, people get exhausted and their speed decreases, so data entry takes around 2 to 3 hours."

"I understand. Give me the weekend to ponder over the information you have given me, and hopefully, I can work something so that this situation will improve."

"I hope so because I have been so exhausted and tired all the time this week. On top of that, I haven't been able to spend time with my newborn daughter and my family as my office timings are not fixed."

Mr. Asif and his friend bid farewell, and the CIO went to his car to drive home. While driving, Asif pondered over his earlier conversation with his friend. It dawned on him that the situation was extremely critical, and he needed to act as soon as possible. If it persists, it will increase the resentment among the salespeople and other employees and can make the organization long-term.

He decided to gather his colleagues and brainstorm some ideas on improving the order-taking system first thing Monday morning.

Company History

Pakistan Beverage Limited was started on the 14th of August 1950 under the direct control and management of Haji Ali Muhammad (late), who is the founder of Pakola. This company started with a small investment in hand, which is currently one of Pakistan's top carbonated soft drink brands. It is situated in the heart of Karachi's Lawrence Road, on a 1000-square-yard plot; this budding company has since blossomed into Pakistan's largest beverage manufacturing and selling company. They successfully launched Bubble Up in 1965 and Apple Sidra in 1982 with lots of effort and market research as most people like to bubble up with their food and apple Sidra for refreshment purposes. (Pakistan Beverage Limited, Ltd.)

Mr. Yassin Haji Kassam joined the beverage industry in 1968 after completing his education. His new ideas and intensifying approach have taken the company to the next level. The company also introduced a few new products such as

Orange and Pineapple Crush in 1976. The Sindh beverages plant was set up in Hyderabad. PBL took the PEPSI, MIRANDA, and TEEM franchises and moved Pakola and allied products to Mehran Bottlers Limited in 1979.

Pakistan Beverage Limited has expanded its network all over the country, which consists of six Factories, as follows:

1. Pakistan Beverage Limited – Karachi
2. Pakistan Beverage Limited – Hyderabad
3. Pakistan Beverage Limited – Quetta
4. Yassir Fruit Juice – SLICE
5. Aquafina – Highway
6. Pakola Product Limited – Highway

Just like any other company that, after its inception, faces many problems, Pakistan Beverage Limited also faces many challenges. The company resolves These challenges over time as it gains experienced professionals through employment, which eventually helps it become the market leader in the beverage manufacturing industry. Pakistan Beverage Limited has maintained its overall performance by ensuring that it provides the same quality and taste to its target audience over time. This enables their customers to demand the company's products in their daily meals, and since the prices of the products are quite affordable for the population, they can be bought by every SEC of people. This attribute allows the company to increase its market share in the industry continuously and not only please the stakeholders already present but also attract other investors and multinational companies to invest and work together with Pakistan Beverage Limited. All these efforts helped PBL get a franchise license from PepsiCo, which allowed PBL to become a Pepsi-Cola bottling partner in 1979 and increase its performance.

In the years that followed, Pakistan Beverage Limited continued to grow as a Pepsi-Cola Bottling Partner and improved its market position. Under the strong and effective leadership of Mr. Yassin Haji Kassam, the chief executive, and managing director, who his brother and son accompanied, have been able to reach immense new heights, such as becoming PepsiCo's 2015 Global Bottler of the Year, this coveted title was awarded to them out of the total PepsiCo bottlers present globally.

Today, In Pakistan, PBL holds the position of being the largest beverage manufacturer. No other competitor is near PBL in terms of the number of customers. Its current operation covers an area of more than 60 acres and spans about three cities. It also boasts 20 state-of-the-art LRB manufacturing lines. That includes bottling facilities for SSRB glass bottles, PET plastic bottles, bulk water, and a canning facility. That allows Pakistan Beverage Limited to produce on a massive scale level, enabling them to cover all of their major PepsiCo beverage brands, such as Pepsi, 7up, Mountain Dew, and Aquafina, among others, to its various customers present in the cities, which includes surrounding areas of Karachi and Hyderabad as well as in the entirety of the province of Baluchistan. Aside from beverages, Pakistan Beverage Limited also produces and sells dairy products under the Pakola Milk brand. Its commitment to excellence can also be seen here, as its milk operation, Pakola Products Limited (PPL), is the market leader in the flavored milk segment in Pakistan with standout flavors like Zaafran and Ice Cream Soda.

To succeed in any industry, a company needs to be proactive in its decision-making and always be forward-thinking to ensure it becomes a market leader. Pakistan Beverage Limited is and has always been a highly innovative and forward-thinking company. Initially, they started by investing in their manufacturing capabilities. Still, as time went by and new technologies started to arrive, they matched themselves with the industry they were operating in and started to invest in various IT projects to decrease their operating expenses.

With their investments, they have started implementing fully integrated IT systems in their company to get all the departments onto one platform and to decrease any internal issues that may arise that can affect their productivity and efficiency. SAP is one of the most-used business applications that are available in the market. Just like any other company, Pakistan Beverage Limited also used SAP as the company's primary business reporting and recording solution. They have also invested in their people, which are the key persons through which Pakistan Beverage Limited can make profits. According to the leadership, if an organization's staff is satisfied and happy with its organization, then only they will prosper; in turn, the company will prosper. Investing in and using technology cannot bring efficiency on its own, but it's the addition of skilled labor that uses that technology that drives the efficiency of the company. This motivates Pakistan Beverage Limited to form a policy that aims at investing in its people and focusing on new technologies.

Asif was born in the area of DHA, Karachi, in 1965. His father was a renowned politician and a businessman, giving him access to all the luxuries of the world from a young age. Despite his upbringing, he remained modest and went on to complete his bachelor's in Pakistan only from a local university. Then, for his postgraduate studies, he went to the UK, where he enrolled and graduated from Anglia Ruskin University. After successfully completing his education, he joined Sunrise Technologies (ST) in 1995 as a Lead IT engineer, where he served software to various customers. His continuous effort and hard-working ability have made him a senior lead IT engineer. After serving ST for eight years, he joined IT Support London, where he worked for seven years, and then he joined Pakistan Beverage Limited. Mr. Asif joined Pakistan Beverage Limited in June 2010 as Chief Information Officer (CIO).

At the time when Asif joined Pakistan Beverage Limited, all of the operations were manual, from sales orders to order dispatch. His first task on the job was to reduce the number of staff working on repetitive tasks and to increase the efficiency of sales in the company and other related departments. The reason for automating the company's existing procedures was an increase in competition for the company and high operating costs.

Background of the Case

Pakistan Beverage Limited has branches across the country, with five plants in total. There were three plants in Karachi with six lines, one in Quetta with two lines, and one in Hyderabad with three lines. The company has been doing all the distribution of its products directly. No other distributors or third party is involved in distribution. Daily, 25 to 30 deliveries were done with 2 to 3 loads of overall Heavy Goods Vehicle (HGV), whereas in peak season, 2 to 3 loads of every HGV are done, consisting of 350 HGVs in total. Moreover, the company gets sales orders of around 3000-3500 (including different lines of the order) on average (off-season), while on-season sales orders increase by 3000, making a total of 5000-6000 on-season. A company's sales orders are the accumulation of the orders of different products (which are referred to as different lines) placed by a store owner.

The CIO of Pakistan Beverage Limited wanted to shift the company's operations from manual to automated because of the major problems that the company was facing. The excessive use of paperwork, employee overtime, and the time-consuming procedure were the reasons that made the CIO want to eliminate the manual system from the company. The CIO and the team realized that by adopting a new system for the company, employees could show some reluctance. However, for their acceptance, extensive training would be required.

In the earlier days, most of the company's operations were done manually. Every step was performed manually, from taking orders from the retailer to recording them into the system. The orders were taken through the receipts provided by the company. Daily, the company had to generate three receipts in total, of which one was supposed to be for the customer (who is a store owner) and the other two were for office use. The company had a team of 30 members to enter the data into the systems, which almost took 45 mins to 1 hour for the settlement of the orders that were completed daily. The data entry team members were supposed to manually record the total sales done each day in the system using the remaining two receipts. Due to the manual recording, sales were recorded at the end of the day, so the company couldn't do the next day's product demand planning. This complete process was costing a lot of paper usage, staff overtime, a fall in efficiency, and human errors due to manually entering data. Another problem the company faced was that the total sales were recorded at the end of the day rather than getting real-time data.

Operations Flow

Procurement Processes

The Purchasing department carries out procurement from local suppliers as well as foreign suppliers. The items include raw, chemical, packing, empty, spare parts, IT, stationery, admin materials, etc. The purchase order is raised when a requirement is generated from the user department, and stock is not available at the store. Thus, the purchase process will begin with requirement identification and conclude with the finance department making payments for the purchases.

Goods Receipt Process

Goods will be received in stores against purchase orders. The movement of the material will depend upon the nature of the material, i.e., whether it is a stock material or a non-stock material and whether the material is to undergo quality inspection or not.

Goods Issue Process

For all issuances, reservations need to be created in the system. Goods will only be issued against the reservation. The reservation can be created manually or automatically. The purpose of a reservation is to ensure that material will be available when it is needed. It also serves to simplify and accelerate the goods issue process and prepare the tasks at the point of goods issue.

Exhibit 1 shows the flow chart of these processes.

Sales Order Processing

ORDER TO CASH PROCESS

There are four main stages of the SAP order-to-cash process: pre-sales activities, order processing, shipping, and billing. Pre-sales activities take place before an actual sale deal has taken place. (See Figure 1)

Figure 1: Order to Cash Process

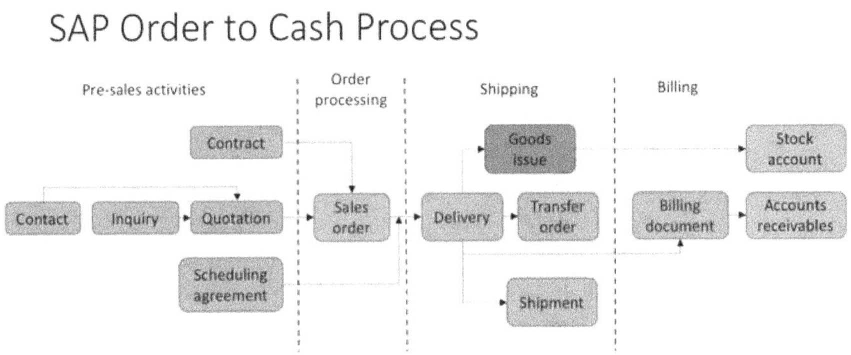

SAP Order to Cash Process

Next, the order processing stage includes activities for capturing and formalizing requests of customers as well as pricing and delivery conditions. After this stage, the customer has committed to ordering goods or services from the company. As soon as goods are ready to be sent to a customer, the shipping stage of the SAP order to cash process begins. It involves the creation of an outbound delivery document, dispatch of goods, and customer invoices in SAP are created using billing documents.

The overall sales Process of PBL Karachi is divided into two types:

1. Spot sales
2. Pre-sales

Spot Sale

- CR prepares manual demand notes based on the previous buying history or demand from the customer on the telephone.

- Physical stock is loaded on trucks using manual demand notes as shown in the above picture.

- After that, the DPG computer dept. Issues empty/filled stocks from the DPG floor location to the virtual storage location (truck) using stock transfer order and issued printed gate pass.

- The truck is checked by a gate concerning the stock mentioned on the gate pass, and stock is loaded on the trucks.

- In the sales area, C.R. visits individual customers and records the sales order by using a hand-held device.

- Once the sales order is finalized, CR performs post-good issues and billing using a handheld device.

- On the day's end, trucks came back to DPG 3 & 5 from respectively the sales area with the remaining stock of filled and empty loads.

- After that computer dept., the record returned empties & filled stock from virtual storage location trucks to referencing the same store. (See Exhibit 2)

Pre-Sale:

- Order bookers go to the market on the mentioned route for order booking for the next day using a hand-held based on sales orders created by the order book. A manual demand note is created for loading stock into the truck.

- After that, the DPG computer department issues empty/filled stocks from the DPG floor location to a virtual storage location (truck) using stock transfer order and issue printed gate pass.
- To deliver stock to customers, delivery men collect printed gate passes and invoices from the DPG and sales department respectively.
- The truck is checked by a gate checker concerning stock mentioned on the gate pass and stock loaded on the trucks.
- Stock is delivered on the customer site with pre-printed invoices.
- On the day's end, trucks returned to DPG- 3 & 5 from respectively the sales area with the remaining stock of filled and empty loads and customers receiving receipts.
- After that, computer department records returned empties & filled stock from virtual storage location trucks to the DPG referencing the same store
- After that, the DPG sales department performs post-good issue activity in the SAP system using the receipt of the customers to clear the route, and billing is performed. (See Exhibit 3).

History of Information System at PBL

When the CIO joined the company, nearly every other procedure was done manually, from taking orders from the retailer and then recording them into the system. This system generated physical copies of receipts to take orders from the distributors. Each day three copies were printed. Two receipts were kept for office use to record data for the day, while the remaining one was given to the customer. This resulted in the sales being recorded at the end of the day, which affected the supply forecasting mechanism for the company. This complete process was costing the company a lot of paper usage, staff overtime, and human errors due to manually entering the data.

As the years passed, the CIO and his team made drastic changes to prevent any problems with the company's processes by developing and introducing new software. It was a difficult task given the company employees lacked Enterprise Resource Planning (ERP) concepts and hardly any Information Technology present. Hence, before shifting towards any ERP system, the company first started using the FOX PRO system, which it used to develop a data-centric desktop application with its own internal database. At that time, sales that were done regularly were recorded manually by the staff by entering each store's order, which was then uploaded into the system. A bunch of staff was required to enter data in the system, of daily sales of each truck that was sent for the delivery of the products of PBL. Entering data of each receipt took approximately 40-45 mins with around 30 staff members.

In 2010, Pakistan Beverage Limited adopted SAP ERP with the database MAX-DB to record its total sales. The company used two SAP modules: sales & distribution and material management. Later, in 2015, the company changed its database and migrated from MAX-DB to SAP HANA. Currently, the company's IT department focuses on implementing SAP S/4 HANA, a successor of SAP ERP.

Operations Flow

The operation flow of the company consists of the following steps:

- Sale Forecast

- Production Planning

- Material Resource Planning

- Raw Material Purchasing

- Raw Material Issuance for Production

- Finished Goods Received at the warehouse.

Sales Forecast

The first and foremost step of the operation flow is the sales forecast, in which the system forecasts the total sales of all the company's products. That might be seasonal forecasts or demand forecasts. Before automation, sales forecasts were done manually on Excel sheets by the finance team, but after automation, the forecasted sales were automatically calculated on the system by seeing past trends without any hassle or dependency on a particular person. Based on last year's analysis, a sales forecast is given to the production team. The sales forecast is done monthly, and the system calculates how much sales need to be done for the upcoming month.

Production Planning

Once the sales forecast is done, the next step is to plan the production. Depending on the sales that have been forecasted for the upcoming month, the production of the products is planned. Relevant ingredients were ordered from the suppliers, and a proper setup was done to store the finished products.

Material Resource Planning

A separate material resource planning department is present, which plans the availability of material for the production of beverages within the warehouse. Excess inventory increases the cost and chances of expiry, and so inventory of a maximum one month is made available for production purposes.

Raw Material Purchasing

For the production of beverages, the raw materials that PBL requires are the container, materials used for the packaging & labeling, and all ingredients (e.g., flavors, water, sugar, juices, etc.). We have the best quality suppliers of beverage products. Our team regularly checks the raw material availability, and if there is any shortage or excess demand in the market, then our procurement team works actively on it.

Raw Material Issuance for Production

The raw material purchased in bulk quantity is placed in the warehouses where there is a proper arrangement for storing and managing the raw material. On a weekly basis, the raw material from the warehouse is sent for production purposes to the production site. The factory is working on a 24/7 basis as demand for beverages is present for the whole year.

Finished Goods Received at the Warehouse

Once the product is produced, it is sent to the warehouse through trucks, Mazda, and other means of transport. The warehouse has a proper arrangement for storing the final products. A few items need room temperature, and some can be placed at different temperatures. From the warehouse, it is sent to different locations all over Pakistan. The warehouse is located near Karachi highway, where other competitors' warehouses were also present.

Selecting the System

The company wanted to eliminate the process of recording its sales manually and move towards automating its sales to reduce the paperwork, time, and manual working and increase its efficiency. The competition in the beverage industry was also high at that time. The competitors are using their automated processes to manage their inventory, reduce operational costs, forecast future sales, and get the best of their efforts from their employees. Earlier, when the company was using FOX PRO and had to switch to Enterprise Resource Planning (ERP), they had two options to implement. One was the Oracle financials, and the other was the SAP ERP. Considering the company's intricacies and technicalities, they came up with the decision that SAP was more in line with industry best practices and had a strong technological foundation, hence implementing SAP ERP. Later on, a pro-type module was developed by the information technology (IT) team. It was demonstrated to management with a problem statement and proposed a solution that can help reduce paper, time, and manual working.

Detail of the Solution

System Applications and Products (SAP) is the most demanding in Data Processing. It was founded in 1972. Multiple business functions are performed by SAP software. SAP is the market leader in ERP software and helps companies of all sizes, whether large or small. SAP is the company's primary business reporting and recording solution. The company's integrated applications connect all parts of a business into an intelligent suite on a fully digital platform. All the information is relevant to decision-making is readily available 24/7 with the arrival of SAP HANA and handheld devices, facilitating swift reactions to the ever-changing business environment. That, coupled with a centralized data center, has allowed the massive organization to function more effectively as one unit, one that also hopes to pursue further and more complex methods of sales and operational automation.

To resolve the issue of recording orders, a new application has been aligned/integrated with the existing modules of sales & distribution and material management. It provides hand devices to the sales personnel for quick and early orders. SAP on handheld allows customers to mobilize their business processes for handheld devices, such as Mobile Scanners, PDAs, etc. Handheld applications target users who need to access information while away from the office. Users of handheld devices are sales executives, field service engineers, or delivery personnel.

Implementation Process

The team decided to use the ASAP methodology to implement the hand-held devices, in which they divided the implementation process into five stages in hopes of increasing the efficiency of the new system.

a)   Phase 1: Project preparation

b)   Phase 2: Business Blueprint

c)   Phase 3: Realization

d)   Phase 4: Final Preparation

e)   Phase 5: Go-Live and support

Phase 1 - Project Preparation

For project preparation, initially, there was a high-level meeting between the board and senior management to discuss the possible phases for implementing the project, the departments involved, timelines, possible expenses, pros and cons of the project, etc. After the meeting, a team of senior personnel as well as a junior staff mixture team was announced, which will look after the preparation of the project. Junior staff was responsible for retrieving information from the user. That includes the team members going alongside the delivery truck for the entire working day to get as much information as possible about the salesperson's needs and pinpoint their pain areas.

Simultaneously, they also started assembling resources needed for a Dot net developer for the HHD devices. Some new staff was also hired from the market who have previous experience in automation in the beverage industry. Senior-level management support was important at this stage as they were working here for many years and had experience of the automation of different departments on SAP modules. They have clear project objectives to ensure that the company has a suitable environment for change management and there is no resistance in the implementation process.

Phase 2 - Business Blueprint

After getting the senior management on board with this project, the next stage was to prepare 'TO-BE', also known as the Business Blueprint. These blueprints were in the form of questionnaires that are designed to probe for information that uncovers how a company does its business. This stage also documents the implementation process for the entire team to follow. The business blueprint consists of all the steps for the implementation process using a flow diagram so that the users and the management better understand the processes being followed. The next step after the blueprint is created in this phase is to get approval from the stakeholders.

Approval from the Stakeholders

A meeting was arranged with the stakeholders to get their approval. Multiple sessions were conducted with them to fully explain the process and bring the entire team on board for the new solution. In these sessions, the team explained every single process flow mentioned in the blueprint and informed them how the new system would improve their business. Once the stakeholders are satisfied with the company's new steps, they then show their approval by signing a document giving the team the go-ahead for the next steps.

Phase 3 - Realization

After getting the approval from the stakeholders, the team can then move on to the next phase, which is developing a testing regime to try out the new system and test its efficiency and workability.

Phase 4 - Final Preparation

After a plan is laid out for testing, the team tests the new system. In this phase, not only does the team test out the handheld device (HHD) but also provides training to end-users of the device present in the company's sales area. That is done to ensure the users are comfortable with the new technology once it is live.

Testing the new System

Initially, the team picked around 2-3 routes for this pilot project to test the new system. The idea behind selecting only limited routes in the pilot testing was that the users in these routes would then act as trainers for the remainder of the users that work on the rest of the 3rd issues that the implementation process was facing. These issues can be worked on while implementing the process on other routes. The problems faced were that the users were mishandling the HHD, forgetting to charge their respective devices, writing the wrong information into the systems, or facing connectivity issues in some areas, which were at a great distance as the internet was unavailable in those locations.

Phase 5 - Going Live and Support

This was the last phase of the implementation process, in which the entire system was made live and available to all company and management users. The team also ensured that system support was provided to all those who required it during the operation of the system. This entire implementation process of the new system took around 4-5 months.

Training

For training the users on the usage of handheld devices, the company divided its users into two subdivisions, which were done according to the routes being followed. The first set of users was included in the pilot testing. For which the company provided training in the following manner

The second set of users were those who were given the training after the pilot testing program. For them, the users of the first set acted as trainers, giving them instructions and teaching them the proper way to handle the hand-held device without facing any possible issues.

Project Team

The CIO first needed to make the team to manage the hand-held devices' implementation process and ensure it ran smoothly. Since he was responsible for supervising and making all the necessary decisions, he needed a team that efficiently managed the whole process. This was done during phase 1 of the implementation process.

When the project team was announced, it consisted of 3 members.

- Project manager
- Business Manager
- Developer

The CIO soon realized that to achieve the results he envisioned, he would also need help from other departments. Hence, he included the capability department from the sales side and the infrastructure in the development team from the IT department in the project team to assist in implementing and running the new system.

Implementation Issues

With the implementation of the new system, some issues were coming to light to the CIO that the users of the new system were facing.

For Pakistan Beverage Limited (PBL), the issues were the following:

People

Lower management was not involved in the decision-making process for this new system. It was not included in the implementation process as the major focus was on shareholders and the four-member project team. Hence, the employee motivation levels were low, and they were resistant to trying out the new system.

During the testing period in phase 2, an assumption was made by the project team that each salesperson taking the order would have the same level of capability and ability to utilize the new system efficiently. Hence equal amounts of training were provided to all the users, and few training sessions were done to increase staff competency. This hindered the further training of users as salespeople who lack the knowledge of using the hand-held devices would not be able to transfer their skills to future users after the pilot testing.

In the initial stages of the implementation process, the team saw that users were resistant to adapting to the change in the system, as it was a different system than they were used to. But other users' word of mouth and the incentives provided to those who utilize the new system (such as getting home early) encouraged the remaining users to give the new system a chance.

During phase 4 of the implementation process, it was seen that many users mishandled the HHD (hand-held device). Some users forgot to charge their respective devices, making taking the order harder. Some users made wrong entries. Due to this, the usage of the devices became limited by the salespeople, and some even started to record orders by hand again.

Process

Initially, there was some resistance from the Customer representatives and record punching staff for this process change. There were many different factors involved that resulted in this behavior i.e., firstly, as they had to learn this new system, they were barriers as they were not used to this new practice and technology. Secondly, manual entries can usually be manipulated easily, making it easier to speed up the process to get the work done early, whereas the new system enforces constraints that ensure the data is being punched with integrity in a timely fashion.

The IT Development team was encouraged to learn new technologies to develop this Application in-house, which took time and resources for the company. This process also required multiple iterations to be developed and implemented to mature the process.

Technology

The devices required charging on time to ensure longevity and make the device available for order taking. Hence, the users need to keep an eye on their devices' battery levels and be taught the proper way to charge these devices.

One of the biggest concerns was the security concern of using such technology in the uncertain environment of Pakistan. Given that there is always the risk of snatching of the devices by thieves or hackers hacking the devices through which information about the business can be leaked or orders of the centers can be lost.

Another concern was the availability of the Internet, which was a big issue in ensuring that the system was efficient. Fast Internet connectivity was required to take the orders. Additionally, some route locations in Pakistan do not have good connectivity as they have low levels of data signals, a huge cost borne on a monthly basis by PBL.

Besides facing several issues in implementing the new system, the company did see some benefits from the hand-held devices. These benefits were not limited to only one department but were felt throughout the organization. The company did not have a proper measure in place to judge the productivity of this new system and monitor the rate of investment in this project. However, they utilize these benefits to measure the success of this project and monitor the impact of implementing hand-held devices in the company.

The company saw the benefits in the following manner:

Reduced Waiting Time: Since the orders were taken on hand-held devices, the device automatically updated the order on the system in the company, and the production team made it available on time. That reduced the time for the employee to wait on the office premises in the long queue lines to get their cash receipt for the order taken. That also reduced the waiting time period of the istribution centers that got their order taken at the time promised to them earlier as the salesperson assigned was not involved in lines for the order processing of the previous center for a long time as it was previously done.

Minimum Truck Returns: When the salesperson takes orders from the distribution centers, they return to the center to deliver the required order. Previously, if the order was not complete or correct, then due to data integrity of punching the data, the truck would then have to make returns to the site and then back to the center to complete the required order. This was not only a time-consuming process but also strained the relationship of the company with its distribution centers. With the implementation of the new system, the company was then correctly able to record the order taken into the system with ample time for the truck to be loaded with the correct materials for the order efficiently. Hence, once the truck has gone to the distribution centers, they successfully completed the order with zero truck returns to the site.

Employee Motivation: With the new system in place for the order-taking process, employees were more motivated to work and try out the new system. Not only were they able to perform all of their daily tasks on time, but they were also going home at a suitable time to spend with their families and friends. Previously, they would stay at the office till late hours due to the system's inefficiency in recording the orders and receiving the cash. Hence, they were unwilling to work efficiently and were disheartened as they barely saw their families.

Cost-Saving: A crucial element of a company's operation is the costs associated with running the company. Hence, this new system enabled the company to reduce its costs in various aspects. First, the fuel cost that would have been spent on the fuel of the truck being returned to the distribution centers was reduced as with the new system there were zero to very few returns of the orders being delivered. Next, fixed costs associated with managing the building and running its day-to-day operations (such as electricity and overtime pay to workers) were reduced. Since the order-taking process was efficiently done, people went home at a suitable time, which reduced the amount the company spent on overtime pay. The building didn't have to stay open for long, so electricity usage was reduced. Also, the storage costs of keeping excess inventory not used in the day was reduced as the stock being kept was according to the forecasting and correctly fulfilled the demand.

Forecasting: Forecasting was done by the company to predict the orders for the next day, and then they would know how much stock to hold in their inventory. That was called the pre-sale method in the company. This new system ensured that all the forecasting was done correctly with the presale method, so the stock inventory was done efficiently and accurately. In comparison to the previous system, the system could not predict the orders properly given the tardiness of the orders being entered into the system; hence, the stock inventory was affected. Sometimes, the company would keep an excess of one product that was not required while keeping very limited quantities of the desired product that didn't match the demand. By the implementation of the new system, the system was able to predict the stock needed for the operations for the following day, and hence, all the demands were accurate, and their storage costs were also reduced.

Less Data Entry Errors: Each salesperson has different handwriting through which they take the orders of the distribution centers. With the previous system being followed, the ineligibility of the handwriting caused errors in data entry as sometimes the data entry people couldn't read the writing and inserted wrong orders. Also, it was easier to manipulate the orders with manual entries. However, with the new system being placed through the introduction of hand-held devices, it made it easier to accurately record the data that were exactly as the distribution center required and prevented no manipulation or exploitation of resources.

Transparency: The new system promoted transparency in the transactions being taken place. Previously, there was a usage of fake bills that were not accounted for by the old system, causing problems for the company in the future concerning calculation errors. However, with the new system in place, a code was generated for each distribution center, which had to be written down on the receipt to load the truck to the right orders. The code was known by a limited number of people, including the head of the distribution and the salesperson, so the chance of recording a fake order was reduced.

The Way Forward

Mr. Asif and his team were concerned with some of the problems that the company had been facing for ages, due to which a new system was implemented to eliminate the outdated manual system and enable the company's growth.

In this technological and competitive era, where every other operation in every other aspect has been automated, the CIO also wanted to shift its major operations towards automation, which would be beneficial for the company, its profitability, and the employees. The purpose of implementing an entirely new system was to eliminate the excessive use of paperwork and make the life of staff more flexible. As all the operations were manual, it gave an idea of how much paper was consumed daily, costing the company a lot. The future plan of the CIO for the company was to encourage automation for the operations, with zero manual systems. So. What steps will the company take to eliminate that one receipt that is generated for office use?

Exhibit 1
Operations Flow of the Company

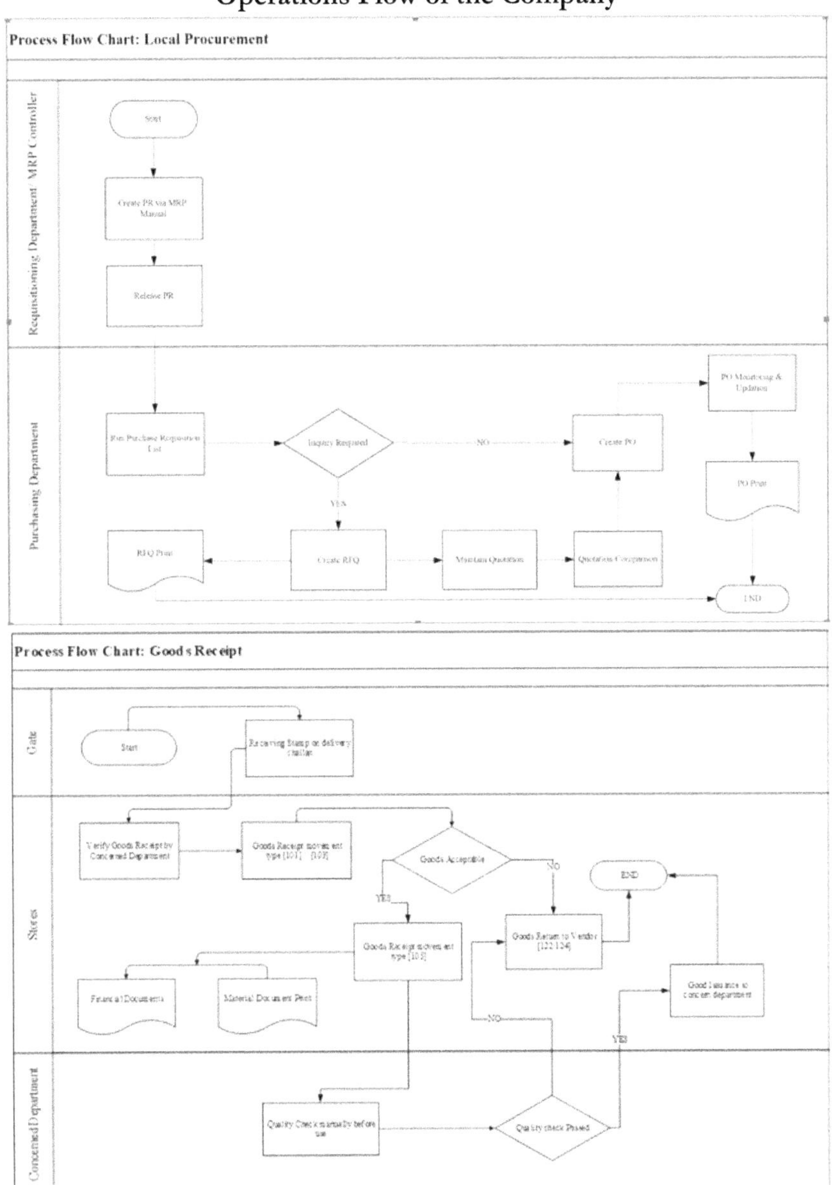

183

Process Flow Chart: Goods Issue

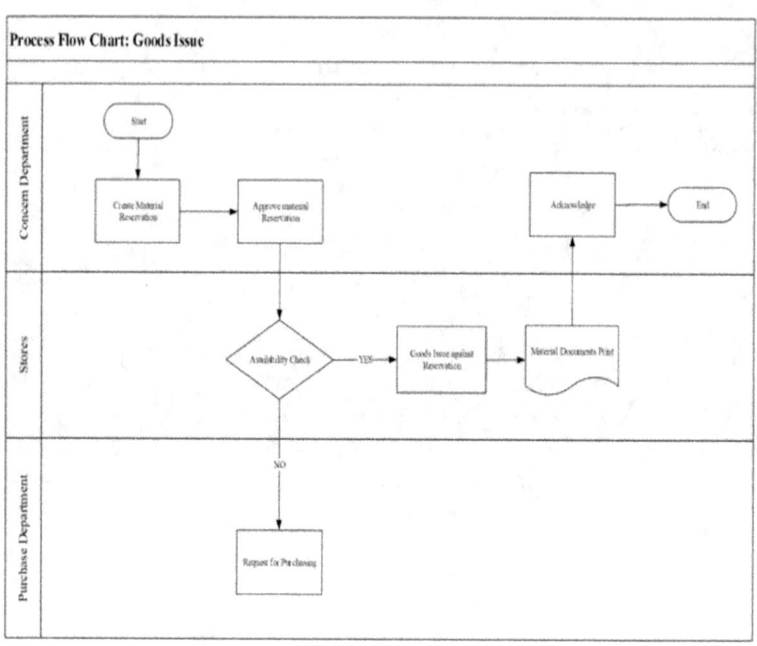
Concern Department
Stores
Purchase Department
Start
Create Material Reservation
Approve material Reservation
Availability Check
YES
Goods Issue against Reservation
Material Documents Print
Acknowledge
End
NO
Request for Purchasing

Exhibit 2
Spot Sales Process

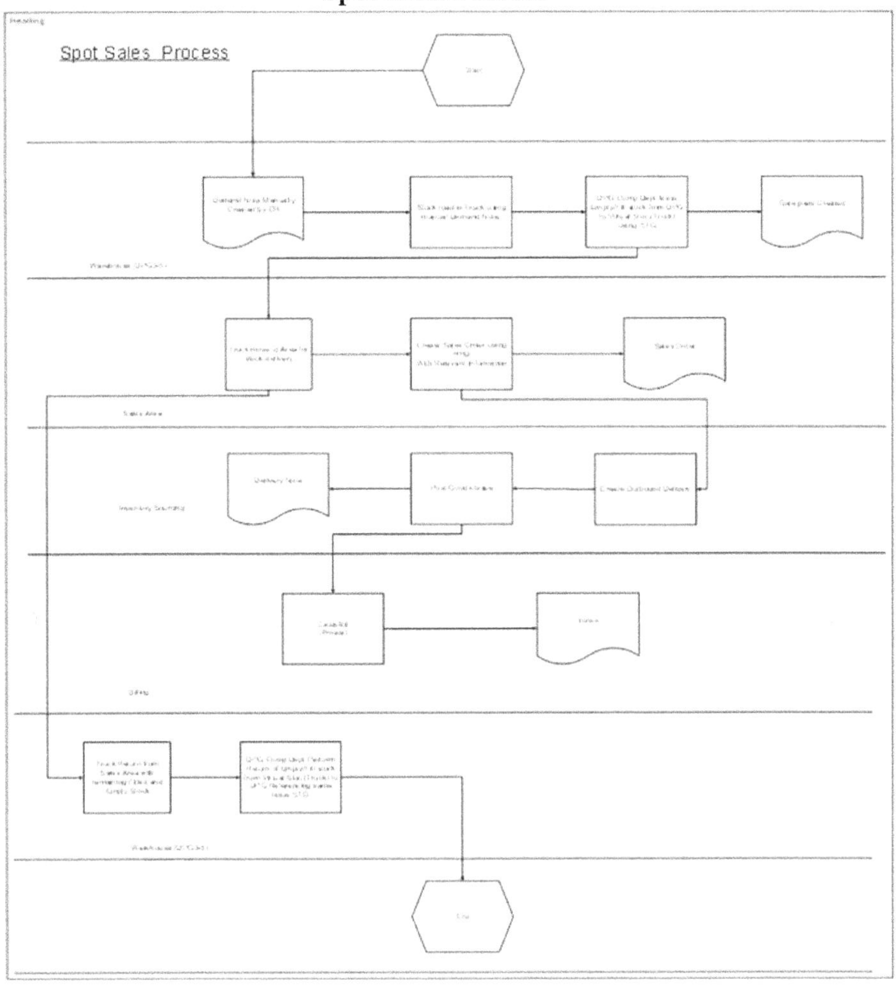

185

Exhibit 3
Pre Sales Process

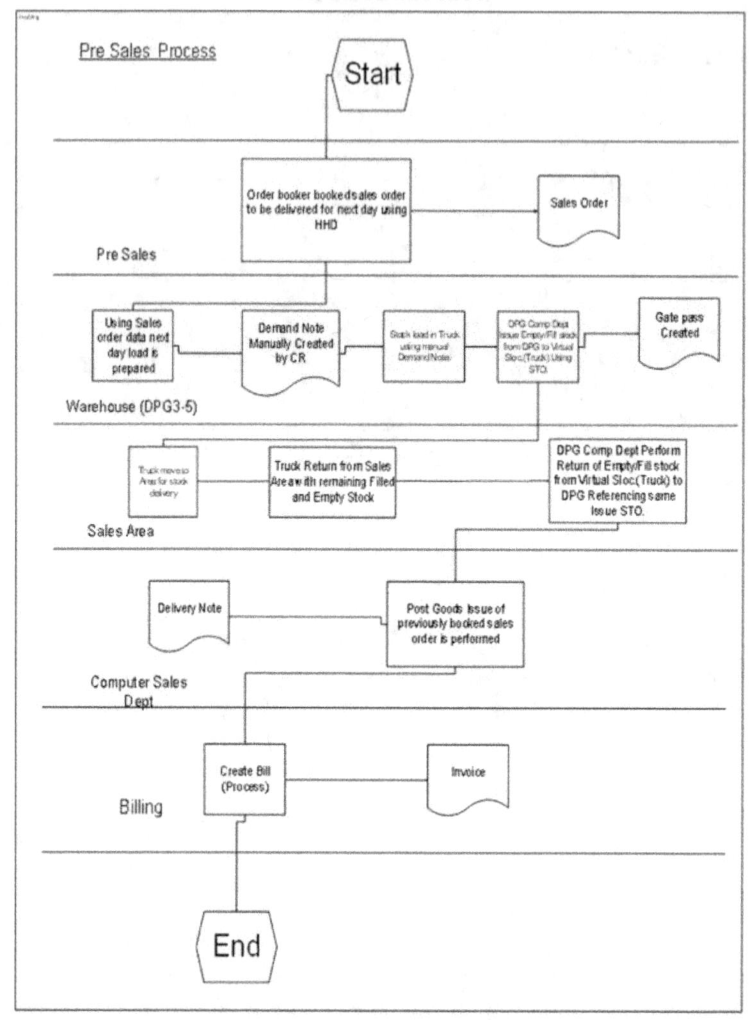

ERP SYSTEMS AT NATIONAL FOODS LIMITED

Muhammad Haider, Syed Saad Mansoor, and Muhammad Arsalan of Karachi School for Business and Leadership (KSBL) prepared this case under the supervision of Dr. Amir Manzoor. The case was prepared solely to provide material for class discussion. The authors do not intend to illustrate either effective or ineffective handling of a managerial situation. Certain names and other identifying information have been disguised to protect confidentiality.

National Food Limited is a multinational company that aims to create food that enriches people's lives everywhere. The company started its operations in 1970 by introducing spices in the Pakistani market. The company initially started recording its activities manually. Still, due to increasing demand, Abrar Hassan soon realized that the company could not sustain its operations by using the manual recording system. So, in 2003, he decided to shift the manual recording to the enterprise resource system and chose SCALA as the better option and gave the title to National Foods Limited of being the first local food company to implement an enterprise resource system. After the successful implementation of SCALA, the company's management recognized that it must shift to another enterprise resource system as the company's size was increasing and they had certain security risks on SCALA. SCALA worked smoothly with the business requirements and increased the company's recording system and overall performance efficiency.

After some time, the company realized that the size of the company was increasing, and SCALA was not a solution to complete the increasing business requirements. So, for that reason, the company started searching for different options and finalized two available candidates: ORACLE and SAP. The company for this hired Abacus Technologies as their business consultant, and Abrar Hassan, along with the IT head of National Foods, Mr. Zahid Sheikh, and Managing partner of Abacus Technologies, discussed the business requirements and available software packages which can solve the existing problems being faced by the company. However, due to the increasing size of the company and Abacus's information about SAP, the company left the option of ORACLE and decided to move on to the solution SAP.

Later, in 2015, they approached Rapid Commute to achieve a cloud-based solution for their ongoing software, and due to this step, their whole software was moved to a cloud-based system instead of onsite software as a solution.

Company History

National Foods commenced its business in 1970 as a small company, a business initiative within a group of friends. The company presented an amazing concept of branded spices in the market of Pakistan. At the start, the company saw the opportunity in well-processed branded spices and planned to develop innovative food products based on convenience and fast preparation per the modern day-to-day lifestyle and yet preserving traditional taste and values.

In 1970, the spice industry of Pakistan was not properly designed, and there were unbranded open-market spices. The present way of operations started when the current management purchased a major stock of a small company called "National Food Laboratories Limited." The company commenced its journey in a rented warehouse in Dinar Chambers, starting sales of only Rs. 16,500 in the first fiscal year. The company inaugurated a spice mill and packaging plant in 1978.

The company introduced branded salt in 1981, which was a profitable move for the business. Most of the facilities are still located in the new plant complex that was built in the Korangi Industrial Area in 1986. Branded pickles, a related diversification that is currently the company's top category, were introduced by the company's expansion in 1991.

In 1988, they decided to operate as a public limited and were listed in all of Pakistan's three stock exchange markets. In 1997, ketchup and jams were added to the product list. In the year 2000, National Foods exported its products to Australian markets. In 2006, the company opened a new facility in Port Qasim with more than 10 acres of state-of-the-art labs and machinery.

Vision and Mission of National Foods Limited

Vision Statement

To be an Rs. Fifty billion food company by the year 2020 in the convenience food segment by launching products and services in the domestic and international markets that enhance lifestyle and create value for our customers through management excellence at all levels.

Mission Statement

- ❖ National Foods must concentrate on serving customers at their doorsteps with high-quality goods at reasonable costs.

- ❖ Our products must not have any impurities and conform to international standards.

- ❖ Our research must constantly result in novel, scientifically tested items that are made hygienically and packaged in a way that is both secure and appealing.

- ❖ We have to create such an environment in our facilities and factories where talent is groomed and is provided an opportunity to advance.

- ❖ We must demonstrate that we are respected as decent corporate citizens, support charitable causes, and pay our fair amount of taxes.

- ❖ Reserves must be built, new factories created, sound profits made and fair dividend paid to our stockholders through building a reliable brand.

Company History

Abdul Majeed is the founder, director, and Chairman of National Foods Limited. He and Waqar Hasan, a former Pakistani test cricketer, inaugurated the company. Waqar Hasan was the company's first Managing Director from 1970 and retired in 2000. Through his leadership, Waqar Hasan set the fundamentals of efficient governance and ethics, which are still within the company.

Abrar Hasan, who graduated from Purdue University in the United States with degrees in business management and industrial engineering, is the MD of National Foods Limited. He joined the company in April 1993. He has been instrumental in revising and redefining National Food's vision and strategy due to his expertise in information technology as a plant director. When Waqar Hasan retired, he was elevated to the role of Chief Executive. Abrar Hasan has always played a key role in continuously growing human resources, and he is strong in developing people for increased performance and higher production. He wants to advance the company by investing in its employees. He said that we have specialists working in all areas and have given them the authority to make decisions on their day-to-day tasks. Strategies are developed by the top management and are approved by our Board which operates the company according to Corporate Governance

An intriguing narrative is how National Food came to be known as a brand. The ultimate brand design reflects loyalty and communicates the business's positioning. The rainbow is a representation of excellence and purity. The Company concentrated solely on quality and purity for the first ten years. Methods of mass marketing were employed to advertise the brand. While the brand's leadership position was upheld, it also evolved into a segment-specific stance.

According to Abrar Hasan, he and his colleagues have put much effort into changing National Foods' image from spice to a food company. We all saw the need to reposition the brand when I started working for the firm. Instead of positioning the brand as a spice brand, we wanted it to become a food brand. "Due to our extensive product mix, we also simultaneously focused on strategic and segmental marketing. Segmental marketing took the role of mass marketing, but the strategic focus persisted. To reposition the brand, the Company needed to be reimagined. Consequently, the new brand identity and packaging were launched".

Through effective planning and efficient operations in expanding its portfolio now, National Foods are offering several products in the following categories:

- Jams

- Ketchup

- Pickles

- Raj masala

- Health foods

- Desserts

- Chinese

- Spices and ingredients

- Salts and Rivaaj past

National Foods felt the need to promote the brand as a concept rather than the company philosophy since they wanted to expand the brand's market outside Pakistan. The mainstream multiples market saw the introduction of the new brand. The new brand, however, was created using an older set of principles. The brand is now promoted as a culinary adventure. However, because the company is aware of the product's strength, they have also made significant investments in technology and packaging.

In 2011, National Foods Limited gained a growth rate of 23% in sales. NFL gross margin have been pressed down because of high inflation in agriculture products and price variability in imported raw material. NFL gross margin went down by 1% in 2011 compared to 2010, from 29.5% to 28.5%.

Chief Executive Abrar Hasan made the decision to re-engineer the company's internal management. In 2011, he launched the "Cost Control & Cost Management Program" to eliminate extra costs. He informed the stockholders that there is substantial ownership at all levels to provide financial value. The Chief Executive personally oversaw and was involved in this endeavor. Compared to 2010, the net profit after taxes for 2011 climbed by 166 percent. The cost control and management program is the only thing that has made this feasible. The main savings came from better supply chain management, which caused a significant decrease in the cost of product delivery.

NFL is always pursuing profitable opportunities domestically and internationally. The salt and Sauce category had 40% growth in 2011. NFL experts have hiked by 21% even in recession at the international level. Financial charges increased by 27% in 2011 compared to 2010, mainly because of an increase in interest rates by the State Bank of Pakistan. NFL's advertising and promotional activities, attractive in-store displays, and successful below-the-line activities contributed strongly to business growth.

Recipe Mix was a particular category with potential and a 34% increase in sales in 2011. It is marked as a star category by the management and includes recipes for the most ethnic dishes. This category brackets Bombay Biryani, Achar Ghost, and fish masala. The advertising campaign "Hamarey Khaney Humarey Tehwar" during Eid and on Sundays has resulted in tremendous sales for the company. Ketchup showed 30% growth. The 2011 chat masala combo pack under the ketchup category was a huge success. National's tomato ketchup, specifically its unique taste, has been a washout success in 2011.

Fruitily was a new powdered drink in orange, lemon, mango, and mixed fruit flavors. It was introduced in 2011 to compete with Tang" and "lemopani," two well-known brands. Lemopani has particularly high sales during Ramadan, while Tang is known for being a highly well-liked orange drink. Although Fruitily's "Stir the Magic" advertising campaign was heavily promoted on electronic media, the results were not very encouraging, given how slowly the product is moving. According to a market expert, the NFL will need to enhance the flavor and make significant investments in this brand to make it successful.

Chief Executive Abrar Hasan said, "We are the leaders of the food industry in Pakistan, and we are leading in almost all the categories we manage. The vision of the company is to achieve PKR Fifty billion sales by 2020 are the biggest challenge my team has to achieve." In 2011, NFL sales revenue was Rs. 5.5 billion. That was a big achievement considering the first year's sales were only PKR 16 thousand forty years back. But now, National Foods has to achieve the goal of 50 billion in the coming eight years.

Abrar said his intuitiveness points out that growth will come from exports, rural areas, and new innovative products, and the Indian market will also direct the growth of the NFL. The vision statement of the NFL directs our strategies, and the mission statement affects all decision-making of the NFL, even decisions taken by our Board. Abrar added that he is aware that Nishat Group is also completing its business strategy to enter the food sector and that Nestle Pakistan is set to enter the market for spices and recipes. Unilever's Knorr is already in direct competition with us. Shan Food is a formidable rival. We always increase the bar when facing fierce competition because we embrace competition.

NFL has always learned from rivals. As the industry leaders in the food industry, they will do all in their power to stay that way. National Foods has an ISO certification and uses HACCP in its production methods. NFL exports to 35 nations; its exports to the United States, Canada, Europe, the Middle East, Asia Pacific, and Australia are growing by 12 percent annually. Australia has a huge market for cooking in pastes sold under the National Foods brand name Revaaj.

According to their chief executive, brand loyalty is always rising. In the 2011 Brand Elections, which were held in 50 cities throughout Pakistan with 10,000 votes, National Foods Limited came out on top in five food categories: Recipes, pickles, spices, ketchup, jams, jellies, and marmalades.

ERP Timeline at National Foods Limited

NFL followed a manual bookkeeping system till 1996, and they recorded all the activities in the physical registers. The company handled different registers for all the departments and activities like payroll, sales, payment, etc. In 1993, Mr. Abrar Hassan joined the NFL as plant director. In 1996, due to changing demand for business and expansion, he recognized that the company could not continue with the manual recording system as it cost time and had more chances for error in increasing demand. Therefore, in 1996, Abrar Hassan led the development of the Human Resource Management system, which was the first of its kind for any national company in the country's history.

Abrar Hassan was elected as the deputy managing director of the NFL in 1997, and soon after, in 1999, he led the development of international marketing infrastructure, which was also the first initiative by any food company in Pakistan. In 2000, Mr. Abrar Hassan was elected as the Chief Executive of National Foods Limited and provided direction and leadership to the company by aiming to become the first Rs. Fifty billion company in Pakistan by setting targets to deliver long-term growth through aggressive international growth and entering into the technological world.

By recognizing the vital growth of information systems and technology in business development, Abrar Hassan bought some IT revolution in the company. In February, National Food achieved the title of becoming the first local food company to introduce the enterprise resource system (SCALA), which was ultimately upgraded to SAP-ERP in a record time deployment of 6 months.

Soon after the implementation of SCALA, the company recognized that the production planning, cost controlling, sales, and distribution elements of the current ERP system were not sophisticated enough to support the company's growth strategy. So, after six months of implementation of SCALA, NFL management started working on shifting to a new ERP solution and evaluated ORACLE and SAP for the business need. With the help of Zahid Sheikh (Head of IT at National Foods), Abrar Hassan recognized that the SAP ERP system was a closer fit to the business requirements and decided to go ahead with the migration from the existing platform.

The previous solution was running on the Microsoft Windows operating system, and the company could not afford the risk of viruses and hacking. The company had to keep patching them to ensure they were secure, which was time-consuming and inconvenient. In 2015, with the help of its technology partner Rapid commute (a cloud division of Cybernet), the company successfully shifted its SAP ERP to the cloud system to secure more of its servers.

Product Solution

Abrar Hassan recognized that SCALA is not enough solution for the growing need of business, and its user interface of Microsoft Windows would not provide a better security solution to the company. So, with the help of Zahid Sheikh (IT Head), he realized that they must implement the better ERP system, which requires the business community's involvement as it was not the only initiative of the information technology department. They must need the best people to complete all the requirements and meet the business needs.

The company hired its business partner, Abacus Consultancy, who saw the opportunity to build the business around these applications. Abacus came with their highly professional staff who have a better experience with these software packages. The team initially came up with different packages of solutions, but NFL and Abacus combined and elected only two feasible options: completing the business need and requirements. Those were ORACLE and SAP enterprise resource systems. Zahid Sheikh informed that the company's size is also an issue in the selection process as the company had already expanded in different corners of the world. Vendors were shortlisted and invited for the software orientation separately. After listening to both solutions, the company and its partner decided that ERP was a better solution in the food industry worldwide and selected that option for their business need.

Building the Implementation Team

With the approval of Abrar Hassan (Chief Executive of NFL), the ERP team started setting up a structure for the implementation. The company initially had a small team of members who were checking the business requirements and software packages. Still, after deciding on a solution, the company had to increase the team, representing every national food community department. The implementation team members were selected based on members' knowledge of business and technology and those who can work on this project as their ultimate goal. The whole team was managed by Abrar Hassan, Zahid Sheikh, and the project manager from Abacus Technology. The committee of these three people was called the steering committee, which overall was responsible for the successful implementation. The major role of that committee was to provide every facility to the team that could directly interfere with the project management and to provide familiarity and motivation to the team.

Mr. Hasan joined the NFL as Plant Director in 1993 and stood firm on that footing for a considerable time. He was chosen as Deputy Managing Director in 1997 and afterward as Chief Executive presently. In 1996, he drove the improvement of a thorough Human Resource Management System, which was the first of its sort for any public organization in the country. He likewise drove the improvement of a global showcasing framework beginning in 1999. As the Chief Executive, Mr. Hasan is giving guidance and initiative to the Company by setting a distinctive vision for future development, which means to turn into a PKR 50 billion organization. The company was set to convey its drawn-out objectives by zeroing in on top brands, developing a client base, and forceful worldwide expansion.

Mr. Hasan has effectively sought after new market open doors and conveyed fruitful procedures to drive NFL's vision, zeroing in on ceaseless development, best expectations of value, and unrivaled customer esteem. He has directed the organization to convey consistent deals development year on year, obviously clear from the emotional extension in deals, from just PKR 200 million in 1993 to Rs.23 billion today, a fortunate development rate, going from 20% to 30% every year, nevertheless intense monetary circumstances.

Through the foundation of the Pakistan Advertisers Society (PAS), Mr. Hasan was important for the group that sent off TAM Peoples meter in Pakistan in September 2007 and the MEMRB Consumer Insight Survey in August 2008, both first of their sort devices in Pakistan. He has likewise pushed for managing ad morals through PAS. As past Chairperson of the Anti-counterfeit and Infringement Forum (ACIF), Mr. Hasan emphatically upholds making mindfulness about fake and IP encroachment among purchasers and different partners.

Mr. Hasan is a big fan of Corporate Social Responsibility. An Adult Literacy Program for Representatives began at NFL as soon as 2000. In 2007, he led the improvement of a Sustainability Strategy, which directs all business capabilities no matter how you look at it today. As a visionary and showcasing pioneer, Mr. Hasan has tended to crowds of different parts of promoting associations, gatherings, classes, instructive organizations, and distributions. He has shown up on a few business TV syndicated programs examining the business climate and economy overall. He has gotten various honors, including the Marketing Excellence Award 2008 from the Marketing Association of Pakistan (MAP).

SCALA

SCALA was founded in 1978 and registered under SCALA Business Solutions. It is a European-based company known primarily for its enterprise resource planning, supply chain, and customer relationship managing solutions. SCALA targets pharmaceuticals, FMCGs, distribution, and transport channels. SCALA was considered to be the most used software at the manufacturing and industrial levels. Later, in 2003, Californian-based firm Epicor, a well-known software firm, announced the merger with SCALA. Epicor's prime business was to provide software solutions for customer relationship management, financials, manufacturing, supply chain management, professional services automation and collaborative commerce, as well as a number of complementary services. With this merger, Epicor's SCALA performed incredibly well, and in 2005, SCALA was honored as the best performing ERP of the year by Microsoft in Europe.

SCALA Business Solutions was implemented at National Foods by SCALA Business Solutions as Mr. Abrar Hassan was inspired by SCALA and its usage during his two-week training in Romania, where he was in the previous firm. SCALA enables large businesses to integrate IT technology and traditional ERP functionality to support and run their business efficiently. The core features of SCALA include Client management, Order processing, Finance, and Human Resource modules. Abrar believed implementing an ERP is his best shot for integrating the departments and improving future efficiency. National Foods became the first FMCG to implement ERP in Pakistan. Along with this badge of upholding IT technology, Abrar has some challenges to face before its implementation. Generally, it is believed to be better to prepare yourself and the firm before implementing ERP software. Hence, as a result, Abrar emphasized cutting down extra lengthy processes, redundant procedures and complexities to make ERP implementation easy for the organization. In the first phase, the Human resource management system was implemented and was a success for Abrar and his team. Later, just after the success of the HRM module, Abrar implemented all three modules, including the finance, purchase, and client management module.

Challenges Faced During Scala Implementation

National Foods pioneered implementing the ERP solution in Pakistan's FMCG industry, so it was new and untested in the industry. As such, ERP implementation carries a substantial risk that it may fail. Abrar carried out a phased approach to implement SCALA across the whole organization. At first, the biggest challenge was training the employees and providing them with knowledge of the system. The employees are usually following cognitive inertia where they are not ready for the new system to be implemented, so the main task was to provide them adequate training regarding the system, also making people believe that the new system is not a threat to traditional workers' jobs.

The second main issue was to integrate the system and departments because too much data was involved, and filtering the data was a heavy task, too, because SCALA was .NET based and transferring the whole data into SCALA, although it was time-consuming and expensive to implement Overcoming these difficulties Abrar implemented the system across the organization.

SCALA, with all its capabilities, worked well for five years. Later, as the operations expanded, Zahid Sheikh was hired as IT head; a new induct brought new values and expanded the company's IT vision.

Looking For Solutions

As National Foods expanded its operation and the corporation grew, it realized that the legacy system, SCALA, was sufficient for the company's requirements. SCALA could not keep up with the company's growth, and National Foods could not scale the solution alongside the company's growth. The main problem, however, that National Foods had with SCALA was not having a single centralized Decision Support System that could handle production schedules for the domestic and international markets.

Pakistan's local or domestic market has production cycles that follow historical market data and MRPs to predict future sales and schedule procurement and production of goods accordingly. In the international market, however, companies follow an order-based or a JIT (just in time) approach. This difference caused difficulties for National Foods to schedule future demand in the international markets because the current SCALA ERP was not sophisticated enough, forcing the company to look for more options.

The Company started looking for other ERP and vendor companies that could provide solutions that better suited the company's needs. National Foods narrowed the search to two ERP software providers, SAP and Oracle, and weighted the benefits and disadvantages of each to decide which one to implement.

SAP

SAP is a product of a German Company called SAP SE. SAP was released in 1972, and it has been running and upgraded since then. It is currently one of the corporations' most prominent and sought-after ERP systems. SAP has become a cloud-based solution with configurations available in more than 50 Languages. It is also a cross-platform software compatible with Windows, MacOS, Linux, and Unix. Its multi-language, multi-currency, and multi-platform compatibility make it a versatile and flexible ERP system. It is well suited for a global business that operates in different countries. SAP is a module-based system, which means it has specially designed modules for various business functions. Billing, Analytics, CRM, Product Design, Financials and accounting, HR, Planning and scheduling, and Supply Chain Management are just some of the modules SAP offers.

While considering the implementation of SAP, National Foods looked at the Advantages and disadvantages of both solutions. Some of the main advantages SAP are:

- Lower Costs: By using SAP, the company can improve its cost efficiency in the long run.

- Cleaner Data: SAP is the best option for reducing data redundancy and redundant data entry.

- Managing Large Volumes of Data: SAP advances the data management system by processing huge amounts of data. Furthermore, it allows the people within the organization to view the shared data.

- Integrating Business Stakeholders: SAP helps Integrate the external stakeholders and value chain members into the ERP, for example, suppliers, customers, retailers, etc.

- Scalability: Allows companies to scale their operations effortlessly while maintaining data security.

Dome of the disadvantages of SAP are:

- The one-time cost of installing SAP is quite high because it includes software, hardware, implementation, consultant, and training.

- SAP often consumes a very long period for full implementation.

- SAP can be quite complicated to use without proper training.

Oracle

Oracle is the third largest software company in the world after Microsoft and IBM. It was founded in June 1977 in Austin, Texas. Oracle first launched its Oracle application suit with financial capabilities in the late 1980s. By 2009, after several upgrades and additions, the ERP offered supply chain management, HR management, Inventory management, Customer relationship management, and many other modules. Oracle's Cloud cloud-based enterprise Resource Planning software was launched in 2012. It has all the functionalities of the legacy Oracle application suite but with the additional benefit of cloud computing and various other modules and add-ons.

Some advantages of ORACLE include the following:

- Configurability with most devices and operating systems and flexibility as a global product.

- ORACLE uses a single database for all data types.

- Offers better identity management and user controls

- Executes quick backup and recovery.

- Includes Flashback technology, a feature that enables undoing a human error and correcting it in the system relatively quickly.

Some disadvantages of ORACLE include the following:

- For the local on-premises version of Oracle, extensive SQL knowledge and administrative experience in database management are required.

- Oracle licensees are costly (Standard Edition approx. 17,000 USD, Enterprise Edition approx. 40,000 USD)

SHIFT TO SAP

National Foods Limited partnered with Abacus Consultancy as their vendor for the implementation of SAP ERP. A six-month accelerated deployment plan was executed, and the complete lifecycle of SAP ERP and Business Objects was completed in June 2010. Completing a full implementation in such a short time was an achievement for this partnership. During the implementation of the SAP modules, even when the deadlines for implementation seemed too ambitious to be completed so quickly, Abrar held his ground and remained persistent on the deadlines. He believed in the capabilities of both the consultancy firm and National Foods, and his persistence bore fruit as the implementation neared its end within the target deadline. Abrar also did his best to ensure there was no downtime or "pause period" for the company while shifting from SCALA to SAP ERP, where the company's business processes were affected and maintained the cost-effectiveness of the ERP implementation.

Challenges Faced During SAP Implementation

As it implemented the new ERP SAP, National Foods faced some challenges that are usually expected to come in any ERP implementation:

Ensuring Quality Standards

The first issue that Abrar and his team faced was maintaining the standardized quality of their database. The company needed to grow and maintain its competitive edge in the market. Hence, it was critical that while implementing the new ERP, they ensure the Database quality is on par with the industry standards and that the records and data are kept safe during the process.

Integration issues

A big challenge in implementing SAP ERP is the integration process. SAP is a highly complex software that requires a cautious point-to-point integration process. National Foods has a long list of divisions and product lines and multiple functions with unique requirements for each. Hence, the implementation of SAP in such an organization needs to be done carefully and skillfully because any leftover bugs or errors in the implementation can cause profit losses.

Resistance to change

The New ERP system SAP had many additional features that could speed up and automate the company's business processes much more efficiently than the legacy system SCALA. This automation threatened many employees who saw this ERP as a replacement for their jobs. The SAP ERP hence faced some initial resistance from the employees that were hesitant to adopt the new ERP.

Employee training

All the employees of National Foods who were potential users of the new SAP ERP had to be given the proper training and skillsets necessary to operate the system in day-to-day operations. Suppose this training is not done properly and employees are not fully ready to implement the new system. In that case, it may lead to massive mismanagement issues, and the implementation can backfire in efficiency and effectiveness.

Shifting To Cloud

At the start of August 2015, NFL took another big step in the company's digital transformation and decided to move its entire SAP ERP Infrastructure and application onto a cloud-based server. In doing so, National Foods became the First FMCG in Pakistan to have a Cloud-based ERP system. National Foods partnered with RapidCompute, a Cloud computing Service provider, to migrate its ERP. RapidCompute Provided NFL with its Cloud Server as an IAAS (Infrastructure as a Service), which means the company provided NFL with a server where National Foods can use the processing power, storage, and all other computing resources of the cloud while using the National Foods own ERP system, which in this case is SAP. Using IAAS, National Foods will only pay RapidCompute for their computation services and storage services and pay SAP for the software, as compared to a SAAS (software as a service) where the NFL would have had to pay for the infrastructure as well as the software to the same vendor. In any case, National Foods has now completely outsourced its ERP Infrastructure and moved SAP to the cloud.

Migration with RapidCompute

RapidCompute is a cloud computing service provider and a subsidiary division of Cybernet. It was established in 2012 and is Pakistan's largest and most trusted cloud operator, operating in multiple cities in Sindh and Punjab. It has a history of working with large banks, SMEs, and FMCGs all over Pakistan to deliver cloud services for mission-critical operations. National Foods chose RapidCompute as its cloud services provider because of its successful past relationship. Syed Zeshaan Ali, General Manager of IT, said, "National Foods has a long-standing relationship with Cybernet as our MPLS connectivity provider". Abrar Hassan added, "Our experience with Cybernet and RapidCompute has been very positive."

As for the implementation plan, National Foods and RapidCompute decided to go with a phased rollout approach where the ERP infrastructure would be moved to the cloud in parts. After completing each phase of implementation, teams from National Foods and RapidCompute performed tests and quality controls to ensure the implementation went smoothly and there were no errors. RapidCompute also provided National Foods with a cloud-based disaster recovery system, a backup measure in case of a crash or data loss.

Benefits of Moving to Cloud

Lower Costs

Running the SAP ERP on a cloud server enabled National Foods to cut down on its hardware expenditure used in the legacy in-house IT infrastructure. It did not need new servers and hardware every time there was a need for expansion of additional storage. The server maintenance fee was eliminated because there was no need for in-house servers when the company was using an IAAS solution.

Flexible Data Storage

As mentioned above, neither was National Foods bound by its own IT infrastructure for its data storage needs nor did it need to buy additional equipment in case it needed to expand its system capabilities. With a cloud-based Enterprise system, National Foods could now increase its data storage capabilities as needed quickly and cost-effectively.

Scalability

The biggest advantage of Cloud computing is its scalability. National Foods struggled with its SCALA ERP because SCALA could not fully support its ever-expanding business, and the NFL had to move over to SAP. Similarly, with in-house infrastructure, there would come a time when the hardwired SAP would become insufficient for the company's needs. Scaling the ERP can cost a lot of hardware investment, but scaling its business up with a cloud server is no challenge for National Foods.

Data Backup and Restoration

The Cloud service vendor provided National Foods with a disaster management and backup system that regularly backs up the company's data on the cloud. That helps the company safeguard any critical data that can cause business processes to halt or disrupt in case of any data breach or loss. Some extreme situations like fire, theft, and hardware failures have caused numerous companies data losses that cause massive downtime in their operations. Such lags can potentially turn into monetary losses for the company.

Remote Accessibility

A significant benefit of cloud-based ERP is that National Foods can now access its ERP system off-site and on-site. The ERP can be accessed from any location on any supported device like smartphones, laptops, or tablets and can be used to collaborate with teams.

Technological Development Post ERP Implementation

In 2018, the National Foods head office shifted to a state-of-the-art building in Bath Island Clifton's posh area. This new building is comprised of highly modernized IT infrastructure. This office IT infrastructure setup involves comprehensive program management skills, having multiple IT Vendors and teams working together to integrate all major departments of the NFL. The overall setup comprises a Data Centre and HVAC solution, a centralized solution and Cisco wall manager, a video conferencing system, and a video wall. The implementation of SAP led NFL towards a higher growth rate and extended from a basic manual quality control process to an automated process to record inspection data. The SAP power was extended to enable efficiency in Finance and Integrated supply chain processes. The processes include Customer Ledger Clearing, Bank Reconciliation, sales and operational planning, Production order automation, and rescheduling processes for automating the delivery, which is priority-based. Also, it supports PO alerts for due and overdue deliveries. Further, the Workflow system was extended to automate the paper-based forms for Finance and HR. NFL implemented portfolio and project management software.

Comprehensive and interactive dashboards were developed to provide actionable insights to National Foods. NFL worked extensively for data analytics for all business functions to gain a competitive advantage over competitors. As a market leader in applying technology in the FMCG industry, the NFL is using the most advanced techniques and smart ways to compete and analyze market strategies. Using visual analytics, integrating modules of businesses to monitor efficiency, identify new opportunities, and better understand customer demand. Visual analytics offered data analysis capability for the management to understand, slice, and dice the data at regional levels, categories, and product-wise. Interactive dashboards enable NFL to integrate the information from Sales, planning, stocks, delivery, and procurement departments. The upgraded SAP version also supports the Quality control and performance monitoring system. Some other IT initiatives involve a partnership with ISC to move the ordering mechanism to a demand-driven dynamic replenishment model using the DBRS system.

The Way Forward

National Foods Limited successfully implemented its enterprise resource system and earned efficiency in its working environment. It has been observed in the NFL that the company initially was using a manual system for recording and maintaining their activities, but after some time, they realized that the company was expanding due to increasing demand and that their manual system was not feasible enough to maintain the flow of activities. In 2003, Abrar Hassan (Chief Executive) contacted Epicor company, which specialized in the planning and implementation of enterprise resource systems for the implementation of SCALA in National Foods Limited.

Abrar Hassan and Epicor successfully implemented SCALA in the company. Soon after the implementation of SCALA, the company realized that its size was increasing, and it would soon be expanding to the Asian market. They analyzed the situation that SCALA won't be enough solution in the company's expansion, so they decided to search for other alternatives. For that purpose, the company hired Abacus Consultancy and discussed the business needs with them. After a successful discussion with the technical partner, the company selected two candidates for the business need: ORACLE and SAP. As per the knowledge and history of Abacus consultancy, the company decided to drop the option of ORACLE and elected SAP ERP as the solution.

For implementation, Abrar Hassan made the steering committee and placed himself as the senior responsible person in that committee. He also selected two more candidates, Mr. Zahid Sheikh (Information Technology Head at National Foods Limited) and the Project Manager from Abacus Consultancy. The steering committee prepared the team for the implementation. They selected employees from all the departments keen to learn about the new technology and are also technology adoptive profiles for the successful implementation of SAP ERP.

The steering committee was responsible for providing everything needed to the team for the implementation, from facilities to motivation. The company successfully implemented SAP ERP software in 2010, and in 2015, they shifted SAP to cloud-based software for better efficiency and security of the system.

Exhibit 1
History of National Foods at a glance

YEAR	EVENTS
1970	National Foods was founded as a small entity that has a broad vision to grow. Initially, the spice lineup have five variants.
1971	National Foods moves its head office location from a small setup to dinar chambers west wharf site area Karachi.
1978	National Foods acquires a spice mill and launches its branded salt.
1986	National Foods inaugurated a new factory at the site area and launched a mix spices brand.
1988	National Foods became a certified supplier of McCormick USA. This certifies excellent quality provided by national foods.
1991	With a constant development vision, National Foods introduces their branded achaar (pickles).
1992	National Foods joined hands with UNICEF to make people aware the use of iodized salt.
1993	National Foods goes for a salt modernization program.
1996	National Foods becomes the first FMCG to launch an ERP system (Human Resource Department)
1997	Ketchup was added to the National foods portfolio.
1998	National Foods became ISO certified and added jam and jelly to their portfolio.
2000	National Foods goes international, launches the products in Australia, and crosses the Rs.1 billion sales mark.
2001	National Foods launches its custard range.
2006	National Foods launches a new factory in port Qasim based on 10 acres. This factory was equipped with the latest machinery.
2009	National Foods revamped its logo, and a fresh and better look was introduced.
2010	On the 40th anniversary of National Foods, Fruity, a juice brand, was launched.
2013	National Foods established a subsidiary in Dubai.
2014	National Foods established a subsidiary in Canada with the name National Epicure Inc.
2015	National Foods launches a state-of-the-art facility in Gujranwala. This factory manages all core operations of the Punjab region.

| 2017 | National Foods revamped its packaging and upgraded all its operations to Microsoft 365. Systems were shifted to the Office 365 office. |
| 2018 | DBRS (Demand-based replenishment system) was introduced. Shifted to new head office at Clifton. |

Exhibit 2
Organizational Structure of National Foods Limited

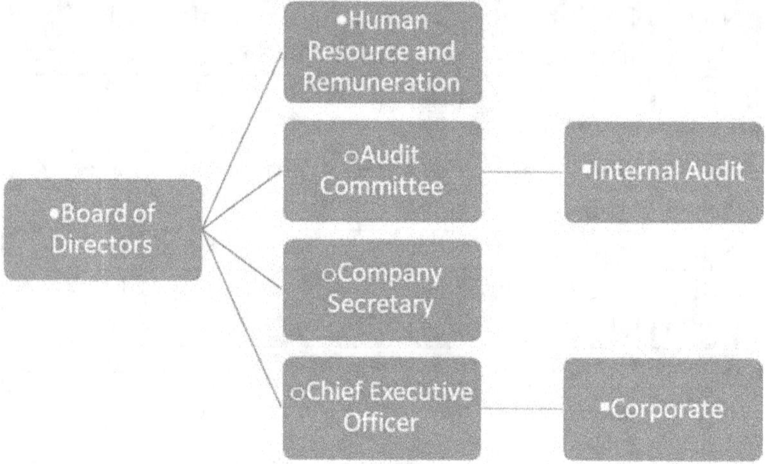

Exhibit 3
Organizational Hierarchy of National Foods Limited

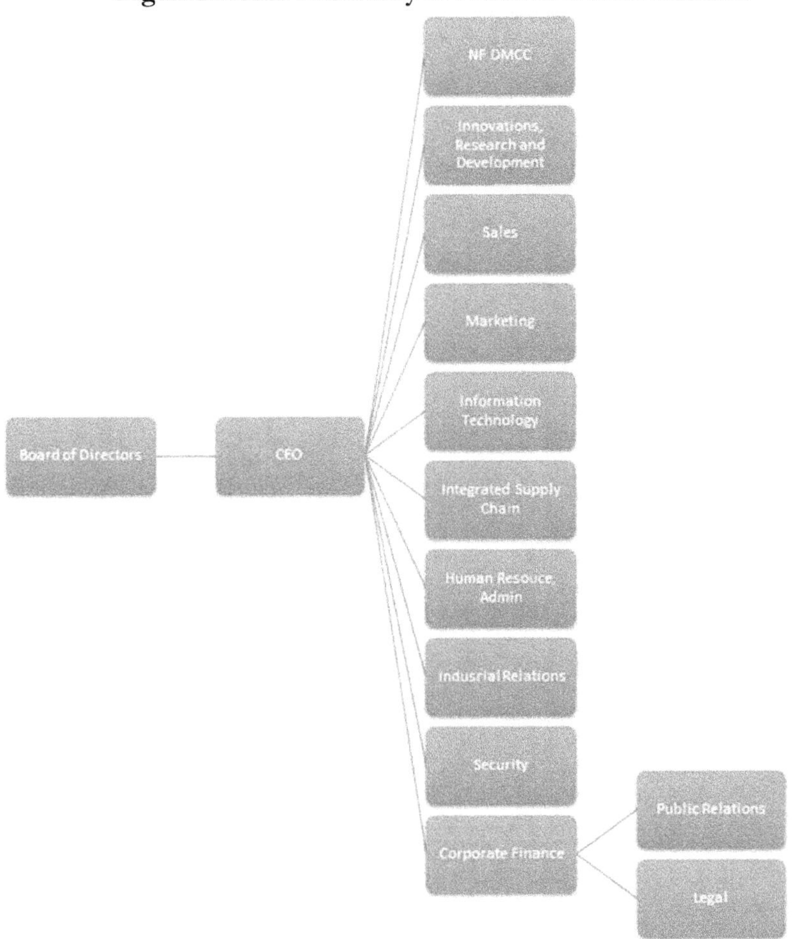

This page was intentionally left blank.

ERP IMPLEMENTATION AT FACO INDUSTRIES

Sameed Ahmed Khan and Jawwad Ur Rehman of Karachi School for Business and Leadership (KSBL) prepared this case under the supervision of Dr. Amir Manzoor. The case was prepared solely to provide material for class discussion. The authors do not intend to illustrate either effective or ineffective handling of a managerial situation. Certain names and other identifying information have been disguised to protect confidentiality.

For many years the accounting, bookkeeping, data storage, and administration work was done manually in the factory office, and it usually took hours of writing and calculations. Every now and then, the CEO, Mr. Aftab, would call his assistant to bring a stack of files from the file room so that he could look at old records of purchases of raw materials or look back at customer order history. It was routine work and had been done for decades, and the staff had grown accustomed to it. Now, the time had come when the CEO was fed up with all this. Being a true believer in upgradation and adopting new technology, he called in his General Manager and asked him to research to get an Enterprise Resource Planning system, as one of their clients had, so that things could be automated and work could be done faster.

General Manager Talha started to look around and found a software company named Future Tech Solutions, with its own ERP named "Bestow." They were providing open-source code software that was up for customization and was not heavy on the budget. After several discussions with the software company and the CEO Of Faco Industries, the GM went on with the planning and customization of Bestow. After months of customization, the software Bestow finally went live on 1st July 2009, and things started to change at the office.

FACO Industries

FACO is Pakistan's only and largest exporter of Flexible Hoses and showers to Europe, the Far East, Gulf countries, and world-renowned OEMs (original equipment manufacturers). It came into existence more than three decades ago with the vision to become a pioneer in this field. Qualified professionals empower Faco's corporate structure. The production facility is equipped with cutting-edge technology with all in-house facilities, from profiling to packing, including all kinds of surface finishing processes.

To meet customer needs, FACO is fully equipped to produce hoses in different metals and finishes, i.e., Brass, Stainless Steel 200 & 300 Series with Nickel Chrome Plating, etc., per EN-1113, EN-13618, and EN-248 standards. Exhibit 2 shows some of the products produced by FACO industries.

FACO has Various Product Certifications such as ACS (Attestation de Conformité Sanitaire), WRAS (Water regulatory advisory scheme), NSF (National Safety Foundation) & KTW (Kunststoffe and Trinkwasser). Their products are 100% anti-microbial and safe for drinking water and water in contact with the human body. FACO's Quality Management System is ISO 90001-2000.

Company History

FACO Industries (FI) was established and started functioning in 1990. The need to establish a manufacturing unit for their product (shower hose) emerged as it was not manufactured locally in Pakistan. The only available products sold in the local market were German, Chinese, and other imported products. Also, the price of these products was high, and there was a big gap to be covered in the market. The company's founder is Mr. Aftab Ahmed Khan, who has over 40 years of experience in this field. He is a true visionary who has put tremendous effort into locally producing these products, benefiting local consumers, and exporting to other countries.

FACO Industries' line of business is diversified and vast. Its primary industry is the sanitary and water-related industry. Its secondary industry is the auto parts industry, as FI also provides chrome-plated parts for Pakistan's automobile giants, such as Honda, Toyota, Yamaha, and Suzuki. The raw materials for their products involve high-quality metals and chromium-plated finish, so they are also deeply rooted in the metal and chemical industry. Annual net sales of the fiscal year 2021-22: 222,679,438 PKR. The factory is located in the Federal B area industrial area, and the head office is located at Shahrae Faisal in Karachi.

FI's employees include 100 workers and 16 admin staff as of 1st June 2022. The main competitors were MASTER Sanitary, SONEX, and FAISAL Sanitary. Other competitors include imported brands such as Grohe, Porta, and unbranded Chinese products.

Corporate Vision & Mission

The vision of FACO is to be initially Pakistan's biggest brand of sanitary ware and then to be the world's biggest brand of sanitary ware products. Its main vision is to produce locally and provide its consumers with products that are in the best interest of their health and make their life easy.

FACO's mission is to promote intelligent and sustainable water usage. FI has been producing its products keeping in mind all international standards promoting saving water and giving high value to human health. Exhibit 1 shows the organizational structure of FACO industries.

Company Strategy

FI's corporate strategy is to emerge as a global sanitary ware brand in the world. Their management practices are strategically designed to achieve both long-term and short-term goals. They manage to maintain worldwide public relations with the biggest brands and traders in many countries. Having a production facility with the latest international technology has allowed them to gain good global strategic partners.

Marketing Strategy: FI's main product is the flexible shower hose and connection hose. Along with it, they also launched a state-of-the-art shower range. The chromium-plated metal shower hose is the main product of FI and is famous throughout the Pakistani market with the jargon of the "FACO chain." This metal connection hose used in faucets and FACO industries is also the sole manufacturer of this product in Pakistan.

All of these products of FACO are available throughout the country in all big sanitary markets. These products have built their name in the market because of their outstanding quality and attractive price range. Faco has its own dealer network through which all these products are distributed to small and medium shops. Faco's marketing and sales team is led by experienced professionals who have been in the field for over a decade.

Financial Strategy: Faco relies on its own retained earnings and savings. It has never taken debt as an investment for any of its plants or machinery. They have a proper payment system for all their stakeholders, which ensures timely payment to all individuals. A payment system and MOU are signed between FI and its dealers. The CEO especially overlooks the finance department as they believe in paying vendors as soon as possible and without any delays.

HR Strategy: The FACO Human resource system focuses on employee benefits and their well-being. They have a monthly bonus for all employees having full attendance. Faco manages its corporate social responsibility with a few members of its team who are self-driven for the betterment of humanity and their own company. All employees get their medical allowance and additional help whenever needed. Ration bags are given to those in need who live in the adjoining areas. Other than that, a yearly bonus is given at the end of each fiscal year. Special Ramadan iftar drives take place every year, which ensures that the community living nearby or any travelers in the area get to eat iftar. Learning and organizational development are encouraged, and the firm supports employees who wish to continue their education.

Critical Success Factors of Business

- Outstanding quality
- A good policy for all dealers
- State-of-the-art machinery and plant
- Fast delivery system
- All in-house processing
- Strong leadership
- Sole manufacturer in Pakistan for flexible pipes and hoses
- Vertical unit
- Strong international relations

Strengths and Weaknesses

Strengths

- The only manufacturer of flexible hoses in Pakistan
- One of the best electroplating plants in Pakistan
- 30 years of expertise in metals and surface finishing
- Highly experienced staff with a proactive approach

Weakness

- Less focus on marketing and advertising
- A bigger sales force is needed
- No specific HR department
- Less working space

Opportunity

- High duty on imported flexible hoses is a chance for FI to grab the existing market.
- No direct competitor for shower hose
- Pakistan's growing economy has a lot of emphasis on construction, which is a related industry.
- Subsidies from TDAP and tax refunds for exporters

Threats

- A high influx of imported smuggled products from Iran and neighboring countries.
- The cost of production is rising daily due to inflation in the economy.
- The threat of new entrants in the local market is moderate

Background of the Case

The CEO wanted to change the manual process to make the work speedy. The manual system was very time-consuming. For example, if one had to check old receipts, it meant going back to the file room, finding files, carrying them to the desk, and checking the values. This process was very irritating as several minutes used to pass by, and the work was still not done.

Including this time-taking process, everything was on paper and registers, which meant high usage of paper and handwriting. As the firm was dealing with big companies like Toyota, Honda, etc., it was sometimes a shame that they were doing everything manually. It was high time that the company had to implement new software, reduce the time taken for work, and reduce paper usage.

Procurement

The purchasing department issues a Purchase order for the vendors. The raw materials include brass, packaging material, PVC tubes, chemicals, stationery, fuel, nuts, bolts, iron, steel, oil, etc. Sourcing for the raw materials is done locally, and some of it is imported as well. Faco Industry imports Stainless steel, showers, plastic, and PVC grains.

The management has set a buffer quantity for the imported raw materials stored in their warehouse. The buffer quantity for the main raw material, Stainless Steel, is ten metric tonnes. The procurement department tries to maintain the quantity levels higher than that. The company imports these directly from China whenever the inventory levels reach the buffer stock levels. For the locally procured raw materials, the particular department issues a requirement form to the purchases department, and a Purchase Order (PO) is generated, following which the raw materials are bought locally, and the finance department then makes payments for those purchases. A purchase requisition form is also available to each department head, and they can fill out their needs and send them to the finance department. From there, the procurement officer instantaneously goes out to procure that product, which are usually petty items, and brings them back.

Goods Receipt Note

The inventory is bought against the purchase orders and stored in the warehouse located alongside the factory. After docking and unloading the goods, a Goods Received Note (GRN) is made, and an invoice is generated for the number of goods that have been received at the time. Many times the orders are in large quantity and not all of the goods reach the factory together. The GRN is made up before a thorough quality check and a physical inspection of the arrived goods.

Goods Issuance

To utilize the available goods, the head of any particular department would have to ask for an inventory reservation form, fill it out, and send it to the procurement department. This will mark that the inventory would be reserved for the said particular department, and they would also mention the number of days it would require for them to move the inventory from the warehouse to the department.

Sales Process

The sales process is very simple. When the sales team receives an order, they make a sales order on which there are all the goods and their quantity with their prices. That sales order is then signed by the CEO and given to the assembly department, which then starts to manufacture the goods. Once goods are processed and are ready to be shipped, a delivery challan is generated along with a gate pass.

Delivery Challan

Faco is involved in providing service to the automobile industry for the surface finishing of its products. So these goods come in by quantity and are counted at the gate. After being processed, the companies pack, count, and then pick up these goods. All billing is based on counting. End of the month, all processed parts are calculated with the quantity of delivery made every day so that the customers can be billed. So, a goods received note is made when the products are received, and a delivery challan and invoice are made when the goods are being sent back to the customers.

History of information systems at FI

Since its inception, all the work has been done manually, and there is no history of information systems at the firm. However, in early 2000, they used computers and Microsoft Excel for accounts-related work. The purchase orders were made on a blank piece of paper and then signed by the CEO, which went forward for payment release from the accounts department and so on. When the CEO asked about previous purchase prices of the materials, the accounts department had to check the files and ledgers, which took time.

System Selection

Faco wanted to shift from a traditional manual working method to an automated and integrated business solution. The manual work wasted a lot of their time, energy, resources, and valuable working hours in data management, and they wanted to increase their efficiency. One of Faco's clients was using Alliance Manufacturing ERP software, and they got to know about it, however, it was very expensive at that time and not suitable for an SME like Faco. The other option they had was Bestow, from Future Tech Solutions Company. Bestow was under 1 million rupees and hence was not very expensive.

Details of the solution

Bestow ERP was a product of future tech. This ERP had been running in many industries because it was an open-source code software, which meant that it was open for customization. It had all modules from import/export to payroll, accounts, sales, and tax. A single server needed to be installed at the site where the software would run. A physical server was selected, which was the need of the time as the technology for cloud servers was nonexistent for SMEs in 2009. The server was physically placed in the IT room which was built specifically for the server. The GM was assigned to oversee the implementation. He was assigned knowing that he had a complete grip on the structure of the company and the business processes that went along with it. Also, in case of any customizations in Bestow, one person overlooking each relevant department and area of expertise was shadowing the software implementation so that all scopes are covered.

Implementation process

The implementation process was led by the general manager who also had a history of software engineering, so it was beneficial for the company as he was the point of contact in the firm and he had knowledge of all the business processes in the firm. He also knew how and what customization had to be done. The implementation technique used was a phased approach.

Until the new system went live, all business processes were manually carried out like

1. **Planning:**
    It was decided that since the GM had the most knowledge about software and no one else had yet worked on an ERP. He would lead everything from planning to going live.

2. **Customization:**
    The implementation started with the customization of Bestow as per the needs of Faco. The charts of accounts were set as they wanted. The

units of measurement were set for the manufacturing costing, raw materials, and finished products as the raw material came into the factory by weight and went out per piece. So, a lot of measurements had to be done and included in the system. Part numbers were made for all of FACO's products. Reports were made as per requirements.

3. **Trial**

   After all the customization was done, it was time to try the software with dummy data so that when the system went live, all the issues would already be resolved.

4. **Go-live**

   When the system was ready, the data was uploaded, and the final trial began. The system did have some bugs, which were resolved as soon as possible.

5. **Training**

   All administration departments were trained by the professionals who implemented the system. The accounts executive was given thorough training as he had the most crucial job, from managing payroll to generating customer payments. After that, the procurement executive was trained on how to issue purchase orders and check reports in the ledger. Later, the sales team was trained on making sales orders, delivery challans, and gate passes. Then came the import and export department.

6. **Support**

   The team from future tech was on call during business hours, and they still used to visit once a week if there were any bugs in the system.

Implementation Issues:

People:

The biggest issue faced by Faco during the implementation was that the person from Future Tech, the company that provided the software, was not performing up to the mark. According to the management, he was not devoted 100% to working on the implementation.

During the implementation, the management for FACO realized that the implementation team was actually not experienced in implementing the software in manufacturing companies. They had previously been implemented in trading companies, but for FACO, which was a manufacturing company, the business processes and the nature of business had to be explained to the Implementation team as well. So, in retrospect, instead of Future Tech training FACO on how to use the software, FACO ended up training the Future Tech team on their business practices, and this meant that the implementation was delayed by a significant time.

The implementation team assumed that all the users were of the same tech understanding, and hence, the training provided to them had to be of different levels as some needed more tutoring and some needed the basic levels. This assumption caused some delays.

The users were hesitant at adapting the new technology, and some even resorted to working the old manual way at the slightest inconvenience. So, getting the end users on board seemed to be a daunting task for the management.

Process

Initially, bugs came up from time to time when the implementation was complete. The management had to request the Future Tech team to process it, and then there seemed to be a delay as their query was sent to the Future Tech office, and then they resolved it. Meanwhile, back at FACO, the operations would face hurdles as they could not work on the system.

Technology

The issue of power and electricity was initially unaddressed, as frequent power disruptions caused the servers and computers to malfunction. This was worked on later after UPS and backups were installed to protect the database.

The entire wiring, fixtures, and the systems of the people who would be working on it had to be upgraded. This cost was an additional burden at the time, and the Future Tech sales team did not consider it when providing a quotation for Bestow.

Bestow was made to be based on Windows XP and compatible with similar programs of that time. With time, when the management upgraded to Windows 7 and Windows 10, Bestow had to be configured in a different way to be able to run on those operating systems. This future hindsight was not taken into account when making the software.

Benefits of the new system

Bestow was a new world for the company. It changed how the company functioned for almost a decade. One major benefit was that the CEO could now check all ledgers and bills on his system or ask the accounts executive to easily tell the figure in minutes. That would allow making the payroll quite fast as all the attendance is uploaded, the salary is automatically updated, and the accounts team just has to check it. The time it took to generate the payroll has been reduced by 80% now. The system could calculate all of it based on formulas set in the design of the ERP.

Ledgers were very easy to maintain as no separate data was needed to be input to make accounts payable and accounts receivable. The data for that was recorded at the time of the goods receipt note and sales invoice. Each month's sales recovery and total sales were at a distance of a click. All these reports were very beneficial for daily critical analysis. This gave new insights into the business perspective of FACO. The employees were a bit excited with the new system and were enjoying it as the work was quicker and more efficient. The daily runs to the file rooms were no more, and getting figures and calculations was very fast, just with a click. There was the ease of access for the CEO, and the system was transparent. There were no entries that were not understandable. All cash and bank transactions were in reports. That gave a new perspective to the CEO, which was more holistic.

FACO did weekly closing of accounts previously, which took a lot of time, and much paperwork was involved. Now, the weekly closing was done in just 2 hours and presented to the CEO. Every document that went out of the company had a standardized design and structure, which was more presentable to the big companies that Faco was working with. Also, this format was constant, making it easy for everyone to understand.

Exhibit 1
FACO Industries Organizational Structure

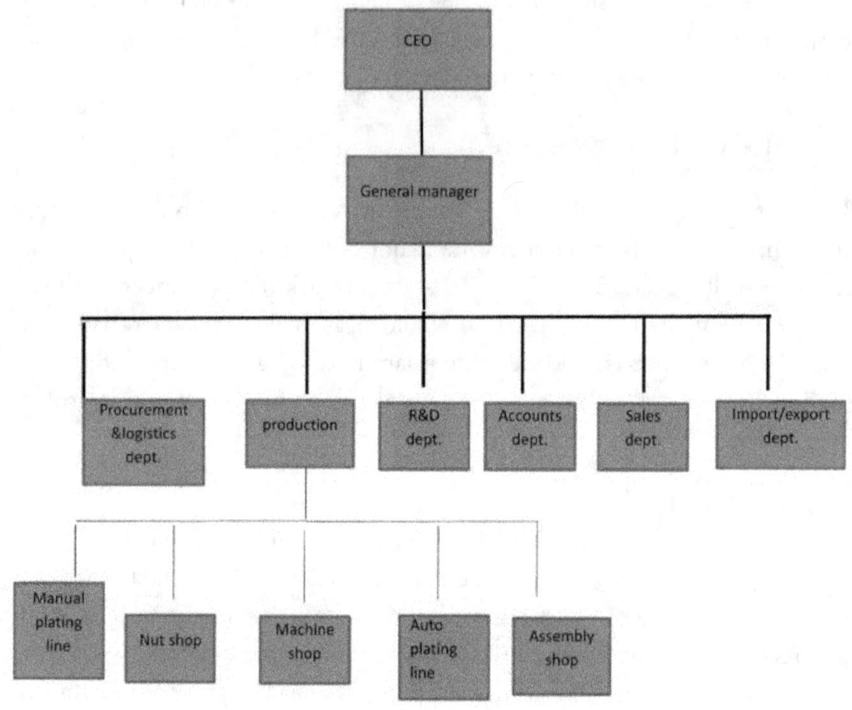

Exhibit 2
FACO Industries Products

This page was intentionally left blank.

9 798858 975311